From Small Places

From Small Places

Toward the Realization of Literacy as a Human Right

Jo-Anne Wilson-Keenan, Ed.D.

SENSE PUBLISHERS
ROTTERDAM/BOSTON/TAIPEI

A C.I.P. record for this book is available from the Library of Congress.

ISBN: 978-94-6300-134-2 (paperback)
ISBN: 978-94-6300-135-9 (hardback)
ISBN: 978-94-6300-136-6 (e-book)

Published by: Sense Publishers,
P.O. Box 21858,
3001 AW Rotterdam,
The Netherlands
https://www.sensepublishers.com/

Printed on acid-free paper

For my father Lucien William Rouillard
who was an avid reader
and for my mother Catherine Fredey Rouillard
who believed, like the woman in this book who fled Darfur,
"Education is the only thing that cannot be taken from us
and upon which
we can build a better life for our children."

Where, after all, do universal human rights begin? In small places, close to home –so close and so small that they cannot be seen on any maps of the world... Unless these rights have meaning there, they have little meaning anywhere.

— Eleanor Roosevelt (Roosevelt, Speech to UN on Tenth Anniversary of the Adoption of the Universal Declaration of Human Rights, 1958a)

Reflection upon the words of Paulo Freire: We do not leave the fight. We simply move to another front.

— (Adapted from Pedagogy of the City, 1993)

TABLE OF CONTENTS

PREFACE

We celebrate the past to awaken the future. —John Fitzgerald Kennedy (August 14, 1960 at the Franklin Delano Roosevelt Birthplace in Hyde Park, NY at the 25th anniversary of the signing of the Social Security Act)

FROM MY SMALL PLACE

The Irish tell of the potato blight of 1846–1850, during which an estimated eight-hundred thousand citizens died of starvation. When the potato crop failed, the Irish in the countryside began to live off what they could find around them including wild blackberries, weeds from the roadside, nettles, old cabbage leaves, seaweed, shellfish, roots, and even grass that turned their mouths and teeth green (Historyplace.com, 2000). In the streams and along the coast, especially the west coast, where the Great Hunger caused the most hardship, fish were abundant. But generally, the Irish did not eat fish (Woodham-Smith, 1962). There does not appear to be a definitive explanation as to why the Irish did not do so. Possible reasons are that many people had no previous history of fishing, no access to fishing, neither the equipment, nor the funds they needed to fish. Most likely, some fish were out of reach in water too deep and dangerous for their little cowhide-covered fishing boats, known as currachs. Those who may have fished in the past possibly pawned their tackle and nets to buy food for their families (Historyplace.com, 2000). The Irish were also accustomed to eating potatoes, the main staple of their diet. As a culture, they may have been reluctant to try new foods. Possibly, forced labor kept them locked into working the land. Extreme poverty and a fatalistic view of life may have led them to simply accept whatever sufferings came upon them. Perhaps they believed that God would provide if they just were patient and waited a bit longer for their plight to end (Kelly, 2012). Regardless of the reasons, hundreds of thousands of Irish starved although they were surrounded by fish, a possible source of food.

All too often, potential solutions to catastrophic problems are within the reach of ordinary people, but people fail to recognize them. The solutions remain hidden in plain sight. This book is about recognizing and using resources that are right in front of us to confront one such problem that impacts nearly 800 million people worldwide.

For the past several years, ordinary people across the globe, from Tunisia, Egypt, Liberia, cities in the United States and other places have been articulating their ideas, communicating through electronic technologies, and taking their future into their own hands. Governments and businesses are being challenged as institutions that are not working for people. More people are awakening to the idea that they can shape their destiny, and they are teaching others to do so. To date, the emphasis of these revolutions has been political. This book considers a different kind of revolution that will sustain changes people seek—the revolution of a world of learners who seek to attain literacy as a human right that begins at birth, extends throughout a person's lifetime, and connects the global community. Approximately twenty percent of the world's population has not realized literacy as a human right. I believe that many solutions to this problem lie in the hands and communities of all people. What is necessary, however, is that we recognize and implement the solutions.

I am a former Director of Reading for the Public Schools in Springfield, Massachusetts, a school system of 27,000 students. In 2006, Springfield had the sixth highest poverty rate of any city of comparable size in the United States. In addition to holding the director's position, I worked as a teacher, literacy specialist, researcher, school principal, professor, and director of a family-school collaboration project. For nearly four decades, I spent a great deal of time in small places with children and other learners. My colleagues and I worked hard and thought deeply about literacy, teaching, and learning. We conducted research, designed instructional systems, drafted curricula, wrote plans, laid out schedules, partnered with parents and the community, won grants, and garnered numerous resources. We engaged in innovative and successful teaching and learning. We were mindful of keeping our focus on the children and advocating for them. We regarded our work as service to the children and their families. But education and literacy as human rights were not ideas that we discussed often. I did not think of myself as a human rights advocate. To me, human rights advocates were doctors, lawyers, and other humanitarians who traveled to distant places to provide medical care, free prisoners, construct housing and schools, or relieve the burdens of child labor. I have changed my view.

One day, a friend who knew that I admired Eleanor Roosevelt gave me a poster with the following excerpt of her words:

> Where, after all, do universal human rights begin? In small places, close to home — so close and so small that they cannot be seen on any maps of the world...Unless these rights have meaning there, they have little meaning anywhere.

I framed the poster and displayed it on the wall of my office. I began to contemplate the words—and the words began to open a new perspective for me. I was aware of the Universal Declaration of Human Rights[1] and when I received the poster, I presumed that Eleanor Roosevelt spoke the words of the quote in 1948, when the Declaration was adopted by 48 member States of the United Nations. Later, I learned that she said the words a decade after that event. This quote has influenced me to bring together global concepts with ways of engaging children in language and literacy within personal settings. While doing so, I discovered that I was also bringing together historical and contemporary research and practices.

By the time I left my position as the Director of Reading in Springfield, I understood that literacy begins long before children first enter the classroom door, and it is deeply embedded in home and community practices. Therefore, the work of fostering literacy extends well beyond the range of schools. I realized that schools need to tailor instruction to meet the needs of children from diverse backgrounds.

In my work, I experienced the consequences of No Child Left Behind (NCLB), the centerpiece of the Bush administration's education agenda. Diane Ravitch, who was Assistant Secretary of Education during that administration, states:

> A well-educated person has a well-furnished mind, shaped by reading and thinking about history, science, literature, the arts, and politics. The well-educated person has learned to explain ideas and listen respectfully to others. (Ravitch, 2010, p. 10)[2]

Ravitch goes on to explain how NCLB became the antithesis of this definition. "NCLB was a punitive law based on erroneous assumptions about how to improve schools" (Ravitch, 2010, p. 110). These assumptions included believing that changes in governance would bring about school improvement and that lazy teachers and principals are to blame for schools with low test scores. Shaming these schools and the people who work in them, and threatening their jobs was seen as the way to bring about higher test scores. Ravitch further states that the most naive assumption of NCLB was that increased test scores on standardized tests of basic skills were viewed as "synonymous with good education." Reflecting on NCLB, Ravitch says, "Its assumptions were wrong. Testing is not a substitute for curriculum and instruction. Good education cannot be achieved by a strategy of testing children, shaming educators, and closing schools" (Ravitch, 2010, p. 111).

As a result of NCLB, I participated in narrowing and scripting curriculum—things I did not believe in and did not want to do. The results of NCLB are explored further in Chapter 4 of this book. The work was disheartening, and the results were disappointing.

That disappointment and a measure of anger, but more importantly, a larger measure of hope, led to the writing of this book. I began to research literacy as a human right studying both the history of the development of the Universal Declaration of Human Rights and the evolution of literacy as a human right. The Declaration was written over 65 years ago. It still has profound significance today. I own a small, bound copy. Within its 50 pages, the document is written in its entirety six times, in English, Spanish, French, Chinese, Russian and Arabic respectively.

To my surprise and dismay, when I first opened my copy, I realized that it was bound upside- down within its cover. Like a flag displayed in this manner, the error in the binding appeared to me to be an international signal of distress. In the years since the Declaration was written, much has changed in the world. Today, we communicate with each other instantly through the use of electronic devices, the Declaration has been translated into over 440 languages, and few areas of the world are left unmapped. But wars, natural disasters, lack of political will, and political posturing have jeopardized human rights to a greater degree than ever. The voices and rights of children who live within in the smallest and economically poorest places are in the greatest danger of all.

Opening my copy of the Declaration, however, was not the first time that I realized that children's voices were endangered. Throughout this book, the reader will find vignettes, each designated as a *View from a Small Place* that give attention to those places where rights and literacy are coming into being or being denied. The first of these views comes from my own experience of failing to hear and value children's voices.

View from a Small Place

> We now know that learning begins at birth and that children acquire a great deal of language and literacy before they enter school. As a teacher of young children, there was a time when I made the mistake of not recognizing and thereby, devaluing the language that children brought with them to school. There was a time when I did not draw upon the resources that I could have gathered from the talk, reading and writing, from the history of literacy, that children acquire before entering school. Over thirty years ago, when I was a graduate student, I was concerned that the children with whom I was working were not making progress on what were called reading readiness tasks—mastery of over one hundred lessons in letter-sound associations before children were given books to read.
>
> In one paper I wrote for a class, I described my students as children who "did not have language." Rudine Sims-Bishop an African American professor, wrote back to me and provided me with a response that changed my career and my life. She countered that the children with whom I worked "had language" or they would not have survived. She explained that language learning is a social process and since the time they were born, the children that I was concerned about had been engaging in learning language with those around them. They had figured out what things are appropriate to eat, how to cross streets safely, and avoid dangers. They had learned many other things as well. She advised that my definition of "having language" was based in the language of the classroom and was too narrow. The children had indeed acquired language, but they may not have been familiar with the limited focus of the language of the tasks that I was presenting to them in school.

It was my intention to support learners, but instead, I was constructing barriers as they tried to fashion their own models of the world. I was working within a banking model, treating students' minds, as scholar Ira Shor describes, as "empty accounts" (Shor, 1992, p. 31)[3] into which I made deposits of information. I restricted children's learning by requiring them to fit their language into the language of my world. These limitations applied to young low-income children and to older students with whom I worked. These beliefs were most harmful to African American and Latino boys in the intermediate grades, who were still reading at primer or early reader levels. The strategy I had employed most often was to attempt to re-teach the same skills until the children passed required reading tests. But the children kept failing the tests, fell farther and farther behind, and were tracked into low reading groups. At the time, I did not understand that children's own words, their own understandings of language, can be the foundation of their instruction.

Since that time, I have been working to gain new understandings of literacy development. Accepting my blindness and underestimation of the language capabilities of the young learners with whom I worked was a difficult lesson for me. But as a result of my professor's response to my misjudgments, I began to learn about the acquisition of oral language and research the connections between children's oral, written language and brain development. I found that trying to reflect on my practices by myself was not enough.

I explored and tried out the ideas of Don Holdaway, an educator who worked in both Australia and New Zealand. He wrote for those who want "to think deeply and to be convinced slowly; those who are prepared to read more widely when in doubt; and those who wish to influence outcomes from an informed conviction which they tested in their own experience" (Holdaway D., 1979, p. 11).[4] Holdaway stated, "There is no more successful example of language learning than that provided by mastery of native language during infancy" (Holdaway D., 1979, p. 19). Holdaway and his contemporaries avoided the "traditional error" of "thinking about reading and writing...as discrete [school] subjects isolated from the world of language and spoken culture and then to teach them as if they had no relationship to listening and speaking" (Holdaway D., 1979, p. 12). I set out to examine my assumptions about learners, observe, read, do research, talk and work with others, get to know students' families and as a result, changed my thinking and practice. I now understand that if speech is denied or viewed as flawed, if home language is denigrated, literacy development is restricted. Furthermore, learners' dignity and rights are disregarded.

As I continued to engage in this inquiry, my questions kept coming. What would happen if people across the world viewed education and literacy as human rights… sought to understand what a child learns from the time of birth until the time they go to school…shared this information with others through social media and other platforms…thought about children's brain development and growth in language and literacy…used children's own words as their first reading material…documented children's language and literacy growth in simple collections stored in envelopes or on electronic devices…brought that documentation to the school as evidence of a child's strengths when the child enrolled…began to see every child's language and literacy from a perspective of strength rather than deficit?

This book extends an invitation for readers to continue seeking answers to these questions.

NOTES

1 The UNIVERSAL DECLARATION OF HUMAN RIGHTS by The Human Rights Commission of the General Assembly. Copyright 1948 United Nations. Quoted and reprinted by permission of the United Nations.

2 From THE DEATH AND LIFE OF THE GREAT AMERICAN SCHOOL SYSTEM. Copyright © 2010 by Diane Ravitch. Usage determined by Perseus Books Group.

3 From EMPOWERING EDUCATION: CRITICAL TEACHING FOR SOCIAL CHANGE. Copyright © 1992 by Ira Shor. Reprinted with permission of the University of Chicago Press. All rights reserved.

4 From the book FOUNDATIONS OF LITERACY by Don Holdaway. Text copyright © Don Holdaway, 1979 First Published by Scholastic Australia, a division of Scholastic Australia PTY Limited, 1979 Reproduced by permission of Scholastic Australia PTY Limited.

ACKNOWLEDGMENTS

With deepest appreciation to:

My publisher, Peter de Liefde, for supporting the publication of this book.

Eleanor Roosevelt for her work that helped bring about the Universal Declaration of Human Rights and her words that continue to safeguard the dignity of people today and will do so into the future.

Eleanor Roosevelt's granddaughter, Nancy Roosevelt Ireland, for continuing to make Mrs. Roosevelt's works available to the world.

My mother's cousin, Suzanne Nédoncelle. During the World War II, she deciphered and distributed messages through unoccupied zones of Paris for the French Resistance. Suzanne was in the process of writing her own book when she died during the war. Her book was lost and never published. Suzanne has been in my thoughts throughout the writing of my book because like her, I try to see and hear messages hidden among words and symbols. I share the publication of this book in her memory.

My aunt, Germaine Rouillard, who envisioned the influence of my work long before I understood that I could accomplish it.

The extraordinary teachers and staff members from the Public Schools of Springfield Massachusetts with whom I worked for many years. These educators are passionate about their work and care deeply about the children and the families they serve.

Judith Solsken and Jerri Willett, Professors Emeritae of Language Literacy and Culture of the School of Education, from the University of Massachusetts, Amherst. For many years, Judy, Jerri and I worked together as a research and teaching team. We would often ponder the writing of a single sentence for an extended period of time. When writing on my own, I often ask myself, "How would Judy and Jerri think we should say this?"

Sonia Nieto, Professor Emerita of Language Literacy and Culture of the School of Education, University of Massachusetts, Amherst, for her encouragement in writing this book.

Rudine Sims Bishop, Professor Emeritus of Education, The Ohio State University, formerly from the University of Massachusetts, Amherst for her knowledge and insight that started me on the road to writing this book .

Femi S. Otulaja, Ph. D., Academic Staff Development Advisor, Faculty of Science, University of Witwatersand, Braamfontein, South Africa who helped me contact educators at the Molteno Institute for Language and Literacy and bridge the distance between Cape Cod and Braamfontein.

Johnson Gaitha from United Nations Publications for his patient assistance in helping me acquire permission to include UN documents in this book.

Cindy Cullen, Assistant Director of the Dennis Massachusetts Public Library, who procured documents for me from databases and university, college, municipal libraries through the Massachusetts Library System (MLS). The MLS promotes equitable access to excellent library services and resources for all who live, work, or study in Massachusetts.

Librarians Jennifer Klump of Education Northwest, Portland, Oregon and Fiona Gray of the National Library of New Zealand.

My brother-in-law Andrew Arnold whose accomplishments taught me that it takes time to appreciate the power and influence of innovators. In 2001, Andy and his team from Kodak won a technical Emmy for an invention they had created in 1984. The project was the 8mm camcorder (video camera and associated electronics in one compact—for 1984—package, something we take for granted today). The invention of this compact handheld video camera changed the way we film home movies. The team did not receive recognition until 17 years later, however, when the effect of the compact camcorder on the home movie industry was evident. Andy's work helped me realize the importance of not just moving on to the next "big thing," but of thinking about the power of integrating valuable ideas from the past with current research and practices.

The Reverend Prince Wreh, Director of the Keenan Institute in Monrovia, Liberia for his support and encouragement.

Jackie and Steve Keenan, Co-Founders of the Keenan Institute, for their careful editing of the book and insights about dynamics of African families and communities. To their colleague Barbara Gibson for her encouragement.

The following individuals, foundations, and information sources for their assistance and contributions: Mark Liberman, Noam Chomsky, Peter Bailey, Donald Kommers, Anne Fernald, Margaret Phinney, Stephen Krashen, David Crystal, Julia Parish-Morris, Grover "Russ" Whitehurst, Hal Varian, Matt Kam, Dorothy M. Neddermeyer Ph. D., Linda Fredericks, Lucia Quiñonez Sumner, Aron Goldman, James Gleason, Kelly Jane Doyle, Jean Canosa Albano, Heidi Hayes Jacobs, Maya Pines, The Schott Foundation for Public Education, The Pew Foundation, The Joan Ganz Cooney Foundation at Sesame Street Workshop, Strategies for Children; Common Sense Media; Henry J. Kaiser Family Foundation, edutopia, What IS MY IP Address.com, www.gmsouthafricafoundation.com, Historyplace .com., newlearningonline.com., and UnitedStatesHistory.com.

Lynn Hallowell who participated in a course I taught for the Springfield Parent Academy. Lynn is an extraordinary educator, grandmother, reader, and friend.

Merri Boone who gave me the "Small Places" poster.

All of my Cape Cod and western Massachusetts friends.

My three wonderful sisters, Catherine Marek, Suzanne Scorzafava, and Mary Arnold for their support throughout the writing of this book.

My nephew, P.J. Scorzafava for his assistance and contributions.

My daughter-in-law Kristin Rivnyak Wilson whose encouraging words helped me to “stay the course.” My son, Noah Wilson, who always encourages me to say what I can say, and believes that I will say it well.

My husband, John Keenan, who made this book project possible. His countless readings, suggestions, and edits greatly improved my writing. His technical expertise rescued me from the brink of disaster several times. His faith in me kept the project going. John’s infinite store of patience, kindness, and understanding enabled me to complete what he has come to call an “ambitious” book.

INTRODUCTION

THE PURPOSE OF THIS BOOK

Nearly seventy years ago, Eleanor Roosevelt, who would become the Chair of the Human Rights Commission that wrote the Universal Declaration of Human Rights, stated, "One of the best ways of enslaving people is to keep them from education and thus make it impossible for them to understand what is going on in the world as a whole" (Roosevelt, 2001, p. 79).[1] Eleanor Roosevelt believed that human rights begin, "in small places, close to home" (Roosevelt, 1958a). Five decades later, reflecting on the future of human rights, law professor and author Mary Ann Glendon said, "...what will be decisive is whether or not sufficient numbers of men and women in 'small places, close to home' can imagine, and then begin to live, the reality of freedom, solidarity, and peace" (Glendon, 2001, p. 241).[2] In his second inaugural address, President Obama spoke of "a little girl born into the bleakest poverty who knows she has the same chance to succeed as anyone else..." (Obama B., 2013).

PEOPLE ARE BEGINNING TO IMAGINE

The intention of this book is to help empower people from small places across the world as they envision literacy as their human right, so they can recognize and use their own resources to attain it, live richer lives because of it, and pass it on the future generations. Declaring that literacy is a human right is not enough to make it a reality. My original vision was that this book would be written mainly for teachers. It will be of value to teachers, teacher educators, early childhood teachers, special education teachers, and teachers of children who speak multiple languages, and it can generate conversation and action across the education community. But this book is not written solely for people who run programs outside the home.

The audience for this book can extend beyond the teaching and care-provider profession. Literacy evolves across a lifetime, therefore, supporting literacy is not the sole responsibility or privilege of teachers or early care-providers. The information in this book is also relevant for parents and caregivers, out-of-school-time providers, members of faith-based organizations, and other people who support families and influence the lives of children every day in both formal and informal settings. Policy makers at all levels, political leaders, human rights advocates, philanthropists, and those who work with children in poverty also make up the audience for this book.

The word "poverty" as used in this book is drawn from the work of linguist and educational researcher, Stephen Krashen, and refers to the condition of having an "inadequate diet, lack of health care, and lack of access to books..." Like Krashen, I believe that "The best teaching in the world has little effect when children are hungry, undernourished, ill, and have little or nothing to read" (Krashen S., 2014,

p. 1). I use the word *books* in the broad sense to refer to texts in a variety of formats and other sources of knowledge.

This book does not attempt to determine what should constitute specific language and literacy practices for people in various parts of the world. These practices function differently according to community and cultural norms and values. In this book, literacy is viewed as a "social practice, not simply a technical and neutral skill." Literacy is seen as always embedded in socially constructed principles. This book takes a "culturally sensitive view of literacy practices as they vary from one context to another." It acknowledges, "The ways in which people address reading and writing are themselves rooted in conceptions of knowledge, identity and being" (Street, 2005, p. 13). Members of communities, within their own social context, determine how language and literacies are meaningful for them.

My book invites people to share knowledge and practices from both the past and present, so that they can continue to define what literacy means. It can serve as a catalyst for conversations about similarities, strengths—both acknowledged and hidden— and differences within and across families and communities. Furthermore, the scope of peoples' educational needs and "how they should be met will vary with individual countries and cultures, and inevitably changes with the passage of time" (World Conference on Education, 1990). Because of these variations, a spectrum of literacies from traditional to new literacies is explored in this book.

The literacy theory and practices in this book grow out of the work of Brazilian educator Paulo Freire's with UNESCO. They also align with the Critical Discourse Analysis (CDA) that has roots in "critical social theory, critical linguistics, sociocultural studies, and critical pedagogy." CDA "includes a set of approaches that emphasize a dialectic process for investigating power relations and how they are constituted through discourse practices" (Rogers & Schaenen, 2014, p. 122).[3] In particular, CDA encompasses the following:

- An interest in the properties of actual language by real language users
- A study of action an interaction among language users
- An extension to non-verbal aspects of interaction and communication including gestures, images, film, the internet, and multimedia
- The study of the contexts of language use (social, cultural, situated, and cognitive) (Wodak & Meyer, 2009, p. 2)

Critical Discourse Analysis focuses on units of language that are larger than isolated words and sentences, including conversations, speech acts or communicative events. Areas of focus include turn taking, expressions of politeness, topics, and other aspects of texts and discourse (Wodak & Meyer, 2009). A recent review of the literature on CDA examines 76 literacy-focused empirical studies and theoretical papers published between 2004 and 2012. The studies took place on six continents. They examine student identity; teacher identity; racism, ethnicity, and diversity; testing, standards, and commerce; social class; and families and empowerment.

(Rogers & Schaenen, 2014). Because this book explores the topic of literacy as a universal human right, many of these topics are addressed and references to the work of several critical discourse analysis researchers are included.

The researchers and educators whose work is described here come from different times and places. The research cited spans several decades. Some of the research presented comes from educators from Australia, New Zealand, and the UK from the 1970's to the 1990's. Like the work of Eleanor Roosevelt and Paulo Freire, their work is timeless. They are innovators because their work has spread and has influence in many parts of the world over time. Some of the innovators and the approaches presented here will be familiar to readers, others are less-known. This book does not endeavor to present a definitive picture of those who engaged in literacy work during the past several decades, but each of the educators included here conducted research or developed curriculum and practices that were drawn from the essence of children's lives—from their personal and cultural background. They include Don Holdaway, John Dwyer, Betty Murray, Rose Duffy, Sylvia Ashton-Warner, Vivian Gussin Paley, Carol Chomsky, Carolyn Burke, and Virginia Woodward. All of these educators honor a child's history of language and literacy and mine them as the basis for future learning. All honor children's dignity, therefore, they contribute to the realization of literacy as a human right.

This book is not simply a means of paying homage to educators, however. It also makes a significant connection that reveals the work of these educators as both truly innovative and highly relevant for teaching and learning today and in the future. Namely, the research and the ways of engaging with children that these educators conceived are highly compatible with what neuroscientists are now discovering about the brain.

In addition to the work of these innovators, the book also presents work by contemporary scholars, such as Patricia Edwards, Alfred Tatum, Janice Hale, Lisa Delpit. The work of some of the researchers including Sonia Nieto, Brian Cambourne, Jerome Harste, Judith Wells Lindfors, and Stephen Krashen has spanned several decades.

I also include notes and findings from my own research. The names of children who participated in my studies are pseudonyms. The only exception is my son Noah's name. Throughout the book, I use the words *child, children, citizens, or people* as often as possible in recognition of both genders. In quotations from other authors, I maintain original gender references and historic terms. Similarly, I maintain spellings of words as written originally by the authors.

Descriptions of UNESCO's Education for All (EFA) goals, the UN Millennium Goals, and the draft of the synthesis report of UN Secretary General, Ban Ki-moon, on the post-2015 sustainable development agenda are also included in this book. Information from EFA Global Monitoring Reports on the progress of the EFA goals, including recommendations for teaching and learning that continue to advance that right for future generations, are also presented.

From Small Places: Toward the Realization of Literacy as a Human Right has fourteen chapters, and is divided into four parts. Each part explores a critical concept that leads to the realization of literacy as a human right. These concepts, described below, are mutually dependent. The chapters in this book move from meeting rooms in Paris, where the Universal Declaration of Human Rights was drafted, to the space between a parent and infant where eyes connect, first words pass, and literacy as a human right begins.

THE PLAN OF THIS BOOK

Part 1—History of Literacy as a Human Right
Chapters 1–3
Critical Concept—Literacy is a human right

The first part of this book focuses on literacy as a human right in itself and a means of achieving all other rights. It begins with Eleanor Roosevelt's role as the Chair of the Human Rights Commission and the writing of the Universal Declaration of Human Rights in 1947 and 1948. These chapters introduce the Declaration and describe the process of the development of education as a human right. Reasons behind the ideas embodied in the Declaration, the struggles and successes of its architects, and ideas for future work, drawn from the nearly impossible task of writing the Declaration, are included here. The ideas are then woven throughout this book.

This part also explores how the Declaration's original goal of providing children with a basic education beginning at age six evolved into fostering literacy as a human right. Covenants, summits, and meetings are described here, including work of the International Symposium for Literacy in Persepolis, Iran, that was sponsored by UNESCO in September of 1975, and influenced by Freire. Here, literacy was viewed as a contribution to the liberation of people and their development. As the Declaration of Persepolis[4] states, literacy "creates the conditions for the acquisition of a critical consciousness of the contradictions of society" and "of its aims." It also stimulates a person's "initiative" and "participation in the creation of projects capable of acting upon the world, of transforming it, and of defining the aims of an authentic human development." Literacy "should open the way to a mastery of techniques and human relations. Literacy is not an end in itself. It is a fundamental human right" (International Symposium for Literacy, 1975).

The information about the Education for All (EFA) goals and the UN Millennium goals is also included in this part.

It is important to note that education is a crucial component of documents other than the Universal Declaration of Human Rights, including the Refugee Convention and related Protocols, the Geneva Conventions, and the Guiding Principles on International Displacement (Women's Commission for Refugee Women and Children). This book, however, focuses on the evolution of literacy as a human right stemming from the Declaration.

Part 2—Barriers to the Realization of Literacy as a Human Right
Chapters 4–5
Critical Concept—The underestimation of children's language and literacy capabilities close down the opportunities for them to succeed in school and in life.

Through the lens of Freire's concept of banking education, barriers that impede the realization of education as a human right are explored in this part. These barriers include the perpetuation of the pedagogy of poverty, pathologizing the language of children who are monetarily poor, and the academicization of curriculum for even the youngest children. Both research and practices that underestimate children's language and learning capabilities and marginalize poor children are explored here. By design, this book begins within my own small place, so initial examples that I cite come from the U.S. I then pair many examples with similar examples from other places in the world.

Part 3—Research that Builds on Strengths and Leads to the Realization of Literacy as a Human Right
Chapters 6–10
Critical Concept—Research from the fields of education and neuroscience affirms the value of talking, storytelling, singing, reading and writing with young children as ways of supporting language and literacy development, and honoring children's inherent dignity and right to become literate citizens.

The evolution of literacy as a human right has come about in part because, in the past sixty-five years, research has shown that extraordinary cognitive growth takes place between birth and age six. Following Freirean theory, these chapters emphasize the importance of continually recognizing, valuing, and building upon children's strengths—their thoughts, language, experiences, memories and literacy. Understandings about how the brain, language, writing, and reading develop are explored in this part. Ways that people support the development of language and literacy within their own communities at little or no cost are also described here. These ways include talking, storytelling, music, reading and writing.

Many others books have been written on each of the individual subjects explored in this book. These books can provide readers with further information. The purpose of the chapters in this book is to show that the development of the brain, language, reading, and writing are interconnected. These chapters contribute to the conversation about language, literacy, and children's capabilities, and support the broader goal of endorsing and informing citizens who strive to help children toward the realization of literacy as a human right. People throughout the world engage children in many of these ways, regardless of the circumstances of their lives or the languages they speak. It is essential that these ordinary ways are seen as valid and valuable means of supporting language and literacy development, and children's dignity and freedom. These ways are simple, timeless, and right in front of us, but they are often overlooked and undervalued. Not all occur in every community. Although adults may not read or write themselves, they still share in many of these ways of advancing children's language and literacy.

Part 4—Practices and Initiatives that Support the Realization of Literacy as a Human Right
Chapters 11–14
Critical Concept—Initiatives that build upon ways of engaging with children and that tap their knowledge of language and literacy can lead to the achievement of literacy as a human right and enhance the lives of citizens and the future of entire communities.

The last part of the book describes community-based literacy practices and initiatives that recognize and build upon learners' language and literacy capabilities. Work within small classroom communities and larger district or country-wide projects are discussed. The use of these initiatives extends over the past five decades, but as people throughout the world focus on the idea that learning begins at birth, there is a need for a resurgence of interest in them today. They were designed by or have grown out of the approaches of the literacy innovators mentioned earlier in this chapter. They are compatible with current brain research. Successful initiatives are presented that support literacy learners who live in challenging environments where funding is scarce, few materials are available, and other approaches have failed. These initiatives reflect the dignitarian rights found in the Universal Declaration of Human Rights. They are rooted in the learner's language and cultural practices, bind the community together, and foster reciprocity. The initiatives also draw on local funds of knowledge, suit local conditions, rely on the use of the learner's own language, develop leadership strengths, reduce rote learning, and foster respect for the learner.

Much of the research and many of the initiatives described in this book began in Australia, New Zealand, and the UK. Some of the information included in this book originated in primary schools, therefore, it focuses mainly on young children. But the information in the book is intended be used in settings beyond schools, and some readers will find support for adolescent and adult learners as well. Two of the initiatives examined in this part, the Concentrated Language Encounter and Breakthrough to Literacy, have gone to scale. These practices have been successful in, sustained by, and adopted throughout developing countries. Some of the nations where these literacy initiatives are taking place include the Philippines, Nepal, India, Egypt, Pakistan, Bangladesh, Laos, Cambodia, Turkey, several Pacific Island countries, and several African countries. Developed nations can take lessons from these successful initiatives as well.

These community-wide efforts promote not only equity and compassion in human relations and acceptance of others, but they also point toward ways that people of the world can learn together. The initiatives described here are rooted in communication, conversation, and collaboration and therefore they integrate well with twenty-first century technologies. This part ends with a description of new literacies that people are taking up today. These literacies are based in new technologies that extend beyond print literacy. These technologies have the potential to support a global literacy community.

WORKING TOWARD NEW UNDERSTANDINGS

Although politicians and others periodically claim that "lack of literacy is the cause of all that ails us and its widespread access will be the solution," there is no clear proof that literacy education could possibly eradicate poverty or unemployment. However, "there is evidence that literacy education can make a substantial contribution to transforming the social distribution of knowledge, discourse, and, with these, real economic and social capital among specific communities, groups, and individuals" (Carrington & Luke, 1997).[5] There are no quick fixes or magic bullets. The task of creating literate communities is lifelong work that demands everyone's time, understandings, reflection, commitment, and willingness to bring about change and continually refine ideas.

The framers of the Declaration recognized that people first come to know and exercise their rights in small places. This book focuses on how the Declaration supports literacy as a human right in these small places.

NOTES

1 From MY DAY: THE BEST OF ELEANOR ROOSEVELT'S ACCLAIMED NEWSPAPER COLUMNS 1936–1962 by Eleanor Roosevelt. Copyright © 2001 by David Emblidge. Reprinted with permission of Nancy Roosevelt Ireland. All rights reserved.

2 Excerpts from A WORLD MADE NEW: ELEANOR ROOSEVELT AND THE UNIVERSAL DECLARATION OF HUMAN RIGHTS by Mary Ann Glendon, copyright © 2001 by Mary Ann Glendon. Used by permission of Random House, an imprint and Random House LLC. All rights reserved. Any third party use of this material, outside of this publication, is prohibited. Interested parties must apply directly to Random House LLC for permission.

3 From Critical Discourse Analysis in Literacy Education: A Review of the Literature in *Reading Research Quarterly*, 49(1) pp. 121–143. doi:10.1002/rrq.61. Copyright © 2013 International Reading Association. Reprinted with permission of John Wiley & Sons Ltd.

4 The DECLARATION OF PERSEPOLIS from the International Symposium for Literacy, UNESCO. Copyright ©1975 United Nations. Reprinted with permission of the United Nations.

5 From Literacy and Bourdieu's sociological theory: A reframing by Vicki Carrington and Allan Luke. In LANGUAGE AND EDUCATION, v11 n2, 1997. Reprinted with permission of the publisher (Taylor & Francis Ltd, http://www.tandfonline.com).

PART 1

HISTORY AND THEORY OF LITERACY AS A HUMAN RIGHT

CHAPTER 1

WHY A HUMAN RIGHTS PERSPECTIVE?

I see disappointment and even outrage. And I believe that out of this frustration hope and action can emerge. —Former Minnesota Senator Paul D. Wellstone, Before the Grassroots Training Seminar at Iowa State, July 11, 1998

HONORING HUMAN DIGNITY

Nicholas Burnett, former Assistant Director-General for Education at UNESCO, describes the global economic devastation that swept across the world in recent years as the worst since the Great Depression. Burnett advises, however, that we should be cautious in drawing parallels to the depression of the 1930's. He believes that this more recent crisis "erupted in a very different world – a globalized world that leaves no country untouched" (Burnett, 2009, p. 4).[1] He notes that when economic crises occur, "Poverty increases and the most vulnerable are hardest hit. Child mortality and malnutrition rise" (Burnett, 2009, p. 5).

Pauline Rose, former Director of the Education for All Global Monitoring Report, raises the concern that global economic slowdown can result in increased job loss, lower pay, and fewer opportunities for generating income. It is also possible that steps taken toward reducing poverty will lag or reverse. When government budgets become overburdened, Rose predicts, "spending in health care and education could be an early casualty" (Rose, 2009, p. 5).[2]

Burnett, reiterating the ideas of the framers of the Universal Declaration of Human Rights, states, "Today's world is built on the ruins of the Second World War and on the conviction that international cooperation and understanding are a defence against extremist ideologies, oppression and tyranny." He also points out that "the world is built on the conviction, in the words of the 1948 Universal Declaration of Human Rights, that '*all human beings are born free and equal in dignity and rights*.' The Declaration establishes education as one of these fundamental rights." He emphasizes, "Investing in education and training is essential to economic recovery" (Burnett, 2009, p. 4).

The Universal Declaration of Human Rights is comprised of thirty articles that focus on civil, political, cultural and social rights. It is intended to be read "as a whole," so that its vision of liberty remains inseparable from its call to social responsibility. This vision was inspired in part by Franklin Roosevelt's famous "four freedoms"—freedom of speech and belief, freedom from fear and want (Glendon, 2001, p. xviii).

Within the present climate of economic threat and social inequity, we are in danger of viewing education and literacy as primarily economic rights. As Glendon cautions:

> The fact that nations and interest groups increasingly seek to cast their agendas or justify their actions in terms of human rights is one measure of the success of the human rights idea… Yet the more the Declaration is pulled apart and politicized, the higher the risk that protection of human rights will become a pretext for imposing the will of the strong by armed intervention or economic pressure. (Glendon, 2001, p. xviii)

At times, an economic perspective can overshadow a human rights perspective.

In his book about the establishment of the Harlem Children's Zone, *Whatever It Takes*, Paul Tough reports on the views of economist James Heckman. According to Heckman:

> … pleas to help solve the problems of disadvantaged families are usually cast "as a question of fairness or social justice." But that's not his argument, he says. He wants instead to make his case on "productivity grounds" –a less heart-stirring angle, perhaps, but for Heckman a politically persuasive one. Yes, he argues, the nation will become more just and equitable if poor children have more opportunities for success—but it will also become wealthier, spending less on welfare and crime prevention and drug treatment and collecting more in taxes from the workers who otherwise might never find a job. (Tough, 2008, p. 193)[3]

Opportunities for success, however, have to be continual. Impressive achievements have been gained by the Harlem Children's Zone, but when it appeared that their middle school students were not going to make the projected gains for standardized assessments, there was a decision to suspend the middle school and send the present students elsewhere. As Tough reports, the principal of the school at that time stated:

> One way to interpret this is we're getting rid of the riffraff so we can move forward. That's how I feel. They were a cancer on the whole school. But you don't want to communicate that to the parents. So, yeah, 'We failed your child.' A lot of people failed the child. The parents failed the child, the child failed the child, and so did we, to a certain extent. (Tough, 2008, p. 249)

Tough also reports that he spoke to one of the school board members who described two other board members as:

> … famously successful stock pickers.And the decision to cut the school's losses and send off the eighth grade displayed a 'very typical trader's instinct.' He explained what he meant. 'When a trader makes a bet on a commodity, and the trader starts losing money, then he or she closes the bet out.' (Tough, 2008, p. 251)

Tough also explains how one board member's profession influenced his decisions:

> [His] history as a marketer also played into his thinking on the board's decision. Pulling back the way they had done looked bad, he admitted. But if the board hadn't trimmed the sails, and a year later the school was still in trouble, it could have been a disaster for the agency's public profile.

Tough quotes the board member:

> … If we had continued for another year and were unable to show dramatic progress, then the middle school would have been placed in a failing bucket. Not failure, but a failing bucket. Which would have made it extremely difficult for us, because it would have affected the Harlem Children's Zone brand, and that is a very important brand to protect. (Tough, 2008, p. 251)

Ironically, after the decision to close the middle school was made, the official scores on the state English and math assessments showed that the students had achieved "significant improvement over the previous year" in reading. In math, "they showed an improvement that was downright startling." The percentage of students in the class who scored on grade level in math rose from 34% the previous year to 70% in the eighth grade year (Tough, 2008, p. 250).

Curtailing any child's education to preserve a brand is unconscionable. Human beings are neither a cancer nor a commodity. They are not riffraff. Categorizing people in these ways, marginalizes and silences them, and ultimately makes them nearly invisible. Engagement with people requires us to see their faces, hear each their voices, listen to their stories, and acknowledge their ideas. When we treat people with dignity, we cannot deny their existence. We cannot deny their rights. These arguments, too, deserve to be regarded as politically persuasive.

Viewing education and literacy as human rights are not just heart stirring or "soft" notions, and should not be dismissed as such. Assuring that "every student has access to the 'opportunity to learn pipeline' is both a human right and a civil right that must be protected by federal, state, and local agencies" (The Schott Foundation for Public Education, 2012, p. 49). The concept of education as a human right rose out of the ashes of World War II. The rights drafted for the Universal Declaration of Human Rights resulted from the study of nearly two hundred years of rights documents. (Glendon, 2001). They pertain to everyone in the world. Article 26 of the Declaration states, "Everyone has the right to education" (UN General Assembly, 1948).

"Today, the aim remains unchanged: to give everyone the chance to learn and benefit from basic education – not as an accident of circumstance, nor as a privilege, but as a RIGHT" (UNESCO-Education, 2010). This right is universal. It is not only for those who win a seat in a school through a lottery, or for those of particular political, religious, or other persuasions. The right to an education applies to girls and boys equally. It is not limited by the color of one's skin. This book is based on the premise that literacy is a human right, a refinement of the right to a basic education that was recognized in the Universal Declaration of Human Rights of 1948. Achieving that right through human engagement lies at the heart of this book.

Furthermore, this book views the Declaration as a "geodesic dome of interlocking principles" (Glendon, 2001, p. xx) with the right to education as an entry way, or essential means, for realizing other human rights. Education makes all other rights, including economic rights, possible. Eleanor Roosevelt was in favor of "the inclusion of economic and social rights in the Declaration, for no personal liberty could exist without economic security and independence" (Black A., 2007, p. 808). At the same time, she believed, "This declaration is based upon the spiritual fact that man must have freedom in which to develop his full stature and through common effort to raise the level of human dignity" (Roosevelt, 1948).

The Committee on Economic, Social and Cultural Rights (CESCR) publishes its interpretation of the content of human rights provisions in the form of general comments on thematic issues. In General Comment Number 13, the CESCR describes not only the power of education to fight poverty and attain other rights, but also the profound human significance of education to enlighten the mind. The first paragraph of the comment reads:

> Education is both a human right in itself and an indispensable means of realizing other human rights. As an empowerment right, education is the primary vehicle by which economically and socially marginalized adults and children can lift themselves out of poverty and obtain the means to participate fully in their communities. Education has a vital role in empowering women, safeguarding children from exploitative and hazardous labour and sexual exploitation, promoting human rights and democracy, protecting the environment, and controlling population growth. Increasingly, education is recognized as one of the best financial investments States can make. But the importance of education is not just practical: A well-educated, enlightened and active mind, able to wander freely and widely, is one of the joys and rewards of human existence. (Committee on Econonic Social and Cultural Rights, 1999)[4]

The realization of literacy as a human right is a daunting task. Yet, while it is difficult to achieve, it is not impossible. As Eleanor Roosevelt wrote:

> …the moment a child enters the world, he is conditioned by his surroundings and that, therefore, there is inequality of opportunity and of development. Therefore, we as individuals should always try to recognize the actual worth of a human being as such and, where opportunities have not been present, make allowances and work toward a world where every individual may have the chance to develop his abilities to the greatest possible extent. (Roosevelt, 1946, p. 120)[5]

Globally, there are still 743 million adults who do not have basic literacy skills (UNESCO, 2013/4, p. 4).[6] "Clearly, refugees and internally displaced people face major barriers to education. The UN reports that over 43 million people have been displaced mostly by armed conflict, though the actual number is probably far higher" (UNESCO, 2010, p. 16).[7] But education provides an asset—sometimes the only asset that people affected by conflict can carry with them. As a forty-year-old woman who fled from Darfur to Chad in 2004 said:

> We had to leave behind all of our possessions. The only thing we could bring with us is what we have in our heads, what we have been taught—our education. Education is the only thing that cannot be taken from us and upon which we can build a better life for our children. (Women's Commission for Refugee Women and Children)

In October of 2009, in the Democratic Republic of the Congo, militias forced 100,000 people, including school children, to flee across the Ubangui River, the border between their country and the Congo. The children had to leave their schooling—and life as they knew it—behind. The 2011 EFA Global Monitoring Report *The Hidden Crisis: Armed Conflict and Education* describes the "striking demonstration of human resilience in the face of adversity" that these people have demonstrated:

> Authorities in the Congo have been able to provide little support. But along the river, village committees have re-established themselves, and getting children back to school is a major priority. With the help of the United Nations High Commission for Refugees (UNHCR), they are beginning to hire teachers. 'We've asked the teachers to cram as much as possible into the lessons to allow us to make up for lost time,' a head teacher commented. At least seventy-five schools have been created along the Ubangui River, from preschool to the secondary level. (IRIN 2010) in (UNESCO, 2010)

The teachers in these schools persevere even though they may be unpaid. They have to "improvise with boards nailed to a tree. There's not a book in sight." One teacher says, "The lack of teaching materials is causing us a problem" (UNESCO, 2010, p. 200).

The 2011 Global Monitoring Report (UNESCO, 2010, pp. 225–226) also states that Liberia has undertaken a major effort to recover its education after years of conflict. By the end of the fourteen-year civil war there in 2003, the net enrollment ratio in primary school was just 35%. At least two generations of youth had been denied an education. In Liberia, however, the post-conflict government, with the support of UNICEF and other organizations, designed an accelerated learning program that enabled children who had lost at least two years of schooling to complete a full primary cycle in three years instead of six. The students received a certificate for completing the program and were eligible to go to seventh grade in a regular school. Within six years, over 75,000 students had been served by the program (Liberia & UN, 2004; Nkutu, Bang, & Tooman, 2010).

The Reverend Prince Wreh is an Episcopal Parish Priest, Executive Director of the Keenan Institute, and a Professor at Cuttington University in Monrovia, Liberia. He describes the importance of education in this way:

> We …want to thank you for sharing our conviction that education is, indeed, potential power which enables the down-trodden to see their condition and do something about it in a positive way. No wonder why human history is so replete with stories of how the dominant and the privileged group of every society jealously protected education and denied it to the underprivileged, under the pretense that the marginalized are morally and intellectually unfit!
>
> Perhaps it is important to share with you how our dream to educate our people, especially the marginalized, began to germinate in the depth of our soul. For some of us who began our life struggle from the lowest rung of society, we share the conviction that if we must ever be grateful to those whose effort and resources brought us thus far, it is our bounding obligation to maintain the very bridge (education) that we used to cross. We believe that education, in addition to faith in God, is one of the fundamental bridges which enable the disinherited to gain their dignity and true image, and be able to throw off the false identity fashioned for them by their society. (Wreh, 2011)

In December of 2008, the occasion of the marking of the 60th Anniversary of the Universal Declaration of Human Rights, a conference entitled *Bringing Human Rights Home* was held at Hyde Park, New York, the former home of Franklin and Eleanor Roosevelt. The work of the conference was based on the premise that Americans often view human rights as issues that pertain to other countries. The task at this conference was to lift the veil on this mistaken belief, and show how many domestic and foreign policy challenges and opportunities faced in the U.S. are in fact human rights issues. The challenge was put forth to revisit the Declaration and the practices that result from it to make better our world today (Franklin and Eleanor Roosevelt Institute, 2008).

A major reason for revisiting the Declaration is that access to education and literacy is not equitable in America today. Nicholas Kristof in a column entitled *Occupy the Classroom* in the NY Times describes two "common" threads in reporting about the education of impoverished students in "New York City or in Sierra Leone." First, "a good education tends to be the most reliable escalator out of poverty." Second, "whether in America or Africa, disadvantaged kids often don't get a chance to board that escalator" (Kristof, 2011).[8]

EVIDENCE OF INEQUALITY

Inequality is a worldwide problem that is evident in many small places. As noted above, the "small place" I come from is Springfield, Massachusetts, a New England industrial city. The written word is an important part of the fabric of Springfield. The G. & C. Merriam Dictionary Company was founded here in 1831. In the early 1900's, Andrew Carnegie donated $240,000 toward the construction of the Springfield Central Library. Theodore Geisel, who is better known as Dr. Seuss, was born and raised here. Jim Trelease, well-known author of the Read-Aloud Handbook, also formerly lived in Springfield.

Among third graders from low-income families, in Springfield in 2014, 63% of grade 3 students tested below proficient in reading. The percentages of students in subgroups who were not proficient are shown in the following chart:

Low income—63%
ELL —69%
Students with disabilites—79%
Hispanic students—66%
African American students—62%
White students—35%
Asian students—32%

(2014 MCAS Results by Subgroup by Grade and Subject, 2014)

Massachusetts is recognized as a national leader in education, but 43% of the state's third graders scored below proficient on the 2014 Massachusetts Comprehensive Assessment System (MCAS) reading test (Massachusetts Department of Elementary and Secondary Education, 2014). Massachusetts also has a wide achievement gap. Among third graders from low income families, 61% scored below proficient in reading, according to the 2014 MCAS.

The consequences of reading failure can be severe. Margaret Blood, president and founder of Strategies for Children, states, "three-quarters of children who have trouble with reading in third grade will continue to struggle in school, substantially reducing their chances of graduating from high school, or pursuing the higher education essential to our knowledge-based economy" (Sege, 2011). National statistics support Margaret Blood's statement. National Assessment of Educational Progress (NAEP) data from 2013 reported by The Schott Foundation for Public Education show that by grade 8, only 12% of Black males and 17% of Latino males were proficient in reading, as compared to 38% of White, non-Latino males (The Schott Foundation for Public Education, 2012, p. 37).

Reaching "proficiency" levels on state or national tests, however, "does not guarantee success in college or the workforce." This fact is "proven by both the rates of incoming college freshmen who need remediation, and the underpreparedness of new college graduates for the literacy demands in the workplace" (Greene & Winters, 2005) in (Lesaux, 2010, p. i).

Furthermore, low academic achievement is not unique to Springfield. Researchers have uncovered several areas of inequity that exist in cities across the nation. In his book, *Teaching Reading to Black Adolescent Males: Closing the Achievement Gap*, Alfred Tatum writes that Black males, particularly those who are learning to read amid turmoil, can reap great benefit from increased reading achievement and literacy development, including "higher levels of college enrollment, lower levels of unemployment, a reduction in violent crime, and lower incarceration rates." He adds, however, that these young men "do not embrace the idea that text can transform their world, because there are too few examples in their neighborhoods to suggest this can be true" (Tatum A., 2005, p. 15).[9]

Nearly two-thirds of low-income families in the U.S. do not own any books for their children. Recent data show that in the U.S., "while the ratio of books to children in middle-income neighborhoods is approximately 13 books per child, the ratio in low-income neighborhoods is 1 book per 300 children" (Edwards P., 2011, p. 16).

Stephen Krashen makes a strong case for promoting quality libraries. He contends that better libraries result in increased reading achievement because reading more helps children become better readers (Krashen S., 2004), and libraries are major sources for finding books (Krashen, Lee, & McQuillan, 2008). He further explains that numerous studies have shown that library quality (number of books available or books per student) is related to reading achievement at the state level (Lance, 2004), national level (McQuillan, 1998) and international level (Elley, 1992; Krashen, Lee, & McQuillan, 2008). He notes that even when researchers control for the effects of poverty, these results are maintained (Krashen, 2008). He adds, "Children of poverty have very few books at home, live in neighborhoods with few bookstores and inferior public libraries, and attend schools with inferior classroom and school libraries" (Krashen S., 2014, p. 3).

The library is often the only source of books for low-income children, however, it is not likely that these children have access to quality libraries (Smith, Constantino, & Krashen, 1996; Di Loreto & Tse, 1999; Duke N., 2000a; Neuman & Celano, 2001) in (Krashen, 2008). Krashen contends that children of poverty have low reading test scores because they have limited access to books. When access is supplied in the form of libraries, these children read about as well as children from more affluent families (Krashen S., 2014).

Researcher Nell Duke noted a dearth of informational texts in primary classrooms and the limited instruction or activities with informational literacy materials. In addition to including informational text in the classroom environment, these texts also need to be part of instructional activities. Duke's study of 10 low- and 10 high-SES 1st grade classrooms showed that students spent an average of only 3.6 minutes each day interacting with informational text during classroom written language activities. The mean time per day that the high-SES classrooms spent on informational text was 3.8% of the total time spent with written language. In the low-SES classrooms, the mean time was only 1.9%. Five of the 10 low-SES classrooms did not spend any time with informational texts on the days of observation for the study (Duke N., 2000b).[10]

In low-SES school districts, she found that classroom libraries were smaller than those in high-SES districts. Furthermore, the number of informational texts in these collections was "much smaller" than in the collections of the high-SES schools (Duke N., 2000b, p. 213).

The 2013–2014 EFA Global Monitoring Report, *Teaching and Learning: Achieving Quality for All*, describes the shortage of books in African nations as well.

Views from Small Places

> Teachers need good learning materials, such as textbooks, to be effective... But many students suffer from a very basic problem: they do not have access to textbooks.
>
> In the United Republic of Tanzania, only 3.5% of all grade 6 pupils had sole use of a reading textbook [SACMEQ, 2010].
>
> In Rwanda, where the government target was one textbook for every two pupils, a 2007 study in two-thirds of districts revealed that there were 143 pupils for every Kinyarwanda textbook in grade 1, and 180 pupils for every mathematics textbook. (Read and Bontoux, forthcoming)
>
> In some countries, textbooks are becoming even scarcer. Between 2000 and 2007, Kenya, Malawi and Namibia experienced rapid increases in enrolment, but the availability of textbooks did not keep pace. In Malawi, the percentage students who either had no textbook or had to share with at least two more pupils increased from 28% in 2000 to 63% in 2007.
>
> Factors that limit textbook availability include low priority on teaching and learning inputs in countries' education budgets, high textbook costs and wastage due to wear and tear. (UNESCO, 2013, pp. 87–88)

Access to electronic technology has also been inequitable for low-income children. Social justice scholar Paul Gorski points out that there is a "popular belief that identity-based discrepancies in physical access to computers and the Internet are disappearing" (Gorski P., 2009, p. 352).[11] But in fact they are not. He reports, "economically disadvantaged children and children of color are more likely than their wealthy and white counterparts to live in households without computers and Internet access" (Judge, Puckett, & Cabuk, 2004) in (Gorski P., 2009, p. 353). Furthermore, technologies are often thought of as the "great equalizers," but they are not. He cautions that although it is tempting to assume that technological progress equals social progress, in schools, "It does not." Gorski believes that systemic inequities in educational opportunity and access between the wealthiest and poorest go unaddressed. He states that before we can view "technology from an authentic multicultural education framework," we must "first acknowledge the inequities that exist in our schools" (Gorski P., 2009, p. 349). These inequities will not go away simply by adding computers, Internet access, and other technologies to classrooms.

As we have moved beyond the Internet to new technologies, access to these technologies alone has not made inequities disappear either. As technology has evolved, a growing concern has been that the rich get richer because those who have access to technology capitalize on the innovations, while those who do not fall further behind. The Pew Research Internet Project documents that there is a 7 percentage point gap still exists in the use of the Internet between Whites and Blacks in the United States. Internet use among older Blacks and Blacks who have not attended college is notably less common compared to Whites in these categories (Smith A., 2014).

Although ownership of smartphones narrows the high-speed access gap between Blacks and Whites, it still does not eliminate it entirely. Two major changes have taken place in the use of technology during the past few years. The first is the introduction of broadband, or high-speed internet access adoption. The second is the increase in use of handheld phones. An article entitled, "How You Connect to the World," states that broadband has replaced old dial-up access services for many users. It eliminates the need for a traditional phone line and allows users to connect to email and their works internet in a matter of seconds. It also provides quick access to popular on-line games (What Is My IP Address.com, 2014). In the U.S., Broadband service, for both Blacks and Whites is nearly universal among young adults, the college educated, and those in higher-income households. Overall, however, there is a 12 percentage point gap for broadband adoption gap between Blacks and Whites (Smith A., 2014).

Cellphone use is an example of an area where Blacks outpace Whites. Ninety-two percent of Blacks own a cellphone of some kind. Cellphone ownership for Whites is 90%. Additionally, smartphone ownership by Blacks exceeds that of Whites by 3% (56% to 53%, respectively). Smartphones have high-speed internet access. When considering the numbers of Blacks and Whites that have either a home broadband connection or a smartphone, their use narrows the 12-point gap mentioned above to 8-points. Nevertheless, a gap remains (Smith A., 2014). Furthermore, in nearly every category, adoption of new technologies for low-income (< $30,000) Whites and Blacks lags behind that of their middle ($30,000 to $74,999) and higher ($75,000+) income households (Smith A., 2014).

According to Zero to Eight: Children's Media Use in America 2013, there has been an "explosion" in the use of mobile media platforms and applications among young children since 2011. Access to devices such as an iPad or similar tablet has increased from 8% to 40%. The percentage of children living in households where they have access to any kind of new mobile media device such as a smartphone or tablet has increased from 52% to 75%. Furthermore, the percentage of children who have used these devices for some kind of media activity has nearly doubled, going from 38% in 2011 to 72% in 2013 (Common Sense Media, 2013). However, the report shows that children in low-income households are much less likely to access educational content on mobile devices and computers than higher-income children. A greater percentage of higher-income children access these devices in six out of seven categories surveyed. The categories include: using educational games or programs on a computer; going to educational or informational websites on line; playing educational games on a video game console, educational device, or handheld game player; playing educational games, apps, or activities on a mobile device like a smartphone or tablet; and watching educational shows on TV. Educational television is the only category in which lower- and higher-income children are about as likely to access educational content. Sixty-three percent of low-income children watch educational shows on television, compared to 56% of higher-income children (Common Sense Media, 2013).

Richard Long, the former Director of Government Relations for the International Reading Association, also expresses concern about the inequities in schools. He asserts that the schools of children in areas with few economic resources are basically different from schools in areas with more resources. He refers to the former as schools where children must still rent textbooks. He refers to the latter as schools where every child has a laptop (Long, 2012, p. 27).

Hal Varian, Chief Economist for Google describes the potential of new technologies and the reason why access to them must be equitable:

> The biggest impact on the world will be universal access to all human knowledge. The smartest person in the world currently could well be stuck behind a plow in India or China. Enabling that person—and the millions like him or her—will have a profound impact on the development of the human race. Cheap mobile devices will be available world wide, and educational tools...will be available to everyone. This will have a huge impact on literacy and numeracy and will lead to a more informed and more educated world population. (Varian, 2014)

Carly Shuler, Industry Fellow at the Joan Ganz Cooney Center at Sesame Workshop, explains that the use of handhelds for learning in some developing countries is significantly ahead of that in developed nations. Shuler interviewed Mike Sharples, from the University of Nottingham, founder of the Learn international conference series. Sharples states that differences in history, cultures, and infrastructure are resulting in differing perspectives on mobile learning around the world (Shuler, 2009). In parts of Africa such as Nigeria, where there was virtually no fixed-line infrastructure, mobile learning has employed standard cell phones. They have been used for management, coordination, and administration of learning (Shuler, 2009, p. 16). In the U.S., the initial use of mobile devices centered on small-scale projects in formal environments. In the U.K., their use focused mainly on learning outside of school, or learning that links formal and informal settings.

THE FAILURE TO EDUCATE AFRICAN AMERICAN AND LATINO BOYS

Pedro Noguera, Professor of Education at NYU, cites research (Noguera, 2012) that reveals, "On all of the indicators of academic achievement, educational attainment, and school success, African American and Latino males are noticeably distinguished from other segments of the American population by their consistent clustering at the bottom" (The Schott Foundation for Public Education, 2010). According to The Schott Foundation, in 2012–2013 the high school graduation rate for Black male students in the United States was only 59% compared with 78% for White male students. The graduation rate for Latino males was 65%. Furthermore, there is a 21% gap between the number of Black and White non-Latino males who graduated during those years (The Schott Foundation for Pubic Education, 2015, p. 7).

Over fifty years ago, Eleanor Roosevelt wrote, "If we do not pay for children in good schools, then we are going to pay for them in prisons…" (Roosevelt, 2001, p. 262). Tragically, her prediction has become reality.

Patricia Edwards, Gwendolyn Thompson McMillon, and Jennifer Turner co-authors of *Change is Gonna Come: Transforming Literacy Education for African American Students* point out that there are more Black males "in prison than in college" (Edwards, Thompson McMillon, & Turner, 2008, p. 35). [12] America is home to 5% of the world's population, but we incarcerate 25% of the world's prisoners. Ten years of data from 1997–2008 shows that by age 23 nearly 50% of Black males in America have been arrested, while the arrest rate for Hispanic males is 44% and 38% for White males (Riggs, 2014).

Other researchers argue that African American youth are in reality "de-educated" (Saddler, 2005) in schools, and…"are being systematically excluded from the education system and/or systematically destroyed within that system" (Edwards, Thompson McMillon, & Turner, 2008, p. 34). The Children's Defense Fund describes this de-education of African American students, particularly boys, as the "Cradle to Prison Pipeline® crisis" (America's Cradle to Prison Pipeline℠, Children's Defense Fund, 2007). Instead of "…investing in properly educating Black boys by providing intense tutoring when their reading scores are inadequate, money is spent on building prisons to house them as adults" (Edwards P., 2011, p. 35).

In 1958, Eleanor Roosevelt wrote:

> We should remember Thomas Jefferson's admonition that democracy, which we have discovered through the years to be one of the most difficult forms of government, cannot function except with an educated electorate. (Roosevelt, 2001, p. 258)

The failure to educate Black boys often leads them to prisons, making them invisible to the larger society. It has another consequence as well. Increased incarceration rates result in a reduction in the number of eligible voters in a community.

Aron Goldman is the author of "Springfield Institute Voter Participation Analysis: Severe Disparities Exist, Lots of Factors." He writes:

> According to a Pew Foundation study, "Between 1987 and 2007, the national prison population has nearly tripled." Nationally, one in every nine Black men between the ages of 20 and 34 are behind bars. One result is a decreased population of eligible voters, and in some cases, participation rates that are "grossly overstated" because they are based on an artificially reduced base number. (Source: University of Washington; Goldman, 2011)

The failure to educate all of the children in the U.S. obstructs their access to education and literacy as human rights. These failures also threaten to erode the very foundation of our democracy.

Teaching and Learning: Achieving Quality for All provides grim statistics for the education of poor children in other parts of the world as well. The report presents data based on household surveys from 74 middle and low income countries (Lange, 2013). It states:

> In many countries, the last mile to universal primary education will not be covered in this generation unless concerted efforts are taken to support the children who are the most disadvantaged. On recent trends, it may be only in the last quarter of this century that all of the poorest boys and girls in more than 20 countries will graduate from primary education – and only next century that they will all complete lower secondary education. (UNESCO, 2013, p. 94)

The summary of the report emphasizes the importance of educating girls:

> Educating girls and women, in particular, has unmatched transformative power. As well as boosting their own chances of getting jobs, staying healthy, and participating fully in society, educating girls and young women has a marked impact on the health of their children and accelerates their countries' transition to stable population growth. (UNESCO, 2013, p. 13)

The report adds that while progress in achieving primary school completion has been made in the world's poorest countries since 2000, the majority of lower middle income countries are not projected to reach the goal until the 2030s or 2040s. Low income countries will only begin to achieve the target from the 2040s onward. Four countries in West Africa: Burkina Faso, Mali, Niger and Senegal will not reach the target before 2070 (UNESCO, 2013, p. 94).

When disaggregated by gender and income, the outlook for girls completing primary school is particularly discouraging. The Report states:

> The differences are even starker when looking at the projected achievement patterns by gender and family income. While rich boys are expected to reach the goal by 2030 in 56 of the 74 countries, this is the case for poor girls in 7 countries. Even by 2060, universal primary completion will not have been achieved for poor girls in 24 of the 28 low income countries in the sample. (UNESCO, 2013, p. 94)

In sub-Saharan Africa, the situation is the most severe. Projections indicate that "… if recent trends continue, the richest boys will achieve universal primary completion in 2021, but the poorest girls will not catch up until 2086" (UNESCO, 2013, p. 7). Even when they complete primary school, however, children are "not necessarily able to read and write". The circumstances are even more dire for children who complete four years or less in school (UNESCO, 2013, p. 97). Seventy-seven percent of these children are not able to read all or even part of a sentence (UNESCO, 2013, p. 21).

This inability to read comes at great cost, but the ability to read reaps great benefits. The "EFA Global Monitoring Report team calculations show that if all students in low income countries left school with basic reading skills, 171 million people could be lifted out of poverty, which would be equivalent to a 12% cut in world poverty" (UNESCO, 2013, p. 13). Concerted efforts are needed to support the children who are most disadvantaged. The roots of that effort are embedded in the Universal Declaration of Human Rights that will be reviewed in the next chapter of this book.

NOTES

1 From LEARNING FROM HISTORY by Nicholas Burnett in the International Institute of Educational Planning (IIEP) Newsletter, UNESCO. Copyright © 2009 United Nations. Reprinted with permission of the United Nations.

2 From THE IMPACT OF POVERTY by Pauline Rose in the International Institute of Educational Planning (IIEP) Newsletter, UNESCO. Copyright © 2009 United Nations. Reprinted with permission of the United Nations.

3 Excerpts from WHATEVER IT TAKES: GEOFFREY CANADA'S QUEST TO CHANGE HARLEM AND AMERICA by Paul Tough. Copyright © 2008 by Paul Tough. Reprinted by permission of Houghton Mifflin Harcourt Publishing Company. All rights reserved.

4 From General Comment Number 13 by the Committee on Economic Social and Cultural Rights, Twenty-First Session, 1999. Copyright © 1999 United Nations. Reprinted with permission of the United Nations.

5 From IF YOU ASK ME by Eleanor Roosevelt. Copyright 1941, 1942, 1943, 1944, 1945, by the Curtis Publishing Company. Copyright © 1946 by Eleanor Roosevelt. Reprinted with permission of Nancy Roosevelt Ireland. All rights reserved.

6 From the EFA 2013/4 GLOBAL MONITORING REPORT, TEACHING AND LEARNING: ACHIEVING QUALITY FOR ALL. UNESCO. Copyright © 2013United Nations. Reprinted with permission of the United Nations.

7 From the EFA 2011 GLOBAL MONITORING REPORT, THE HIDDEN CRISIS: ARMED CONFLICT AND EDUCATION. UNESCO. Copyright © 2010 United Nations. Reprinted with permission of the United Nations.

8 From the New York Times, October 20, 2011. Copyright © 2011 The New York Times. All rights reserved. Used by permission and protected by the copyright laws of the United States. The printing, copying, redistribution or retransmission of this Content without express written permission is prohibited.

9 From TEACHING READING TO BLACK ADOLESCENT MALES by Alfred W. Tatum, copyright © 2005, reproduced with permission of Stenhouse Publishers.www.stenhouse.com.

10 From "3.6 Minutes per Day" by Nell K. Duke in *Reading Research Quarterly*, Vol. 35(2), pp. 202–224. Copyright © 2000 International Reading Association. Reprinted with permission from John Wiley & Sons Ltd.

11 From Insisting on Digital Equity: Reframing the Dominant Discourse on Multicultural Education and Technology by Paul C. Gorski, in Urban Education, Vol. 44(3), pp. 348–364. Copyright © 2009 by SAGE Publications. Reprinted by Permission of SAGE Publications.

12 Reprinted by permission of the Publisher. From Patricia A. Edwards, Gwendolyn Thompson McMillon, and Jennifer D. Turner, CHANGE IS GONNA COME:TRANSFORMING LITERACY EDUCATION FOR AFRICAN AMERICAN STUDENTS, New York: Teachers College Press. Copyright © 2010 by Teachers College, Columbia University. All rights reserved.

CHAPTER 2

REVIEWING THE UNIVERSAL DECLARATION OF HUMAN RIGHTS

"*What other single human being has touched and transformed the existence of so many?*" She walked "*in the slums … of the world, not on a tour of inspection, but as one who could not feel contentment when others were hungry*". —From Adlai Stevenson's remarks at Eleanor Roosevelt's memorial service, Hyde Park, New York, November 10, 1962 (Stevenson, 1962)

ELEANOR ROOSEVELT, CHAIR OF THE HUMAN RIGHTS COMMISSION

President Theodore Roosevelt regarded Eleanor Roosevelt as his favorite niece. He instilled in her the "Roosevelt rule:" Never show fear. By the time she was a young woman, Eleanor Roosevelt developed a strong sense of social responsibility. During her lifetime, she took on various roles, including wife, mother, first lady of New York, first lady of the country, newspaper columnist, author, world traveler, diplomat, and seasoned politician (United States History.com—Eleanor Roosevelt). Eleanor Roosevelt was a prolific writer. She left a legacy of literacy. Long before the dawn of electronic means of communication, she reached an audience of households across the nation. During the 1920's, she wrote columns for *Colliers* and *Redbook* magazines. Six days a week for twenty-six years, 1936 through 1962, she wrote a newspaper column called "My Day." During her years in the White House, the column provided her with the opportunity to communicate with Americans, describing her daily life and commenting on events affecting the country. As a columnist, she reached wide audiences of women. She also wrote a monthly column in *Ladies Home Journal* in which she answered questions on a wide range of topics that were posed by readers (Roosevelt, 1946). During her lifetime, she authored nine books. After she suffered from palsy and was unable to hold a pen, one of her children, "remarking on the frustration their mother must have felt," described her as having been "the writingest woman alive" (Roosevelt, 2001, p. vii).

Her work as chair of the Human Rights Commission that wrote the Universal Declaration of Human Rights would become her most important work. Eleanor Roosevelt considered her position on the Commission to be one of ambassador for the common man and woman. She stated, "I used to tell my husband that, if he could make me understand something, it would be clear to all other people in the country, and perhaps that will be my real value on this drafting commission!"

(Roosevelt, 1947).[1] Her role in the United Nations began in December of 1945 when President Truman asked her to become a member of the United States' delegation to the organizing meeting of the United Nations to be held in London in January, 1946 (Roosevelt, 1958b).[2] She described the UN as a "…bold new concept of an organization that might be our only hope of avoiding future wars" (Roosevelt, 1992, p. 302).[3]

Her thinking aligned with that of other world leaders who had endured two world wars within a span of less than 30 years. As a member of the U.S. delegation, Eleanor Roosevelt attended sessions of the General Assembly and large briefing meetings. Although she participated in the large public meetings, she believed that the important, hard work was done in the small continuous meetings of the various committees. While Eleanor Roosevelt came to appreciate the value of the committee work, she struggled with her role as part of the U.S. delegation (Roosevelt, 1958b). She began to think of small ways in which she could build relationships. She invited women from the other delegations, many of whom were the only woman in their delegation, to join her for tea at her hotel. Sixteen of them accepted. The event was so successful that she asked the women back, either together or a few at a time. She began to understand the value of working in small places within global settings. These kinds of small social events became a custom that Eleanor Roosevelt would rely upon in the years ahead (Roosevelt, 1958b).

While in London, Eleanor Roosevelt was assigned to the Third Committee of the General Assembly that focused on humanitarian, educational, and cultural questions. One issue that surfaced in her committee was the fate of the displaced war refugees in Germany at the time of the signing of the armistice. When her work in London concluded, Eleanor Roosevelt wanted to see for herself what happened to the refugees in Germany. Before returning to New York, aided by the U.S. Army that controlled occupied areas, she visited Germany. As she flew over the bombed-out ruins of Cologne, Frankfurt, and Munich, she was "stunned and appalled" by the devastation. She "felt that nobody could have imagined such utter, horrible destruction" (Roosevelt, 1958b, p. 68). She described her mind on the flight back to New York as being "as busy as the aircraft's big motors as we roared along through the night." She added, "The faces of the women in the black market in Berlin kept crowding into my mind." She reminded herself "again and again, there was also hope in the air. There had to be hope" (Roosevelt, 1958b, p. 73).

Once back in New York, Eleanor Roosevelt wrote a note of thanks to the President and Secretary of State for making it possible for her to serve on the committee. At that time, she considered her work for the UN complete. In fact, her work there had just begun (Roosevelt, 1958b).

In the spring of 1946, the UN Economic and Social Council (ECOSOC) created a small, nuclear, commission on human rights. The purpose of this preliminary commission was to make recommendations regarding the formation of the UN Human Rights Commission. During this time, she was also nominated and confirmed to serve as a member of the United States delegation to the UN, a position she held until 1952. The nuclear commission on human rights decided that the major task of the Human Rights Commission would be to "write an International Bill of Rights." It would prevent atrocities, like those that had recently taken place during WWII, from ever occurring again. As Eleanor Roosevelt describes, the document would consist of three parts: the Declaration, a Covenant or Covenants, and a system for implementing or enforcing the rights. The Declaration would "name and define all human rights, not only the traditionally recognized political and civil rights, but also the more recently recognized social, economic and cultural rights. Since the General Assembly is not a world parliament, its resolutions are not legally binding on member states." Nonetheless, the Covenant(s) "would take the form of a treaty and would be legally binding on the countries that accepted them" (Roosevelt, 1958b, pp. 90–91).

The nuclear commission also recommended that the Human Rights Commission be composed of eighteen members. In addition to her other duties, Eleanor Roosevelt was nominated by President Truman as the United States' representative on the Human Rights Commission. She was elected chair of the Human Rights Commission that held its first meeting in January 1947. Members of the commission included John Humphrey of Canada, René Cassin of France, Charles Malik of Lebanon, P.C. Chang of the Republic of China, and Hansa Mehta of India.

A small group of members, Malik, Humphrey, Chang, and Mrs. Roosevelt were assigned the task of writing the first draft of the Declaration. Their work would require approval by the larger Commission. Member states would then comment on the draft, and it would be returned to the drafting committee for revisions. The draft would then go back to the full committee for final consideration. Next, the Economic and Social Council would review the draft and decide if it should be recommended to the General Assembly. If recommended, it would then be examined by The Third Committee on Social, Humanitarian, and Cultural Affairs. After that, the General Assembly would consider it for adoption. Due to the extent of this process, it would take until at least the fall of 1948 until adoption of the Declaration could take place (Glendon, 2001).

DRAFTING THE UNIVERSAL DECLARATION OF HUMAN RIGHTS

At a small gathering at Eleanor Roosevelt's apartment, it was decided that John Humphrey would draw up the initial draft (Roosevelt, 1958b). Drafting the Articles took place over a period of several months. First, Humphrey and his staff at the UN Secretariat spent four months preparing the document and studying "all the world's existing constitutions and rights instruments" (Glendon, 2001, p. 56) as well as documents that had been sent to the UN by governments, private organizations, and individuals. Additionally, the Secretariat gave the drafting group "a review of the most fundamental and widely shared principles to have emerged over humanity's long, ongoing process of reflection on freedom" (Glendon, 2001, p. 56).

Exhaustive study resulted in Humphrey's draft that was a "distillation of nearly two-hundred years of efforts to articulate the most basic human values in terms of rights" (Glendon, 2001, p. 57). The result was a total of four hundred pages of commentary. Glendon notes that the UN announced in its *Weekly Bulletin* that it had brought together "the most exhaustive documentation of the subject of human rights ever assembled" (UN, 1947).[4] Cassin then reworked the structure of Humphrey's draft to include "a Preamble, six introductory articles, thirty-six substantive articles grouped analytically under eight headings and two concluding provisions on implementation" (Committee, 1947).[5] During the next 18 months in the drafting committee, the wording of the document went through numerous changes, but the majority of ideas in Humphrey's draft and the structure of Cassin's draft remained (Glendon, 2001). Reflecting on the enormity of this work, Eleanor Roosevelt stated, "In the period that I presided as chairman of the Human Rights Commission we spent most of our time trying to write the Universal Declaration of Human Rights and the Covenants, and there were times, it seemed to me, when I was getting in over my head" (Roosevelt, On my own, 1958b, p. 94). She also found that the slow and arduous work of the committee was fraught with quarrels and disagreements (Black A., 2007).

At times, writing a Declaration appeared to be a seemingly impossible task. Members of the commission struggled to determine the very purpose of the Declaration and how and by whom it would be implemented. They also debated the rights of the individual in relation to the rights of states or societies as a whole. Underlying the disagreements were divisions "...between the philosophically inclined and the more practical-minded members; between representatives of small or weak nations and the major powers; and between proponents of enforceable instruments and of a declaration of principles" (Glendon, 2001, p. 43). The deepening of the cold war increased the tensions among the members of the committee. When Eleanor Roosevelt attempted to explain American understandings of their Bill of Rights, delegates of the U.S.S.R. and her Satellites drew upon the racial strife in the U.S., manifested through the actions of the Ku Klux Klan, to discredit her positions (Black A., 2007).

Concerns about the possibility of any group of people ever being able to agree upon a corpus of human rights were so deep that the UN's Educational, Scientific and Cultural Organization (UNESCO) formulated the Committee on the Theoretical Basis of Human Rights, chaired by Cambridge political historian E.H. Carr. Jacques Maritain, French social philosopher, was rapporteur and one of the most active members. The committee distributed a "questionnaire to statesmen and scholars around the world—including such notables as Mohandas Gandhi, Pierre Teilhard de Chardin, Benedetto Croce, Aldous Huxley, and Salvador de Madariaga (Glendon, 2001, p. 51). The committee received replies "...from Chinese, Islamic, Hindu, and customary law perspectives, as well as from American, European and socialist points of view" (Glendon, 2001, p. 73).

Based on the responses to the questionnaire, the committee identified practical concepts across widely separated ideologies. These concepts were viewed as a common denominator among these ideologies. Therefore, the committee concluded that the members of the United Nations shared common convictions that underpin human rights. They were also aware that these convictions are expressed through different philosophical principles and are based on diverse political and economic systems (Glendon, 2001). The work could go forward based on the idea that "If there are some things so terrible in practice that virtually no one will publicly approve them, and some things so good in practice that no one will oppose them, a common project can move forward without agreement on the reasons for those positions" (Glendon, 2001, p. 78).

The Declaration was influenced more by the modern dignitarian rights tradition of continental Europe and Latin America than by the more individualistic Anglo-American documents.

Dignitarian rights instruments place emphasis on the family. They focus on duties, and therefore are "more compatible with Asian and African traditions." In dignitarian rights documents, "rights bearers tend to be envisioned within families and communities; rights are formulated so as to make clear their limits and how their relation to one another as well as to the responsibilities that belong to citizens and the state" (Glendon, 2001, p. 227). As professor Donald Kommers explains, "One vision is partial to the city perceived as a private realm in which the individual is alone, isolated, and in competition with his fellows, while the other vision is partial to the city as perceived as a public realm where individual and community are bound together in reciprocity" (Kommers, 1991, p. 867).

Eleanor Roosevelt noted that, during the early work on the Covenants and measures of implementation, it became clear that it would be "exceedingly difficult to agree on articles that would, if accepted, be legally binding on the various nations." She found that agreement on the civil and political rights that had become "fairly well accepted throughout the civilized world" was difficult enough. But trying to agree on the more recent economic and social rights seemed to her at times to be "all but impossible." She attributed this lack of agreement, "in part at least," on the "vast social and economic differences between various countries…" (Roosevelt, 1958b, pp. 95–96).

Additionally, within the United States, the delegation could act only in regard to matters that were under the jurisdiction of the federal government. In other matters that were under the control of the states, the delegation had power only to "recommend" that the states take appropriate action.

Notes from the discussion of the draft at the Eighty-ninth meeting of the Third Committee state:

> The draft declaration was not a treaty or international agreement. It was not legally binding. It was a statement of basic principles of inalienable human rights, that established a common standard of achievement for all peoples and all nations. Although Member States were not legally bound by it, the Declaration would carry considerable weight. Its adoption would commit Member States, in the words of the preamble, "to strive by teaching and education to promote

> respect for these rights and freedoms and by progressive measures, national and international, to secure their universal and effective recognition and observance, both among the peoples of Member States themselves and among the peoples of territories under their jurisdiction." (Third Committee—Eighty-ninth Meeting, 1948)

Between September 28 and December 9, 1948, the Third Committee, composed of representatives of all 58 UN member nations, debated every article of the draft of the Declaration in over 85 working sessions (Sears, 2008). It was clear that while the Declaration could be completed to go before a vote by the end of the UN session, the other two tasks of the Human Rights Commission, drafting the Covenants and planning the implementation, would not be completed. It was decided that the Declaration alone would be presented to the General Assembly at this time. The work on the Covenants and the system for implementation and enforcement of the rights would continue. Although Eleanor Roosevelt was not one of the major writers of the document, her leadership sustained the work (Sears, 2008). Her political influence in the United States kept the State Department involved, and through her personal attention, she demonstrated respect for the individuals on the Commission (Glendon, 2001). Her meticulous preparations for meetings led to her success as the Chair of the Commission (Sears, 2008).

THE FINAL VERSION OF THE UNIVERSAL DECLARATION OF HUMAN RIGHTS

The final version of the Declaration is comprised of the Preamble and 30 Articles (See Appendix for the full text of the Universal Declaration of Human Rights). The first words of the Preamble state, "Whereas recognition of the inherent dignity and of the equal and inalienable rights of all members of the human family is the foundation of freedom, justice and peace in the world" (UN General Assembly, 1948).

The first two articles establish the foundation of human rights as equal and universal. Articles 3 through 21 describe civil and political rights including life, liberty, personal security. They prohibit slavery, torture, and arbitrary arrest. The articles also uphold the right of everyone to recognition everywhere as a person before the law. They also include the right to be presumed innocent until proven guilty. Freedom of expression, freedom of movement, and freedom of assembly are also guaranteed (UN General Assembly, 1948).

Articles 22 through 27 describe economic, social and cultural rights. These rights are essential for free and full personal development. They include the fundamental right of every member of a society to have social security; the right to work and gain fair remuneration; the right to leisure; the right to a standard of living adequate for the health and well-being of himself and his family, including food, clothing, medical care and necessary social services; and the right to participate in the cultural life of the community. Mothers and children are entitled to special care and assistance (UN General Assembly, 1948).

The final three articles, 28–30, provide a protective framework in which all human rights are to be universally enjoyed (UN General Assembly, 1948). The framework describes the social and international order that enables the realization of human rights and fundamental freedoms, the obligations that human beings have to their communities and the protection of the rights from outside interference.

Article 26 centers on education and is one of the few articles in the Universal Declaration of Human Rights that was directly influenced by the European holocaust (Glendon, 2001, p. 189). For the most part, the Human Rights Commission saw their task as defining conditions for peace and left the discussion of Nazi atrocities to writers of the Nuremberg Principles and the Genocide Convention as part of the law of war. Members of the Commission agreed that education was vital to bringing about "freedom, justice, and peace in the world" (UN General Assembly, 1948). They drafted the first paragraph in the article as a manifestation of that belief. The first paragraph reads:

> 1. Everyone has the right to education. Education shall be free, at least in the elementary and fundamental stages. Elementary education shall be compulsory. Technical and professional education shall be made generally available and higher education shall be equally accessible to all on the basis of merit. (UN General Assembly, 1948)

Comments on the drafting of the article, however, suggested that the wording was insufficient. As Glendon describes, an observer from the World Jewish congress noted that the article was a technical structure that failed to address the spirit behind the governance of education. He argued that lack of attention to that essential matter in Germany had been the major reason for two catastrophic wars (Glendon, 2001). Therefore, he recommended the language for the second paragraph of Article 26. The Third Committee added the wording about the activities of the United Nations when they reviewed the document. Paragraph 2 of Article 26 reads:

> 2. Education shall be directed to the full development of the human personality and to the strengthening of respect for human rights and fundamental freedoms. It shall promote understanding, tolerance and friendship among all nations, racial or religious groups, and shall further the activities of the United Nations for the maintenance of peace. (UN General Assembly, 1948)

The third paragraph of the article was "influenced directly by recollections of the National Socialist regime's efforts to turn Germany's renowned educational system into a mechanism for indoctrinating the young with the government's program" (Glendon, 2001, p. 159). Glendon reports that Leo Beaufort, the Dutch delegate, described how the German schools had been used to weaken the role of parents. As a result, the following third paragraph was added to the article:

> 3. Parents have a prior right to choose the kind of education that shall be given to their children. (UN General Assembly, 1948)

This is one just example of a place in the Declaration that the framers specifically attended to the needs of people in small places.

Fifty-eight member states of the United Nations General Assembly, containing four-fifths of the world's population approved the Universal Declaration of Human Rights. Twenty-two of the countries were from the Americas, sixteen from Europe, five from Asia, eight from the Near East or Middle East, four from Africa, and three from Oceania (Glendon, 2001, p. 50). There were forty-eight votes in favor of the Declaration, eight abstentions and no opposing votes against the Declaration. The Soviet Union and its satellite countries, Byelorussia, Czechoslovakia, Poland, the Ukraine and Yugoslavia abstained, as did Saudi Arabia and South Africa. Yemen and Honduras were absent and did not vote (Glendon, 2001, pp. 169–170).

In her speech on the occasion of the adoption of the Declaration of Human Rights, Eleanor Roosevelt said in part:

> In giving our approval to the declaration today it is of primary importance that we keep clearly in mind the basic character of the document. It is not a treaty; it is not an international agreement. It is not and does not purport to be a statement of basic principles of law or legal obligation. It is a declaration of basic human rights and freedoms, to be stamped with the approval of the General Assembly by formal vote of its members, and to serve as a common standard of achievement for all peoples of all nations.
>
> We stand today at the threshold of a great event both in the life of the United Nations and in the life of mankind, that is the approval by the General Assembly of the Universal Declaration of Human Rights recommended by the Third Committee. This declaration may well become the international Magna Carta of all men everywhere. We hope its proclamation by the General Assembly will be an event comparable to the proclamation of the Declaration of the Rights of the Man by the French people in 1789, the adoption of the Bill of Rights by the people of the United States, and the adoption of comparable declarations at different times in other countries. (Roosevelt, 1948)

Law professor Peter Bailey states the Declaration has "come to be regarded as possibly the single most important document created in the twentieth century and as the accepted world standard for human rights." It is viewed as drawing "life-preserving messages from the past," and forming "an essential foundation for building a world in which all human beings can, in the centuries to come, look forward to living in dignity and peace" (Bailey P., 1998, p. 1). We cannot lose sight of the importance of the Declaration today. It has "become accepted (often rather reluctantly, it is true) as an influential statement of standards, even by countries that are doubtful about the whole human rights enterprise." It has also "become almost an extension of the UN Charter." It is now standard to regard the Declaration "as setting out the content" of the "rights and freedoms" included in the Charter (Bailey P., 1998, p. 4).

Also, "most if not all of the provisions of the UDHR have almost certainly become part of international customary law." The rights stated in the Declaration are also "commonly recognised as well founded in moral and good practice terms." Therefore, there are now "virtually unchallengeable grounds for asserting that the UDHR rights have become part of international customary law. That means that, unlike treaties, which only bind a country once it has accepted the treaty obligations, all countries in the world are bound, whatever their particular view may be. A country cannot repudiate international customary law, as it can a treaty obligation" (Bailey P., 1998, p. 4).

While the adoption of the Declaration was a momentous occasion, it was only the overture to the work of guaranteeing universal human rights. Only one of the three goals set for the Human Rights Commission, the writing of the Declaration, had been met. Writing the Covenants that would be legally binding and designing a system for the implementation and enforcement of the rights were yet to be accomplished. The Covenants would not be completed for nearly two decades. The work of implementing and enforcing the rights continues to this day. Eleanor Roosevelt and the other "framers did not imagine in 1948 that they had discovered the whole truth about human beings and human rights. They never claimed that the document they had produced under difficult circumstances represented the last word." They thought of it as "an important milestone on a long and difficult journey. They were content to have advanced the quest and confident that experiences gained in implementing the Declaration's principles would lead to deeper understanding in the future" (Glendon, 2001, p. 231).

As noted previously, drafting the Universal Declaration of Human Rights often appeared to be a seemingly insurmountable task. As I read about the process of drafting the Declaration, I found that in addition to contributing to the creation of the document itself, the framers and philosophers reveal ideas for others who attempt to take up seemingly impossible tasks. Securing literacy as a human right is one of those tasks. The ideas that I have mined from their writings are listed below. These ideas point toward how to accomplish the task of securing literacy as a human right. They are woven into the fabric of this book.

IDEAS FOR ADDRESSING SEEMINGLY IMPOSSIBLE TASKS

Derived from the Process of Writing the Universal Declaration of Human Rights

- Human rights begin in small places within global settings.
- Some things are so destructive that nearly everyone will reject them. Other things are so clearly beneficial that nearly everyone will endorse them. Therefore, work within communities can go forward even if people do not agree on the reasons that underlie the positions they take (Glendon, 2001).
- There must be a willingness to undertake extensive study so work can be built upon knowledge.

- Rights bearers reside within families and communities. Their rights should be based upon reciprocity, rather than competition.

NOTES

[1] From My Day by Eleanor Roosevelt. Copyright © 1947 by United Feature Syndicate. Reprinted with permission of Nancy Roosevelt Ireland.

[2] From ON MY OWN by Eleanor Roosevelt. Copyright © 1958 The Curtis Publishing Company. Copyright © 1958 by Anna Eleanor Roosevelt. All rights reserved. Reprinted with permission of Nancy Roosevelt Ireland.

[3] From THE AUTOBIOGRAPHY OF ELEANOR ROOSEVELT by Eleanor Roosevelt. Published by Da Capo Press. Copyright ©1937, 1949, 1958, 1961 by Anna Eleanor Roosevelt: Copyright 1958 by Curtis Publishing Company; Copyright renewed 1989 by Franklin D. Roosevelt Jr. All rights reserved. Reprinted with permission of Nancy Roosevelt Ireland.

[4] From (1947). International Bill of Rights to Be Drafted in *UN Weekly Bulletin*, 639. Copyright ©1947 United Nations. Reprinted with the permission of the United Nations.

[5] From The Report of the Drafting Committee (E/CN.4/21, p. 4). Copyright © 1947, United Nations. Used with Permission of the United Nations.

CHAPTER 3

LITERACY BECOMES ACKNOWLEDGED AS A HUMAN RIGHT

> *Through education and publicity, we have developed a human rights conscience which is perhaps the strongest factor in the progress we have made... We intend that these advances shall continue.*
>
> —Secretary of State John Forster Dulles. Letter dated April 3, 1953, from Secretary of State Dulles to Mrs. Oswald B. Lord, United States Representative in the Human Rights Commission, released in Geneva on April 7, 1953. Re-printed in *In Your Hands*. (Church Peace Union now known as Carnegie Council for Ethics in International Affairs, 1958, p. 2)[1]

IN YOUR HANDS

By 1958, the Declaration had been translated into 72 languages and dialects and influenced the constitutions of many countries. The ten years following the adoption of the Declaration, however, were viewed as "the raising of the curtain on the first act. The greatest moments in the human rights drama" were "yet to come" (Church Peace Union now known as Carnegie Council for Ethics in International Affairs, 1958, p. 7). A special U. N. committee planned a wide observance for the anniversary that had several goals:

> To demonstrate to the world the great step forward which the adoption of the Declaration represented... To serve as a vivid illustration of the work accomplished by the United Nations in defining the rights proclaimed... To afford an opportunity for making better known the rights and freedoms set forth in the Universal Declaration... To awaken renewed interest in understanding these rights and freedoms, thus encouraging increased respect for them. (Church Peace Union now known as Carnegie Council for Ethics in International Affairs, 1958, p. 2)

On March 27, 1958, the UN Commission on Human Rights met in NYC to authorize a booklet called *In Your Hands: A Guide for Community Action for the Tenth Anniversary of the Universal Declaration of Human Rights*. The guide was a reminder that "On December 10, 1948, the word went out to nations big and small, rich and poor. And men and women raised their heads a bit higher, looked at their children with new hope, felt a new dignity. The United Nations, in a Universal Declaration, had just dedicated itself to advancing the inherent and equal rights 'of all members of the human family' " (Church Peace Union now known as Carnegie Council for Ethics in International Affairs, 1958, p. 4).

Eleanor Roosevelt resigned from the Commission on Human Rights in 1952, but in 1958, she gave the speech to introduce *In Your Hands*. She spoke on "behalf of the thirty-two national organizations representing millions of citizens—of all faiths; of every complexion; in all parts of the United States." She presented members of the Commission on Human Rights a copy of the booklet as "...a token of our faith that, under your leadership, the communities of every country will bring human rights to full reality in the community of the world" (Roosevelt, 1958a). Eleanor Roosevelt connected the duties of national leaders and the responsibilities of ordinary citizens. She put forth the challenge to all people to recognize and uphold the inherent dignity and the equal and inalienable rights of all members of the human family as the foundation of freedom, justice and peace in the world. This message was especially important for the United States. In the decade since the adoption of the Declaration, the political climate in the U.S. had changed radically. U.S. forces had engaged in war with Korea. McCarthyism held scores citizens hostage by creating a culture of intimidation. It was within this political context that Eleanor Roosevelt, girded by the "Roosevelt Rule:" Never show fear, delivered an address that included her famous words, "Where, after all, do universal human rights begin?" A portion of her speech from this event reads:

> Where, after all, do universal human rights begin? In small places, close to home—so close and so small that they cannot be seen on any map of the world. Yet they are the world of the individual person: the neighborhood he lives in; the school or college he attends; the factory, farm or office where he works. Such are the places where every man, woman, and child seeks equal justice, equal opportunity, equal dignity without discrimination. Unless these rights have meaning there, they have little meaning anywhere. Without concerted citizen action to uphold them close to home, we shall look in vain for progress in the larger world.
>
> Thus we believe that the destiny of human rights is in the hands of all of our citizens in all our communities. (Roosevelt, 1958a)

In Your Hands encourages us as citizens to "join together, as we have done wholeheartedly in the past, to check up human rights in our own home town." The work is seen as on-going. The guide emphasizes that "'Only a free people can continually question and appraise the adequacy of its own institutions'" (To Secure These Rights: The Report of the President's Committee on Civil Rights, 1947). The word *continually* is of major importance in this document. It states, "Only by working *continually* in our nation, state and our town, can we improve the world" (Church Peace Union now known as Carnegie Council for Ethics in International Affairs, 1958, p. 9).

Education is addressed in the guide and would become an integral component of this continual work. The guide affirms the idea from the Declaration that education should "'…promote understanding, tolerance and friendship among all nations, racial or religious groups…'" (UN General Assembly, 1948, p. Article 26) and adds, "In other words, it is no longer enough just to teach children the three R's. Today they need 6R's—the traditional Readin', Ritin' and 'Rithmetic plus training in Rights, Responsibilities and Relationships with their neighbors of all backgrounds, races and creeds. They need it for their own happiness, indeed for human survival, in this rapidly shrinking world" (Church Peace Union now known as Carnegie Council for Ethics in International Affairs, 1958, p. 13).

In Your Hands also includes a section entitled "Spotlight on Us" that encourages Americans to plan observances to study and discuss the Declaration. Within their own communities, they are charged with the tasks of examining human rights and planning an observance on the Tenth Anniversary that will result in taking action. Although free public education had been available for more than one hundred years in the U. S., access was not equitable. By the time the Declaration was completed in 1948, the U.S. had become immersed in "vast soul-searching." In 1946, President Truman had appointed a Committee on Civil Rights. The committee was charged with assessing the democratic processes in the U.S. The questions the committee explored included, "Was racial and religious discrimination standing in the way of equal opportunity in employment, in housing, in education?" (Church Peace Union now known as Carnegie Council for Ethics in International Affairs, 1958, pp. 8–9).

In 1946, seventeen states and the District of Columbia maintained separate schools for Blacks and Whites. Reflecting upon the responsibility facing the U.S., Eleanor Roosevelt wrote, "…all children should have an equal opportunity for education in whatever community they live, and this holds good for the whole of the United States" (Roosevelt, 2001, p. 148). In 1958, *In Your Hands* noted progress made toward equal education in the U.S. This section could have served as a response to the criticism of the Soviets during the drafting of the Declaration decade earlier. Racial segregation in the public schools had been banned by the U.S, Supreme Court in the Brown vs. the Board of Education decision of 1954. *In Your Hands* acknowledges, "This decision provoked sharp controversy in some localities and tragic outbreaks in others." But the guide also documents progress. Before Brown, segregated schools existed in 17 states and the District of Columbia. During the 1957–1958 school year, the picture changed, and "350,000 Negro children and two million white children in this area were enrolled in integrated schools" (Church Peace Union now known as Carnegie Council for Ethics in International Affairs, 1958, p. 14).

But providing seats in integrated schools alone would not be enough. *In Your Hands* states, "The Universal Declaration of Human Rights stresses equal educational opportunities for all, which means that youngsters of all races and creeds should be given the same chance to enjoy the best school facilities in your community." Ten years later, *In Your Hands* continued to emphasize, "It's got to be equal" (Church

Peace Union now known as Carnegie Council for Ethics in International Affairs, 1958, p. 14).

However, the struggle to provide equal opportunities for education in the U.S. continues to this day. As Edwards, Thompson McMillon, and Turner state:

> Institutional racism continues to erode the foundation of America's promise to its children. Statistics illuminate pronounced differences in education (assessment scores, graduation rates, college admission rates, retention rates, special education referrals, gifted program referrals, etc.), employment (hiring, salaries, promotions, etc.), and other areas between Whites and minorities". (Edwards, Thompson McMillon, & Turner, 2008, p. 24)

THE COVENANTS

The Universal Declaration of Human Rights as adopted in 1948 defined education broadly, beginning with compulsory elementary or primary education. As early as 1949, the United Nations General Assembly envisioned the minimum requirements for fundamental education as including domestic skills, knowledge of other cultures, and an opportunity to develop personal attributes such as initiative and freedom (Jones, 1990) in (UNESCO, 2005). In 1958, the emphasis was still given to basic education and the UNESCO definition of a literate person was "one who can, with understanding, both read and write a short simple statement on his or her everyday life" (UNESCO, 2005, p. 153). During the next five decades, the UN would hone that definition. The work would not be straightforward or easy. The complicated tasks of crafting covenants, conventions, and future declarations would follow. The refinement of education and literacy as human rights would be embedded within this work.

After Eleanor Roosevelt resigned from chairmanship of the Human Rights Commission, "work on the Covenants proceeded with a painful slowness" (Glendon, 2001, p. 206) and was "stalled for decades during the cold war years" (Glendon, 2001, p. 213). It was not until 1966 that the two detailed covenants, 1) International Covenant on Economic, Social and Cultural Rights (ICESCR) and the 2) International Covenant on Civil and Political Rights (ICCPR), were completed and opened for signature. It took an additional ten years until there was a sufficient number of ratifications by individual nations for the covenants to go into effect (Glendon, 2001). At that time, the ICESCR and the ICCPR, together with the Universal Declaration of Human Rights, formed the International Bill of Human Rights that took on the force of international law. The ICESCR requires its parties to work toward granting individuals economic, social, and cultural rights, including education. Article 13 of this covenant requires that "primary education shall be compulsory and available free to all" (International Covenant for Economic, Social and Cultural Rights). The General Comments on Article 13 describe education as "both a human right in itself and an indispensable means of realizing other human rights" (Committee on Econonic Social and Cultural Rights, 1999).

CONVENTION ON THE RIGHTS OF THE CHILD

In 1989, thirteen years after the adoption of the ICESCR, world leaders voiced concern that "children needed a special convention just for them because people under 18 years old often need special care and protection that adults do not" (UN General Assembly, 1989). The leaders wanted to make sure that the world recognized that children have human rights too. In response, in November of that year, the UN General Assembly adopted a separate treaty, the Convention on the Rights of the Child[2] (CRC), that is:

> Built on varied legal systems and cultural traditions, the Convention is a universally agreed set of non-negotiable standards and obligations. These basic standards—also called human rights—set minimum entitlements and freedoms that should be respected by governments. They are founded on respect for the dignity and worth of each individual, regardless of race, colour, gender, language, religion, opinions, origins, wealth, birth status or ability and therefore apply to every human being everywhere. (Uganda UNICEF, 2014)[3]

The convention supports the concept that "Children's rights are human rights. Children's rights are not special rights, but rather the fundamental rights inherent to the human dignity of all people" (Jamaica UNICEF, 2010).[4] This document is "the first legally binding international instrument to incorporate the full range of human rights—civil, cultural, economic, political and social rights" (UN General Assembly, 1989). Paragraph 1 of Article 29 of the CRC addresses education. It reads:

> State Parties agree that the education of the child shall be directed to:

1. The development of the child's personality, talents and mental and physical abilities to their fullest potential;
2. The development of respect for human rights and fundamental freedoms, and for the principles enshrined in the Charter of the United Nations;
3. The development of respect for the child's parents, his or her own cultural identity, language and values, for the national values of the country in which the child is living, the country from which he or she may originate, and for civilizations different from his or her own;
4. The preparation of the child for responsible life in a free society, in the spirit of understanding, peace, tolerance, equality of sexes, and friendship among all peoples, ethnic, national and religious groups and persons of indigenous origin;
5. The development of respect for the natural environment (UN General Assembly, 1989).

According to UNICEF, the CRC has become the most universally accepted human rights instrument in history (UNICEF Uzbekistan, 2006). By the end of 2009, 192 countries had ratified the CRC. The United States government assisted in drafting the Convention and signed it on February 16, 1995, but has not ratified it. Somalia is the only other country belonging to the UN General Assembly that has not ratified the Convention (United Nations, 2012). Regardless of whether the Convention has been ratified or not, as a matter of human dignity, human rights must be realized in the United States, as well as in other countries.

The CRC affirms the child's right to primary education that was described in earlier documents and includes particulars regarding the child's freedom of expression. The emphasis at the time it was written, however, was on the elimination of illiteracy rather than the development of literacy. The framers of this convention understood that ratifying the CRC alone would not make a difference. "One of the convention's key strengths is that it recognizes that rights must be actively promoted if they are going to be enforced - awareness isn't enough" (Amnesty International Publications, 2012).[5] Strategies for implementation and oversight are built into the concluding articles of this convention.

THE INFLUENCE OF PAULO FREIRE AS LITERACY BECOMES A HUMAN RIGHT

During the 1970s, a major shift in the definition of literacy took place with the introduction Brazilian educator "Paulo Freire's theory of 'conscientization' which stated, among other things, that social awareness and critical enquiry are key factors in social change…" This theory "…gained popularity in developing countries. It also heavily influenced evolving conceptions of literacy in UNESCO and other international organizations" (UNESCO, 2005, p. 154).

"In 1975, during an International Symposium for Literacy held in Persepolis [Iran], Freire was awarded the Mohamed Reza Pahlavi Prize for literacy by UNESCO." International recognition of Freire's approach to literacy was considerable during this period, and The Persepolis Declaration reflects the influence of Freire's theories. It proposes that "literacy must go beyond the process of learning the skills of reading, writing and arithmetic, and contribute to the 'liberation of man' and to his full development" (UNESCO, 2005, p. 154). As stated below, literacy is proclaimed to be a human right in this document. (See the Appendix for the full text of the Declaration of Persepolis.)[6]

> Thus conceived, literacy creates the conditions for the acquisition of a critical consciousness of the contradictions of society in which man lives and of its aims; it also stimulates initiative and his participation in the creation of projects capable of acting upon the world, of transforming it, and of defining the aims of an authentic human development. It should open the way to a mastery of techniques and human relations. Literacy is not an end in itself. It is a fundamental human right. (UNESCO, 1975)

Freire determined that a major goal of the meeting was the evaluation of literacy campaigns from different areas of the world. In comparing these campaigns, he saw an obvious problem. He acknowledged that in some societies literacy campaigns empowered members of subordinate classes to transform their lives with fervor and hope. While other campaigns prevented members of subordinate classes from participating in transforming their society (Freire, 1993).

Freire opposed what he defined as the banking model of teaching. As stated earlier in this book, this is the model that I worked under at one time. As Shor describes:

> Banking educators treat students' minds as empty accounts into which they make deposits of information, through didactic lectures and from commercial texts. The material deposited into students is drawn from the "central bank of knowledge." The central bank in any society is a metaphoric repository of official knowledge. As a store of cultural capital, the central bank is comprised of the standard syllabus in schools and colleges; traditional canons in academic disciplines; established scientific and technical knowledge; "correct usage" considered to be standard for writing and speaking…It is material selected by those with the power to set standards. (Shor, 1992, pp. 31–32)

Furthermore, Brian Street, professor from King's College in London, contends, "The rich, elaborate and varied meanings and uses of literacy in different cultures across time and space become marginalised and treated as failed attempts to access the dominant, standard form represented by western-type schooling" (Street, Preface, 1996, p. 4).[7] Street further states that the "real ways" that could support people "in extending their own prior experience and uses of literacy to adapt to changing circumstances are lost in formalised and hierarchic procedures." He agrees with researcher Catherine Kell (1994) who argues that these procedures "infantilise" people (Street, 1996, p. 4).

Banking education is a deficit model of education. Examples of this model are presented in the next part of this book. Later parts include examples of the work of educators and researchers whose work reflect Freire's work and definition of literacy. This work is child-centered and resists imposed practices that silence learners' voices.

EDUCATION FOR ALL

The implementation of literacy as a human right received support in 1989, when the UN General Assembly proclaimed International Literacy Year. The UN welcomed the convening of the World Conference on Education for All (WCEFA), to be held in Jomtien, Thailand in March 1990. One thousand five hundred delegates from 155 countries and representatives from 150 organizations met at the WCEFA in response to "widespread concern about the deterioration of education systems during the 1980s" (The World Declaration on Education for All: Meeting Basic Learning Needs, 1993/1994).[8] Here, the world community composed the World Declaration on Education for All, and thereby renewed its commitment to ensuring the rights of all people to education and knowledge. UNESCO, UNDP, UNICEF, and the World Bank launched this movement that endorses an 'expanded vision of learning' and pledges to universalize primary education and massively reduce illiteracy by the end of the decade.

The preamble lists "daunting problems" that restricted progress in achieving basic learning needs. The barriers include: "mounting debt burdens, the threat of economic stagnation and decline, rapid population growth, widening economic disparities among and within nations, war, occupation, civil strife, violent crime, the preventable deaths of millions of children and widespread environmental degradation." These problems were compounded because "the lack of basic education among a significant proportion of the population prevents societies from addressing such problems with strength and purpose" (UNESCO, 1990).[9] Although the least developed countries experienced the greatest setbacks, poverty and cutbacks in funding in developing and industrialized countries led to the decline of education in those countries as well. Yet, in 1990, Education for All acknowledged that the world was about to enter a new century, with "all its promise and possibilities..." and that there was "genuine progress toward peaceful detente and greater cooperation among nations" (UNESCO, 1990) (See Appendix for EFA Overview and Goals).[10]

The World Declaration on Education for All is composed of ten articles. The realization of universal primary education as set forth in the Declaration in 1948 is viewed as the centerpiece of EFA. Sections of Articles 5 and 6 introduce three pivotal ideas that redefine and expand the scope of basic education. The first of these is the recognition that "learning begins at birth." The inclusion of this brief phrase signals a major shift from a focus on basic education in primary school. This declaration specifies that "...early childhood care and initial education... can be provided through arrangements involving families, communities, or institutional programmes, as appropriate." It also focuses on a second change because it states that "literacy is a necessary skill in itself and the foundation of other life skills." The third change is a focus on enhancing the environment for learning. EFA acknowledges, "Learning does not take place in isolation" (UNESCO, 1990).

To emphasize this last point, this section states:

> Societies, therefore, must ensure that all learners receive the nutrition, health care, and general physical and emotional support they need in order to participate actively in and benefit from their education. Knowledge and skills that will enhance the learning environment of children should be integrated into community learning programmes for adults. The education of children and their parents or other caretakers is mutually supportive and this interaction should be used to create, for all, a learning environment of vibrancy and warmth. (UNESCO, 1990)

Ten years later, in April of 2000, The World Education Forum was held at Dakar, Senegal. This forum was the first and most important event in education at the dawn of the new century. The 1,100 participants welcomed "the commitments made by the international community during the 1990s, and particularly the rights-based approach to education supported by the Universal Declaration of Human Rights" (UNESCO, 2000, p. 3). The Forum acknowledged that Education for All began a global movement to "universalize primary education and massively reduce illiteracy before the end of the decade" (EFA documents). Furthermore, it reported that there had been "significant progress" in many countries and that the vision of Education for All "remains pertinent and powerful." But "tragically, reality has fallen far short of this vision: millions of people are still denied their right to education and the opportunities it brings to live safer, healthier, more productive and more fulfilling lives." Participants considered the progress of the previous decade as "uneven and far too slow." They concurred, "Without accelerated progress towards education for all, national and internationally agreed targets for poverty reduction will be missed, and inequalities between countries and within societies will widen" (UNESCO, 2000, pp. 8, 12).

They cited "weak political will, insufficient financial resources and the inefficient use of those available, the burden of debt, inadequate attention to the learning needs of the poor and the excluded, a lack of attention to the quality of learning and an absence of commitment to overcoming gender disparities," as reasons for the failures (UNESCO, 2000). The Forum resulted in a document entitled the Dakar Framework for Action.[11] (See Appendix for the Dakar Framework for Action.) It states that the role of government is "indispensable," but it has to "be supplemented and supported by bold and comprehensive educational partnerships at all levels of society." It also declares, "Starting from early childhood and extending throughout life, the learners of the twenty-first century will require access to high quality educational opportunities that are responsive to their needs, equitable and gender-sensitive." Furthermore, the Framework emphasizes, "These opportunities must neither exclude nor discriminate. Since the pace, style, language and circumstances of learning will never be uniform for all, there should be room for diverse formal or less formal approaches, as long as they ensure sound learning and confer equivalent status" (UNESCO, 2000, p. 12).

By its conclusion, the World Education Forum adopted the Dakar Framework that identified six key measurable education goals which aim to meet the learning needs of all children, youth and adults by 2015. These goals, called the EFA goals, extend the work of EFA a decade earlier. The goals address the following concerns: improving early childhood education, supporting complete free and compulsory education for girls, ensuring equitable access to appropriate learning and life skills programmes, increasing percentages of adult literacy, and addressing gender disparities in primary and secondary education. The final goal focuses on improving the quality and ensuring the excellence of all aspects of education, so that recognized and measurable learning outcomes are achieved by all, especially in literacy, numeracy and essential life skills (UNESCO, 2000).

THE MILLENNIUM SUMMIT

Later that year, the Millennium Summit[12] convened at United Nations Headquarters in New York. One hundred forty-nine Heads of State and Government and high-ranking officials from over 40 other countries attended. They unanimously adopted the *Millennium Declaration*, a document which contained a "statement of values, principles and objectives for the international agenda for the twenty-first century. It also set deadlines for many collective actions" (UN, 2000).

The Millennium Declaration accomplished the following:

> The Millennium Declaration affirmed Member States' faith in the United Nations and its *Charter* as indispensable for a more peaceful, prosperous and just world. The collective responsibility of the governments of the world to uphold human dignity, equality and equity is recognized, as is the duty of world leaders to all people, and especially children and the most vulnerable. (UN, 2000)

The leaders at the Summit determined that "the central challenge of today is to ensure that globalization becomes a positive force for all, acknowledging that at present both its benefits and its costs are unequally shared." As a result of the Summit, world leaders "committed their nations to a new global partnership to reduce extreme poverty, and set out a series of time-bound targets, with a deadline of 2015." These targets have become known as the Millennium Development Goals (MGD's).[13] The eight Millennium Development Goals are to: (1) eradicate extreme poverty and hunger; (2) achieve universal primary education; (3) promote gender equality and empower women; (4) reduce child mortality; (5) improve maternal health; (6) combat HIV/AIDS, malaria and other diseases; (7) ensure environmental sustainability; and (8) develop a global partnership for development (UN, 2000). (See Appendix for additional details of the Millennium Development Goals.) While these goals include universal primary education, literacy is not a specific goal.

The United Nations Literacy Decade (UNLD) was implemented from 2003–2012. The mandate for the UNLD focuses on literacy for all which is described as being "at the heart of basic education for all." The mandate also calls for the creation of "literate environments and societies" that are described as "…essential for achieving the goals of eradicating poverty, reducing child mortality, curbing population growth, achieving gender equality and ensuring sustainable development, peace and democracy" (United Nations, 2002).

In 2010, the United Nations Summit on the Millennium Development Goals (MDGs) was held. This meeting concluded with the adoption of a global action plan to achieve the eight anti-poverty goals by their 2015 target date and the announcement of major new commitments for women's and children's health and other initiatives against poverty, hunger and disease. The document that resulted from the three-day Summit was *Keeping the Promise: United to Achieve the Millennium Development Goals*. This document reaffirms the commitment of world leaders to the MDGs and sets out a concrete action agenda for achieving the Goals by 2015 (UN Summit on Millennium Development Goals, 2010).

Together, the EFA goals and the and MGD's create an "ambitious roadmap for the global community to follow. They offer a long-term vision of reduced poverty and hunger, better health and education, sustainable lifestyles, strong partnerships and shared commitments." The EFA goals and MDGs are complementary. Irina Bokova, UNESCO's Director-General, states, "When you fund education, you are securing progress towards all the Millennium Development Goals" (United Nations, 2015).

In December of 2014, the Synthesis Report on the Post 2015 Agenda was released. The report by Secretary General of the United Nations, Ban Ki-moon, is entitled, *The Road to Dignity by 2030: Ending Poverty, Transforming Lives and Protecting the Planet.* The report includes a proposal of seventeen goals drawn up by the Open Working Group on Sustainable Development Goals. The General Assembly decided that this proposal will be the main basis for the Post-2015 intergovernmental process. Goals include ending poverty and hunger; ensuring healthy lives and well-being for people of all ages; building resilient infrastructure; making cites and other human settlements inclusive, safe, resilient and sustainable; and conserving protecting, restoring, and sustaining terrestrial and marine ecosystems. Goal number 4 addresses education. It states, "Ensure inclusive and equitable quality education and promote lifelong learning opportunities for all" (UN Secretary General, 2014).

Over several decades, UNESCO has been a global leader in promoting both access to basic education for children and education programs for adults. During this time, UNESCO also published reports on literacy rates. The language of assessment and instruction that informs the quality of teaching and learning was not a focus of these reports. Since these elements were missing, both policy-making and implementation of programs were more challenging (Wagner, 2010). Since the World Education Forum in Dakar, however, UNESCO has published extensive annual EFA Global Monitoring Reports that track progress toward the goals of the Dakar Framework. Monitoring Reports are issued for the Millennium Development Goals as well.

The 2006 EFA *Global Monitoring Report: Literacy for Life* states that since 2000, when the EFA goals were adopted, the main focus of the reports had been placed on two goals, primary education and gender parity. At this point in time, literacy was still denied to "about one-fifth of the world's adult population" (UNESCO, 2005, p. Foreword).[14] Literacy was seen as "one of the most neglected goals of the six goals adopted…by 164 countries at the World Education Forum in Dakar (Senegal) in 2000" (UNESCO, 2005, p. 27).

Literacy for Life states:

> The fact that some 770 million adults– about one-fifth of the world's adult population – do not have basic literacy skills is not only morally indefensible but is also an appalling loss of human potential and economic capacity. The Report makes a powerful case to end this neglect by affirming that literacy is a right in itself, essential to achieve all the EFA goals and critically important for development. The emergence of knowledge societies makes literacy even more critical than in the past. Achieving widespread literacy can only happen in the context of building literate societies that encourage individuals to acquire and use their literacy skills. (UNESCO, 2005, p. 5)

The report includes the following statement:

> Literacy is a right. It is implicit in the right to education. It is recognized as a right, explicitly for both children and adults, in certain international conventions. It is included in key international declarations. (UNESCO, 2005, p. 136)

The Foreword to this report provides several reasons why literacy is at the core of Education for All. It states, "...a good quality basic education equips pupils with literacy skills for life and further learning; literate parents are more likely to send their children to school; literate people are better able to access continuing education opportunities; and literate societies are better geared to meet pressing development challenges" (UNESCO, 2005, p. Foreword).

The Universal Declaration of Human Rights first defined basic education as a human right. The Executive Summary of Literacy for Life states, "Definitions and understandings of literacy have broadened considerably over the past fifty years, influenced by academic research, international policy agendas and national priorities. In all understandings, literacy embodies reading and writing skills" (UNESCO, 2005, p. 22).

Chapter 6 of the report continues:

> As definitions of literacy shifted—from a discrete set of technical skills, to human resource skills for economic growth, to capabilities for socio-cultural and political change—international organizations acknowledged broader understandings of literacy, which encompass 'conscientization,' literacy practices, lifelong learning, orality, and information and communication technology literacy. (UNESCO, 2005, p. 159)

Literacy for Life documents the significance of "growing international awareness of the broader social contexts in which literacy is encouraged, acquired, developed and sustained." It clarifies that "literacy is no longer exclusively understood as an individual transformation, but as a contextual and societal one." It also defines "rich literate environments" as "public or private milieux with abundant written documents (e.g. books, magazines and newspapers), visual materials (e.g. signs, posters and handbills), or communication and electronic media (e.g. radios, televisions, computers and mobile phones)." Literate societies are seen as places that "enable the free exchange of text-based information and provide an array of opportunities for lifelong learning" Regardless of the setting—home, school, or workplace— the "quality of literate environments affects how literacy skills are practised and how literacy is understood" (UNESCO, 2005, p. 159). Accessing "scientific and technical knowledge, legal information, culture and the media" are also benefits of living in a literate society. Additionally, and importantly, "literacy has been recognized as a mechanism for the pursuit of other human rights" (UNESCO, 2005, p. 22).

The 2013/4 EFA Global Monitoring Report *Teaching and Learning: Achieving Quality for All*, describes a "shift in emphasis" from universal primary education towards "quality and learning." This shift is necessary because "250 million children have not had the chance to learn the basics, even though 130 million of them have spent at least four years in school" (UNESCO, 2013, p. 85). This report states that a "global-post-2015 goal will be set to ensure that, by 2030, all children and youth, regardless of their circumstances, acquire foundation skills in reading, writing, and mathematics" (UNESCO, 2013, p. 89).

This report also describes successful models for teaching and learning. Some of the components of these programs include:

- Trained community teachers provide welcoming, inclusive atmosphere
- A timetable that reflects the children's and communities' realities
- Child-centered learning methods
- Continuity with the same teacher to help foster a friendly, supportive learning environment
- An absence of physical punishment
- Teachers who are generally recruited from surrounding communities, ensuring a common cultural and linguistic background and enhancing accountability to community members
- Curriculum that is taught in a language that children understand to ensure that children from ethnic and linguistic minorities acquire strong foundation skills
- A bilingual approach that ensures continued teaching in the child's mother tongue alongside the introduction of a second language—ideally throughout the primary grades—can improve performance in the second language as well as in other subjects (UNESCO, 2013, pp. 282–283).

Later in this book, the work of many educators who incorporate many of these principles will be explored. Before examining those models, however, it is necessary to identify some of the barriers that get in the way of ensuring education and literacy as human rights in small places.

NOTES

1. From IN YOUR HANDS: A GUIDE FOR COMMUNITY ACTION by the Editorial Committee for the Tenth Anniversary of Universal Declaration of Human Rights copyright © 1958 the Church Peace Union (now know as the Carnegie Council for Ethics and International Affairs). Reprinted with permission of the Carnegie Council for Ethics and International Affairs. All rights reserved.
2. From THE CONVENTION ON THE RIGHTS OF THE CHILD. UNICEF Copyright © 1990, United Nations. Reprinted with permission of the United Nations.
3. From Oveview: Convention on the Rights of the Child (CRC). Copyright © UNICEF Uzbekistan 2006. United Nations. Reprinted with permission of the United Nations.
4. From 20th Anniversary: Convention on the Rights of the Child. UNICEF Jamaica. Copyright © 2010, United Nations. Reprinted with permission of the United Nations.
5. Used by permission of © Amnesty International Publications, 1 Easton Street, London WC1X 0DW, United Kingdom. http://www.amnesty.org.

[6] THE DECLARATION OF PERSEPOLIS from the International Symposium for Literacy. Copyright ©1975 United Nations. Reprinted with permission of the United Nations.

[7] From the Preface by Brian V. Street in THE SOCIAL USES OF LITERACY (1996) Mastin Prinsloo and Mignonne Breier, (Eds.). Copyright © 1996 by Sached Books and John Benjamins Publishing Company. Reprinted by permission of John Benjamins Publishing Company.

[8] From the Coordinator's Notebook, No. 14, 1993/4 by The Consultive Group Secretariat. Copyright © 1993/4 United Nations. Reprinted with permission of the United Nations.

[9] From the WORLD DECLARATION ON EDUCATION FOR ALL, MEETING BASIC LEARNING NEEDS. World Education Forum. Copyright © 2000 the United Nations. Reprinted with permission of the United Nations.

[10] From Education for All (EFA) Overview. Resources for Speakers. Copyright ©2015 United Nations. Reprinted with permission of the United Nations.

[11] From THE DAKAR FRAMEWORK FOR ACTION, EDUCATION FOR ALL: MEETING OUR COLLECTIVE COMMITMENTS. UNESCO. Copyright © 2000 United Nations. Reprinted with permission of the United Nations.

[12] From Millennium Summit (6-8 September 2000), United Nations Conferences, Meetings, and Events. Copyright © 2000 United Nations. Reprinted with permission of the United Nations

[13] The Millennium Development Goals by the Millennium Goals Committee. Copyright ©2000 United Nations. Reprinted with permission of the United Nations.

[14] From EFA 2006 GLOBAL MONITORING REPORT, LITERACY FOR LIFE. UNESCO. Copyright © 2005 United Nations. Reprinted with permission of the United Nations.

PART 2

THINGS SO DESTRUCTIVE: BARRIERS TO LITERACY AS A HUMAN RIGHT

CHAPTER 4

THE LEGACY OF THE BANKING MODEL OF EDUCATION

> *One of the most durable and destructive legacies of discrimination is the way that we have internalized a sense of limitation.* —Barack Obama (Obama B., 2009)

THE UNDERESTIMATION OF LEARNERS' CAPABILITIES

As described in the previous chapter, banking education practices limit opportunities for learning and can lead to an internalized sense of limitation—a dehumanization of people. This barrier can get in the way no matter where people live in the world. It can lead to a devastating sense of both individual and collective powerlessness. This is an idea so destructive that virtually no one would endorse it publicly. The focus of the this part of this book will center on this often invisible factor, the underestimation of the capabilities of learners.

Psychologist Albert Bandura states:

> The psychological barriers created by beliefs of collective powerlessness are more demoralizing and debilitating than are external impediments. The less people bring their influence to bear on conditions that affect their lives the more control they relinquish to others. People who have high collective efficacy will mobilize their efforts and resources to surmount the obstacles to the changes they seek. But those convinced of their collective powerlessness will cease trying, even though changes are attainable through perseverant collective effort. (Bandura, 1998, p. 69)

In her research with children in Head Start, Janice Hale, author of *Learning While Black*, found that three-year olds just entering Head Start performed better on a measure of children's overall cognitive abilities than five-year-old children who had been in Head Start for two years. Hale's findings are of particular importance because we have come to realize that children learn from birth. The children in Hale's study have learned a great deal by age three, but that learning is no longer evident at age five. Hale also notes that the reading scores of African American children fall below grade level at grade five, and then the scores continue to drop, so that between grades seven and ten, the scores are two years below grade level. She states that it is as if the longer children stay in school, the greater the deterioration in their performance. Hale argues that African American children do not "enter school disadvantaged," but "they leave school disadvantaged." She concludes, "There is nothing wrong with the children, but there is clearly something wrong with what happens to them in school" (Hale, 2001, p. 46).[1]

Linguist James Gee also questions the nature of schooling. He points out that children from certain minority groups are good at learning when they enter school. But school somehow changes them, so that they are no longer effective learners (Gee J. P., 2004).

When I began teaching, I was operating from a banking perspective of education. The instructions that were written in red print in my teaching manual composed the script for my lessons. It began with the words, "And now say." I tried dutifully to follow the directives in the manual. In their book, *Affirming Diversity*, Sonia Nieto and Patty Bode state, "Because critical pedagogy begins with the experiences and viewpoints of students, it is by its very nature multicultural" (Nieto & Bode, 2008, p. 56).[2] Critical pedagogy is not based on an imposed culture. In my early years as a classroom teacher, I was imposing a culture on students— and it was not working.

When I became a reading teacher a few years later, I tried to help other teachers to follow the directives as well. But as I recorded the scores for stacks of reading tests, I soon began to realize that the script was not working for many of our students. The children were divided into groups according to their performance on the tests. The students who failed a part were held in a lower reading group and re-taught specific skills. These exercises that were part of a skills approach to reading left little time for actual reading. Once the lessons in the readiness program were learned, children would move on to the first pre-primer, a book that contained stories that were comprised of approximately eight different words. Writing was confined to practicing letter formation or filling in a blank on a worksheet. Some children completed the readiness program in about four to six months. For others it took a year, or possibly two or longer, until they were given even primer stories to read in school. Primarily because of the belief that children must be taught reading readiness skills before they engage in reading and writing activities, the skill/reading time ratio was typically the highest for children of the lowest reading ability.

Working within this approach led me to make incorrect assumptions about children I taught, their capabilities, the strength of language that they had brought with them from home, and the power of their minds. I made what Holdaway described as the "traditional error." I viewed reading and writing as school subjects. I did not connect them to children's language and spoken culture (Holdaway D., 1979). As noted in the Introduction to this book, when I became aware of this error, I began to engage in research. At that point, I began to recognize the error of underestimating children's capabilities was taking place in other classrooms as well.

View from a Small Place

While doing one research project, I met George, a first-grade student, who was disempowered in school. When I suggested that he write a story with me,

> he commented "This ain't easy." His words summed up not only the writing he was attempting to do at the moment, but his view of reading and writing in general. That day, he made a stick-figure drawing of a robot and a picture of a heart. He also wrote two words in which the sequence of letters did not match the sequence of the sounds. He glanced around the room frequently and hesitated to write. I encouraged him to "pretend to spell," using any letters or sounds he knew. But he said "I don't know how to spell that stuff." "Nah, I'm still beginning to read. I'm still in the one group in school.in the first book." George did not see himself as a reader, and he did not think of himself as a writer. I asked George if he might write down a story from his reading book. He said "There ain't no stories in my reading book." I asked him what was in his reading book. He said, "Just work to do."

George knew about stories. He knew that stories are found in books. He understood that words were spelled in specific ways. But his knowledge of written language went untapped. George regarded reading and writing as tasks that were still beyond his capabilities. He was not given a choice of materials or books that matched his interests. He was waiting until someone moved him to another book so he could learn to read and write. He was not allowed to make decisions about what he should focus on as he learned. In his classroom, language was broken down into bits that were spoon-fed to him. George was not viewed as a reader or writer. Some children completed the school's readiness program in kindergarten. It was March of first grade, and George was still mired in learning letter names and sounds and filling in blanks in a workbook. The "work" that George was doing required him to learn dozens of letter and sound associations. His reading program emphasized the sub-skills of letter names, letter formation, and spelling patterns. He encountered words in isolation. They were not part of sentences or longer text. Much of his time was spent making lines to match columns in workbooks and filling single letters into blanks. When he mastered these lessons, he would move on to books containing stories designed from a limited number of controlled vocabulary words. These stories were designed to teach these specific words. They were not real, meaningful stories. Even children who came into school reading fluently had to work their way through these activities before they read actual books. Little time was spent reading. Reading materials were designated for the reader by a pre-ordained program. Reading was viewed as a separate subject that happened in a specific time-slot during the day. Writing, if it took place at all, was limited to single words or short phrases to be filled in to worksheets. Handwriting exercises took precedence over expressing meaning through writing. George's classroom was not the only place where these kinds of practices were being implemented.

UNESCO's 2006 EFA Global Monitoring Report, *Literacy for Life*, (UNESCO, 2005, p. 152) documents that Freire's work influenced literacy in Africa:

> In francophone Africa, scholars such as Joseph Ki-Zerbo from Burkina Faso have documented mobilization for an 'Africanized' literacy that would directly

> respond to the pressing communication needs of the continent. This movement has motivated the introduction of Freirean methodologies by several NGOs. (Fernandez, 2005)

As seen in the following account of an adult learner in a night-school program in Cape Town, South Africa, however, Freire's work did not influence all areas of the country. Therefore, other learners had to endure the same kind of pedagogy as George.

View from a Small Place

> The learners worked exclusively from photocopied materials produced by two different English and literacy organisations in Cape Town. The literacy group mainly seemed to do word building from syllables on the theme of personal information, and I watched Tsotso writing out her name over and over again. I never saw any materials being brought into the classes which were not part of the pre-planned curriculum: not one text, or even one written word from the context of the learners' lives entered the classroom. (Kell, 1996, p. 248)[3]

PRESCRIPTIVE PROGRAMS

In the U.S. in the 1950's, reading was taught through a series of practices that were drawn from a variety of sources. The implementation of these practices came to be called the eclectic approach. The purpose of this approach was to meet the needs of readers who learn in different ways. The practices were not consistent and coherent, however, and there was no clear understanding about why they were being implemented. The situation led to chaos and confusion (Holdaway D., 1979, p. 30).

Holdaway explains in response to this situation, "During the fifties, a determined effort was made in the United States to solve the literacy problem in the schools once and for all." To accomplish this end, "Teams of very experienced and talented academics worked with publishers in creating 'basal' reading programmes supported by massive guidance to teachers in the shape of manuals and resource books of an extremely detailed nature…" Holdaway viewed these programs as "almost offensively prescriptive of every word the teacher should utter." He states the "… programmes reflected the best of informed opinion from many sources, presenting eclectic approaches in a coherent and systematic bundle" (Holdaway D., 1979, p. 30). The authors of these programs attempted to explain conflicting underlying theories, but they were not able to eliminate the confusion brought about by the eclectic approaches.

As described above, in my early teaching experiences, using one such program, readers were expected to work successfully through a predetermined sequence of sound-symbol lessons, then frequently-used words, and then stories with controlled vocabulary. The learners were trapped. They did not encounter actual books. These practices continued to disempower students, especially marginalized students, for decades.

In the 1990's, researchers Carole Edelsky, Bess Altwerger, and Barbara Flores stated, "The notion of reading as word identification (whether accomplished through a whole word or phonics approach) is based on a behaviorist view of language and oral and written language acquisition" (Edelsky, Altwater, & Flores, 1991, p. 29). They explain at that time, it still influenced some methods and that were used to teach reading. In some places, the behaviorist perspective is still being promoted today.

In Australia and New Zealand during the 1970's, there was also a "great deal of speculation about 'reading readiness.'" Holdaway reports that "people began talking about teaching 'pre-reading' skills, and setting up 'readiness programmes,' without reference to the learning situations that actually produce the most literacy-ready children at school entry." He notes that "there have even appeared a number of 'pre-literacy' programs beginning with text-less books!" (Holdaway D., 1979, p. 39). He cites the work of Marie Clay and Margaret Clark, concluding that "More responsibly, research has begun to indicate that many of these purported pre-reading skills and activities which have been speculated into our schools seem to have little relationship to actual progress in reading" (Clay, 1972, p. 75; Clark, 1976, p. 100). Holdaway and other educators from Australia and New Zealand believed that reading at school should be part of the continuous process of language and literacy growth that takes place before children enter school. As we'll see in Chapter 10, Holdaway developed the shared book approach in response to concerns that "populations of Native Polynesian and Maori children were not succeeding in traditional reading and language programs" in New Zealand schools (Hirst & Slavik, 2012, p. 5).[4]

Sylvia Ashton-Warner, who developed innovative ways of teaching Maori children, was struck by the lack of challenge in the reading materials that commercial programs offered her children. She said, "The distance between the content of their minds… and the content of our reading books is nothing less than frightening" (Ashton-Warner, 1963, p. 62).[5]

In the United States, in the early 1970's, Professor Jerome Harste of Indiana University observed the teaching of reading in classrooms. He argued that teachers had theoretical notions about reading that they transmitted to their kids through the kinds of engagements they had. These engagements revealed what the teachers believed about the reading process, and these beliefs affected how they went about teaching reading. At this time, Harste had young children of his own. He was "amazed" by what his children knew about language. However, he was "stunned" by the kinds of assumptions that the teachers were making about kids not having language (Harste J., 2012). As a result of his findings, he and his colleagues Carolyn Burke and Virginia Woodward conducted a 10-year longitudinal study examining what children ages 3–6 knew about reading and writing prior to going to school. The study resulted in the publication of *Language Stories & Literacy Lessons* in 1984 (Harste, Woodward, & Burke, 1984).[6]

Harste believes that the terms “readiness,” “developmental stages”, “emergent reading” and “scaffolding” are problematic because they do not acknowledge what children learned prior to formal instruction. Harste states:

> At its most demeaning level the argument runs: If ‘little children’ have ‘little thoughts’ and attend to ‘easy cues’ in written language, then structured environments need to be designed which recognize these differences and facilitate literacy learning. In more sophisticated form the instructional assumption runs: Complex processes, like written language and written language learning, must be simplified in order to be learned.
>
> This position, in whatever form, inevitably leads to a distortion of the linguistic context…Further, the position fails to explore, acknowledge, or appreciate what the young child has learned about written language prior to formal instruction. (Harste, Woodward, & Burke, 1984, p. 70)

THE PERPETUAL PEDAGOGY OF POVERTY

In 1958, Martin Haberman, a professor of curriculum and instruction at the University of Wisconsin, identified the pedagogy of poverty. This poverty encompasses specific examples of banking education. It has been written about extensively, but it bears repeating here because over several decades it has continued to exist and grow. Haberman states, “An observer of urban classrooms can find examples of almost every form of pedagogy: including direct instruction, cooperative learning, peer tutoring, individualized instruction, computer-assisted learning, behavior modification, the use of student contracts, media-assisted instruction, scientific inquiry, lecture/discussion, tutoring by specialists or volunteers, and even the use of problem-solving units common in progressive education.” Yet, in spite of this wide range of options, a “typical form of teaching has become accepted as basic.” This pedagogy is “not supported by research, by theory, or by the best practice of superior urban teachers” (Haberman, 1991, pp. 290–292).[7] It limits the possibility of success for children who attend schools that embrace it.

These practices denigrate the language, culture and literacy of those who are monetarily poor. The perpetual repetition of ineffective practices that fail to acknowledge children’s language and literacy strengths and comply with existing conditions are elements of the pedagogy of poverty. Haberman named 14 specific acts that are expected practices in most urban schools, and if not performed would constitute evidence of not teaching. The teaching acts are: “giving information, asking questions, giving directions, making assignments, monitoring seatwork, reviewing assignments, giving tests, reviewing tests, assigning homework, reviewing homework, settling disputes, punishing noncompliance, marking papers, and giving grades” (Haberman, 1991, p. 291).

Haberman contends:

> Taken separately, there may be nothing wrong with these activities. There are occasions when any one of the 14 acts might have a beneficial effect. Taken together and performed to the systematic exclusion of the other acts, they have become the pedagogical coin of the realm of urban schools. They constitute the pedagogy of poverty not merely what teachers do and what youngsters expect, but for different reasons, what parents, the community, and the general public assume teaching to be. (Haberman, 1991, p. 291)

The acts of the pedagogy of poverty are not unique to a single, classroom, school, or school system. Many of these practices exist in rural and suburban schools, but they are the typical form of teaching that has become accepted as a basic component of the culture of urban schools. Harold Raynolds, Jr., former Commissioner of Education in Massachusetts, observes that inadequate schools underserve poor children. He argues that if affluent children are in an inadequate school, they can survive because their other advantages can make up for the short-comings of the school. Raynolds also notes that the number and percentage of poor children both in the United States and across the world is increasing. He believes that the fight against illiteracy remains a losing cause (Freire, 1993).

Initially, it may appear that the pedagogy of poverty manifests itself in the schooling of older students. But I found that the onset of the pedagogy of poverty affects the education of children from the earliest days of school by perpetuating the under-estimation and under-utilization of students' understandings, including young children's knowledge of oral and written language.

Haberman sounds the following warning about the nature of the pedagogy of poverty:

> The pedagogy of poverty is sufficiently powerful to undermine the implementation of any reform effort because it determines the way pupils spend their time, the nature of the behaviors they practice, and the bases of their self-concepts as learners. Essentially, it is a pedagogy in which learners can 'succeed' without becoming either involved or thoughtful. (Haberman, 1991, p. 292)

Although the pedagogy of poverty was first described over a half-century ago, the work of several researchers shows that it continues to this day. The following examples demonstrate how the pedagogy of poverty still plays out in the lives of young children.

School literacy typically involves reading, writing, speaking, and listening skills. These skills represent the mainstream practices sanctioned by schools. There are however, limitations to this definition. This view of literacy is esteemed in schools, and is often regarded as "more literate" than other ways of talking, writing, and drawing from texts (Spears-Bunton & Powell, 2009, p. 5). However, this view is both limited and limiting. It marginalizes students who have different forms of cultural practices, experiences, and literacies. As researchers Spears-Bunton and Powell note, "pre-packaged literacy programs often promote ritualized, mechanical responses that have little to do with students' lived experiences" (Spears-Bunton & Powell, 2009, p. 9).

Author and professor, Lisa Delpit, contends that those who employ "skills-based approaches can teach less by focusing solely on isolated, decontextualized bits." She cautions that when children are not allowed to "use their minds to create and interpret texts, [they] will focus on low-level thinking and their school-based intellect will atrophy" (Delpit, 2006, pp. 173–174). She explains that children are often given these activities in reaction to low scores on standardized tests, but the activities rob children of the literacy opportunities they really need. Delpit states:

> [Children] end up spending so much time matching circles and triangles that no one ever introduces them to actually learning how to read. Should anyone doubt it, I can guarantee that no amount of matching circles and triangles ever taught anyone how to read. Worse, these activities take time away from real kinds of involvement in literacy such as listening to and seeing words in real books. (Delpit, 2006, p. 174)

In *Lives on the Edge, Single Mothers and Their Children in the Other Americ*a, Valerie Polakow writes about remedial classes where children are given "endless worksheets" in place of actual reading. She questions how children can ever develop comprehension when they never encounter "an actual children's book" (Polakow, 1993, p. 151).[8] She describes children who can read, but fail constantly because they do poorly on tests of sub-skills and worksheets. Polakow observes that an appropriate pedagogy is seldom found in places where children are considered to be at risk. She states, "Rarely are at risk children given extra doses of talk-time, of expressive activities, of discovery-oriented projects that they themselves control" (Polakow, 1993, p. 157).

Polakow (Polakow, 1993, p. 152) cites the work of Jean Anyon who, in her study of instruction in elementary classrooms from divergent socioeconomic communities, found "distinctions of social class" were "evident in both differentiated curriculum and process." As Anyon describes, "Activities and tests for poor children were geared to lower-level thinking skills, to retention of subject matter, while activities in affluent schools tended to foster creativity and independent thought" (Anyon, 1981). The classrooms of these children, the small places where they reside, become part of a larger culture that disempowers learners. Polakow further notes, "Teachers do not live above their culture; they too are participants in the pervasive poverty discourse that conceals economic and educational inequalities, state-induced destitution" (Polakow, 1993, p. 146).

Delpit asserts that, when teachers do not understand or recognize the knowledge and language competence that children possess, they will "underteach" the children, regardless of the methods they use. She maintains that teacher education programs bear responsibility for shaping teachers' attitudes about monetarily poor children, because these programs typically focus on research that links failure to socioeconomic status, cultural differences, and growing up in a single-parent household. Delpit believes that this intense negative indoctrination shapes teachers attitudes and limits children's chances for success significantly (Delpit L., 2006).

As seen in my example in the introduction to this book, failing to value children's language, a deficit view of children's language and abilities, can lead to lower expectations of many students. Furthermore, the low-level, rote tasks that students encounter as a result of these low expectations can close down opportunities for children to engage in reasoning and reflection. These tasks are apt to make less sense than tasks that require deeper thought (Resnick, 1987).

Linda Darling-Hammond, professor of education at Stanford University, calls the results of these low expectations "institutionally-sanctioned discrimination" (Darling-Hammond, 1995, p. 465). This discrimination "draws power from the wider society." Additionally, "normalized talk that stereotypes racial, cultural, and linguistic groups" increases the power of this discrimination (Lopez-Robertson, Long, & Turner-Nash, 2010, p. 95).[9] This power is also fueled by "destructive media images" (Zentella, 2005, p. 1).

The pedagogy of poverty does not go away. Time and time again, it resurfaces in different guises. In 2010, Haberman addressed the state of work in classrooms. He writes, "in the present system, teachers are accountable only for engaging in the limited set of behaviors commonly regarded as acts of teaching in urban schools — that is, the pedagogy of poverty." He adds, "It's painful to report that the teacher acts I described in this article 20 years ago are still the typical acts of teaching performed by all teachers" (Haberman, 2010). Professor Susan Ohanian adds that Haberman's description of the pedagogy of poverty from 1991 is "even more distressingly accurate in 2011" (Ohanian, 2011, p. 1).

A RECENT GUISE OF THE BANKING MODEL OF EDUCATION

During the time I was writing this book, I was contacted by a teacher who was following the prescribed program for her school, drawing reading material from a library of leveled books. But several of her children were mired—not in lessons about letters and sounds this time—but stuck at the same book level for months. The children were not progressing. Reading, as it was being presented, was not meaningful for them. The teacher considered the situation an emergency.

Concerns about leveling books have been the focus of the research of Kath Glasswell and Michael Ford. They describe a classroom in which children are prevented from attempting to read a book that is even one level above their assessed level, another example of banking education. They also report their concerns about a school in which 50% of the students, who were instructed through leveled reading during the primary grades, entered the intermediate grades reading below grade level

(Glasswell & Ford, 2011).[10] Additionally, researchers Dzaldov and Peterson state, "We seem to be in the midst of leveling mania in which massive amounts of time, money and energy are devoted to organizing books by reading levels. It appears that teachers are driven to attach a level to every text that students encounter during their school day" (Dzaldov & Peterson, 2005, p. 222).

Glasswell and Ford view the problems with leveling as a bad thing that has happened to a good idea—a rigid orthodoxy that has grown up around a useful practice. They argue, as Shannon and others have in the past, that commercial materials lead to less teacher reflection and a reification of certain reading practices. Furthermore, the design of the texts can lead to heavy dependence on the materials at the expense of professional judgment (Shannon, 1992). In the case of leveled books, readers are often identified by their level. For example, a child may be referred as a "Level J." Consistently labeling the reader in this manner can mask the reader's strengths and instructional needs and close down the teacher's reflection on them. Glasswell and Ford (Glasswell & Ford, 2011) concur with Pearson who suggests that such instructional tools can create the illusion of "scientific cachet" (Pearson, 2006), and this makes the tools attractive to users who allow materials to drive decision—making in instructional planning. In other words, the materials become the focus rather than the reader.

THE FAILURE OF READING FIRST

In 2008, the final report of Reading First, an integral part of the 2002 No Child Left Behind law, was issued. Reading First was a $1 billion-a-year reading program, or a $6 billion dollar program over 6 years, designed to strengthen children's reading skills.

The following are three major findings of the study:

- Reading First did not produce a statistically significant impact on student reading comprehension test scores in grades one, two, or three.
- There was no consistent pattern of effects over time in the impact estimates for reading instruction in grade one or in reading comprehension in any grade. There appeared to be a systematic decline in reading instruction impacts in grade two over time.
- There was no relationship between reading comprehension and the number of years a student was exposed to Reading First (Gamse, Jacob, Horst, Boulay, & Unlu, 2008, pp. xv–xvi).

Prior to the implementation of Reading First, the National Reading Panel identified five components or "pillars" of reading: phonemic awareness, word identification skills, vocabulary knowledge, reading rate, and comprehension. In their book, *Accessible Assessment*, Opitz, Ford and Ereksen make the case that four of the five "pillars" are local knowledge outcomes, a level of what they call cognitive outcomes (Opitz, Ford, & Erekson, 2011). These outcomes focus on the small parts of the reading process, including concepts of print, phonemic awareness, alphabetic knowledge, sound-symbol relationships, and high frequency sight words. While these outcomes are necessary, "visible," and easy to assess (Opitz, Ford, & Erekson, 2011, p. 157), analyzing a reader's knowledge and use of these outcomes does not provide a complete picture of the reader. Readers do employ phonemic awareness, alphabetic knowledge, and attend sound-symbol relationships, or graphophonics. Problems arise, however, when instruction focuses solely on these aspects in isolation while delaying other aspects of reading, and denying the reader's language, knowledge, and culture. These problems do not exist, however, when phonics refers to understanding about sound-symbol relationships within language use (Mills, O'Keefe, & Stephens, 1992).

Along with local knowledge outcomes, Opitz, Ford, and Ereksen describe other outcomes that are necessary for comprehensive assessment of a reader. Global outcomes, another level of cognitive outcomes, assess the following: ways of thinking about the content being learned; mental processes, such as higher order levels of thought; response; understanding; comprehending; interpreting; and monitoring of strategy use. Affective outcomes determine how learners see themselves as readers and writers, how well readers and writers think they read and write, and how much they want to read and write (Opitz, Ford, & Erekson, 2011, pp. 155–156). This approach to reading outcomes is influenced by the work of Fitzgerald (Fitzgerald, 1999) and Hall (Hall, 2005).

Opitz, Ford, and Ereksen explain that the Bush Administration's Reading First Initiative mandated under NCLB emphasized the pillars of reading, four of which were local knowledge outcomes. This emphasis did not yield results. These researchers describe the impact study as actually illustrating "the startling facts" (Opitz, Ford, & Erekson, 2011, p. 157) that program evaluators could not find statistically significant differences in the area of comprehension between classrooms in which teachers were using Reading First programs and those that were not (Gamse, Jacob, Horst, Boulay, & Unlu, 2008).

Opitz, Ford, and Erekson clarify that there were no significant differences on a widely used comprehension measure, despite the fact that teachers in schools with Reading First programs received more time in professional development programs compared schools without Reading First—twenty-five versus thirteen hours. Eighty percent of the teachers in Reading First schools also received coaching, while only 60% in non- Reading First schools did. In addition, teachers in Reading First classrooms spent about ten minutes more each day on instruction in the five areas emphasized by the program than teachers in schools that didn't receive the grants. Opitz, Ford, and Erekson state, "They 'pumped up' everything obvious, everything visible, and got *no statistically significant results*!" (Opitz, Ford, & Erekson, 2011, p. 158).

At the time of the study, Grover J. "Russ" Whitehurst was Director of the Institute of Education Sciences, the Education Department's research arm. He notes, "There was no statistically significant impact on reading comprehension scored in grades one, two, or three." Whitehurst adds, It's possible that, in implementing Reading First, there is greater emphasis on decoding skills (i.e., local knowledge outcomes) and not enough emphasis, or maybe not correctly structured emphasis, on reading comprehension (i.e. global knowledge outcomes) (Whitehurst G., 2014).

Opitz, Ford, and Erekson (Opitz, Ford, & Erekson, 2011, p. 159) drawing on Schutz conclude:

> This is but one finding that helps us underscore that if teachers are spending more time doing something and getting the same or worse results—if they are spending all their time counting what doesn't count—they are worse off than when they started. (Schutz, 2009)

Furthermore, the discreet skills-based assessments and instruction of Reading First were isolated from the reader's "world of language and spoken culture." They were another example of Freire's concept of banking education. Additionally, NCLB left a legacy of a test-driven environment requiring teachers to justify how they use classroom time in relation to predetermined and measurable outcomes.

This legacy is now deeply entrenched in American education. In a conversation at Harvard University with European neuroscientist Bruno della Chiesa and developmental psychologist Howard Gardner, linguist Noam Chomsky stated that Freire's description of banking education "is contemporary schooling in the US today—teaching to tests" (Discussion of Pedagogy of the Oppressed: Noam Chomsky, Howard Gardner, Bruno della Chiesa, 2013). Noting the need to return to critical pedagogy, della Cheisa adds, "in the world we live in today," especially in the U.S. and the western world, Freire's work is "more relevant than ever" (Discussion of Pedagogy of the Oppressed: Noam Chomsky, Howard Gardner, Bruno della Chiesa, 2013).[11]

Professor and author, Anne Dyson, describes how this deficit model is playing out:

> In the current politics of accountability in the U.S., writing is a collection of skills, particularly in financially strapped urban schools.... Traditional 'basics' (e.g. writing conventions) loom large at least in part because they are easily tested by grade-level benchmark assessments and by school-wide achievement tests required by federally supported reading programs. In this basic-skills approach, children are invisible, indexed only by their achievement test scores. These scores are themselves treated as a kind of scrapbook artifact, indexing effective or ineffective instructional programs. (Dyson A., 2007, p. 115)

As Edwards, Thompson McMillon, and Turner point out, "Rather than offering immediate assistance to schools with low scores, extra funding is withheld and threats of future takeover by the State Department of Education force many administrators into a 'teach to the test' mode." Low scores on tests result in "reactionary teaching" in which teachers emphasize what "they think students need to know for their assessments." Further, the researchers state that many schools that serve minority students take on this reactionary stance in their efforts to boost low test scores.

"As a result, minority students, who were already suffering from inequities in their education, are now falling further behind in areas that are not covered in a 'teach to the test' curriculum" (Edwards, Thompson McMillon, & Turner, 2008, p. 34).

THE COMMON CORE

In the United States, the Common Core State Standards (CCSS) may hold promise because they emphasize foundational skills, language, and reading both informational texts and fiction. The foundational reading skills standards are directed toward fostering students' understanding and working knowledge of concepts of print, the alphabetic principle, and other basic conventions of the English writing system. The CCSS note that these foundational skills are "not an end in and of themselves; rather, they are necessary and important components of an effective, comprehensive reading program designed to develop proficient readers with the capacity to comprehend texts across a range of types and disciplines" (2012 Common Core Standards Committee).

The CCSS emphasizes:

> Instruction in foundational skills should be differentiated: good readers will need much less practice with these concepts than struggling readers will. The point is to teach students what they need to learn and not what they already know—to discern when particular children or activities warrant more or less attention. (2012 Common Core Standards Committee)

The CCSS standards for literature, nonfiction, and language engage children in reading and making evidenced-based arguments from their reading. There is the danger, however, that emphasis on the foundational skills could be the initial and major focus of instruction for poor children. Furthermore, "higher order levels of thought, response, understanding, comprehending, interpreting, and monitoring of strategy" (Opitz, Ford, & Erekson, 2011, pp. 155–156) could be cast into rigid formulas designed to increase scores on tests. If that happens, teachers of low-income children will continue to carry out the banking model of education and pedagogy of poverty.

The 2008 Schott Foundation Report, *Given Half a Chance*, voices similar concerns. It describes the Common Core as a "good tool," but "not the vehicle capable of providing the supports needed to significantly narrow high school graduation gaps." They argue, "More is needed than a standards movement," because a "standards-based reform agenda is focused on raising the bar and assessing who makes the cut." They argue instead for a "support-based" reform agenda that has the primary goal of providing and strategically aligning "the necessary resources so that each student will have the opportunity to reach the bar" (The Schott Foundation for Public Education 2008, p. 11).

This chapter has focused on the impact of underestimating children's literacy capabilities in the early years of schooling. The next chapter explores the underestimation of the capabilities of children before they even enter school.

NOTES

[1] From Hale, Janice E. Foreword: V.P. Franklin. LEARNING WHILE BLACK: CREATING EDUCATIONAL EXCELLENCE FOR AFRICAN AMERICAN CHILDREN. p. 46. Copyright © 2001 Janice E. Hale. Reprinted with permission of Johns Hopkins University Press.

[2] From NIETO, SONIA; BODE, PATTY; AFFIRMING DIVERSITY: THE SOCIOPOLITICAL CONTEXT OF MULTICULTURAL EDUCATION, 6th, ©2012. Printed and Electronically reproduced permission of by Pearson Education, Inc., Upper Saddle River, New Jersey.

[3] From Literacy practices in an informal settlement in the Cape by Catherine Kell THE SOCIAL USES OF LITERACY (1996) Mastin Prinsloo and Mignonne Breier, (Eds.). Copyright © 1996 by Sached Books and John Benjamins Publishing Company. Reprinted by permission of John Benjamins Publishing Company.

[4] From *Effective Language Education Practices*, by Lois A. Hirst and Christy Slavik. Copyright © 1990 by Effective Language Education Practices and Native Language Survival, pp. 133–142. Reprinted by permission of Jon Allyn Reyner, Professor of Bilingual Multicultural Education, Northern Arizona University, Flagstaff.

[5] Reprinted with permission of Simon and Schuster, Inc. from TEACHER by Sylvia Ashton-Warner. Copyright © 1963 by Sylvia Ashton-Warner. Copyright renewed 1991 by Eliot Henderson, Ashton Henderson & Jasmine Beveridge. All rights reserved. And Teacher ©[1963] by The Estate of Sylvia Ashton Warner. Used by Permission. All rights reserved.

[6] From LANGUAGE STORIES & LITERACY LESSONS by Jerome C. Harste, Virginia A. Woodward, and Carolyn L. Burke. Copyright © 1984 by Jerome C. Harste, Virginia A. Woodward, and Carolyn L. Burke. Published by Heinemann, Portsmouth, NH. Reprinted with permission of the publisher. All rights reserved.

[7] From The Pedagogy of poverty versus good teaching by Martin Haberman in *Phi Delta Kappan* Volume 73, Number 4, December, 1991. Usage determined by Phi Delta Kappan.

[8] From LIVES ON THE EDGE; SINGLE MOTHERS AND THEIR CHILDREN IN THE OTHER AMERICA by Valerie Polakow. Copyright © 1993 by The University of Chicago. Reprinted with permission of the University of Chicago Press. All rights reserved.

[9] From First steps in constructing counter narratives of young children and their families in *Language Arts* Volume 88, Number 2, November 2010. Use determine by the National Council of Teachers of English.

[10] From Let's start leveling about leveling by Kath Glasswell and Michael Ford in *Language Arts*, Volume 88, Number 3, January 2011. Usage determined by the National Council of Teachers of English.

[11] From a discussion of *Pedagogy of the Oppressed*, by Noam Chomsky, Howard Gardner, Bruno della Chiesa, at the Askwith Forum, Harvard University, Cambridge, Massachusetts, May 1, 2013. Excerpts used with permission of Noam Chomsky, Massachusetts Institute of Technology.

CHAPTER 5

PATHOLOGIZING THE LANGUAGE OF YOUNG CHILDREN

...young children from diverse backgrounds bring diverse experiences to symbol-producing—talking, drawing, playing, storytelling and, in our society, some kind of experience with print, all of which are resources with which both teachers and children can build new possibilities. —Anne Haas Dyson (Dyson A. H., 1993, p. 6)

THE ACADEMICIZATION OF PRESCHOOL

As Anne Dyson states in the above quote, children have diverse experiences that can be used to shape new possibilities. One of the concerns about focusing on learning from birth, however, is that the underestimation of children's capabilities will begin in the years before schooling and children's strengths will not be built upon in schools. Many researchers and educators believe that this underestimation is already occurring in the preschool years.

Vivian Gussin Paley taught preschool children for 37 years, much of that time at the University of Chicago's Laboratory Schools. She is the only kindergarten teacher to ever receive a MacArthur "genius" grant. In addition to teaching, Paley wrote more than 10 books about life in the classroom. During the years that Paley taught, she took the stories that children tell as part of their play and made them part of her daily curriculum. Her curriculum was not limited to learning the alphabet and other sub-skills. She engaged in critical literacy with children. Her curriculum included thinking about larger questions, such as fairness and justice, and the purpose of school—both for teachers and children. Patricia Cooper, literacy professor at New York University has written an extensively about Paley's curriculum. The following information is drawn from her work.

Paley's curriculum has been designated as a "model of the integrated developmental learning historically associated with early childhood education in America and other western countries" (Williams, 1992) in (Cooper P. M., 2005, p. 230).[1] Children who engaged in the curriculum used language to express and create meaning. Many researchers have pointed out that "the holistic nature of the storytelling curriculum is evident in the learning it promotes in almost all areas of development, from using language to express and shape intention to making friends" (Cazden, 1992; Clay M., 1991; Cooper P., 1993; Dyson A., 1997; Hurwitz, 2001; Katch, 2001; Katch, 2003; McNamee, McLane, Cooper, & Kerwin, 1985; Niccolopolu, Scales, & Weintraub,

1994; Sapon-Shevin, 1998; Sapon-Shevin, Dobbelaere, Corrigan, Goodman, & Mastin, 1998; Wiltz & Fein, 1996) in (Cooper P. M., 2005, p. 230).

There is a concern, however, that the innate "richness" of this curriculum may bring about its demise in U.S. classrooms. For the past three decades, the "academicization of preschool (4–5 years) and kindergarten (5–6 years) curricula has been steadily moving into the early childhood classrooms in America (Cooper P. M., 2005, p. 230). By 2005, the situation had become formally entrenched and more severe under the No Child Left Behind Act."

As Cooper writes:

> Driven by new state and federal standards, school districts around the USA are rapidly replacing their traditional early childhood programs with more academically oriented ones that give over large chunks of the school day to literacy sub-skills.

Perhaps "many experienced teachers would question the appropriateness of such goals, and object to the concomitant reduction in playground time, singing, cooking, and other hallowed habits of the early childhood classroom…" But in reality, few teachers would actually be "willing to risk the implications for the children or themselves if they ignore mandated directives" (Cooper P. M., 2005, pp. 230–231).

The richness of the curriculum is not the only loss, however. The academicization of preschool subjects young children to regular assessments of progress in the five pillars of reading—phonemic awareness, phonics, fluency, vocabulary, and comprehension. Researcher Karen Wohlwend contends, "This climate of high-stakes testing makes it seem risky to set aside the scripted basal, to make room for play, and to encourage children to explore technologies in school" (Wohlwend, 2010, p. 147).[2] The situation of teaching and learning within a narrow curriculum is similar to the one I found myself in decades ago. The materials have changed, but the issues remain the same—or in the case of younger children have gotten worse.

The examples that I cite in this chapter are from the U.S. However, UNESCO's 2007 EFA Global Monitoring Report, *Strong Foundations: Early Childhood Care and Education*[3] shows that the problem of the academicization of preschool taking place in other parts of the world as well. The following is an example from Kazakhstan.

View from a Small Place

> In Kazakhstan, pre-primary education classes prepare 5- or 6-year-olds who have never attended preschool (especially in rural areas) for formal schooling through a 32-week crash course in school readiness. There is some concern that such classes focus too narrowly on academic skills; it is important to focus as well on children's emotional well-being, which is vital to their adjustment to primary schooling. (Choi, 2006; UNESCO, 2006, p. 164)

PATHOLOGIZING THE LANGUAGE OF YOUNG CHILDREN

In 1979, Holdaway wrote, "Thankfully, the home, where the infant learns to speak, is not an arena for factions or public debate" (Holdaway D., 1979, p. 25). When Holdaway wrote these words he did not anticipate that an extremely influential study of the vocabulary development of infants and toddlers would take place in the U.S. about fifteen years later. This study by researchers Hart and Risley is the primary source for the claim that poor children grow up in linguistically impoverished environments that limit their vocabulary development and, ultimately, their success in school (Hart & Risley, 1995). Due to the far-reaching and negative impact of this study, I will report on it at length.

Researchers Betty Hart and Todd Risley from the University of Kansas collected 1,260 hours of recordings, transcribed and coded them in many ways, and then followed the same children through their subsequent careers in school. They determined that the amount of conversation that children hear matters and varies according to socioeconomic status. There were 42 families in the study categorized as follows: 13 professional, 23 working class—10 middle and 13 lower socio-economic status (SES)— and 6 welfare families. The study began when the children were between 7–9 months of age. Longitudinal data on the families examined what accounted for enormous differences in rates of vocabulary growth. Their study showed that by age 3, children from professional families have heard more than 30,000,000 words, children from the average working family have heard 20,000,000 words, but children from underprivileged families have heard only 10,000,000 (Hart & Risley, 1995).

Drawing on the findings of the study, Mark Liberman (Liberman, 2006), a linguist from the University of Pennsylvania, notes, "Children turned out to be like their parents in stature, activity level, vocabulary resources, and language and interaction styles." Additionally, "follow-up data indicated that the 3-year-old measures of accomplishment predicted third grade school achievement" (Hart & Risley, 2003). The introduction to the study describes the collecting and processing of the data as "heroic" (Hart & Risley, 1995, p. xii). Liberman notes that the study has been deemed an "epic analysis" (Toynbee, 2004). It has also been cited at Congressional hearings (U.S. Congress, 2003), in the popular press, and in over 600 articles in scholarly journals (Dudley-Marling & Lucas, 2009).[4]

Hart and Risley's findings were based on a one-hour period of observation per month in the family's home over a period of two-and–a half years. They conclude that there was a significant relationship between the quantity and quality of language used by parents and children based on a families' socioeconomic status (SES). They state that "competence as a social problem is still with us…" They posit that excessive numbers of poor children become school dropouts. They then "follow their parents into unemployment or onto welfare, where they raise their children in a culture of poverty" (Hart & Risley, 1995, p. 2).

Curt Dudley-Marling, and Krista Lucas from Boston College, conducted an extensive critique of Hart and Risley's study (Dudley-Marling & Lucas, 2009). They note that those who believe that such a culture exists, also believe it "denies poor children the cognitive and linguistic resources needed to succeed in school" (Dudley-Marling & Lucas, 2009, p. 364).

A major point is usually overlooked in the reporting of the Hart and Risley study. As Liberman, points out, the "welfare" group, whose children are at greatest risk of low achievement in school, was based on just "six poor families in 1980's St. Louis" (Liberman, 2006). He argues that 6 participants is too small a sample to provide a "meaningful picture" of the experience of "millions" of people…" He contends that we "wouldn't try to predict the results of a national election based on an in-depth survey of six people in one city." Therefore, Lieberman questions if we should "make national educational policy based on a similarly small sample, even if the data comes from 2 1/2 years of recorded monthly visits" (Liberman, 2006). Liberman's concern takes on even greater significance when we consider that the conclusions drawn from studying this small sample of participants impact the human rights of millions of children. Dudley-Marling and Lucas share Liberman's concern that making strong, broad-stroke claims about the language and culture of families living in poverty should not be based on the small number of families in the study. They describe many failures in the study and raise several other concerns.

First of all, they state that there was no explicit theory of language and culture that underpinned the analysis of the findings. They contend that Hart and Risley engaged in "unreflected action and holding magical beliefs they conduct research without questioning why they do what they do or how their actions are connected to understandings of knowledge, people, or language" (Bloome, Carter, Christian, Otto, & Shuart-Farris, 2005).[5]

Secondly, the study never considers the "language of poor families on its own terms" (Dudley-Marling & Lucas, 2009, p. 366). The purposes, strengths, and cultural influence of the language of the poor families are not analyzed. The language and identities of the poor families are simply held up for evaluation against those of the upper- and middle-class families. This evaluation is similar to mine when I stated that the children I was working with "did not have language." I was not considering that they had language capabilities that were unlike mine—capabilities that I was not tapping in school.

Dudley-Marling and Lucas see this failure as the "fatal flaw" of the study (Dudley-Marling & Lucas, 2009, p. 366). That flaw led Hart and Risley to transform "the linguistic *differences* they found among the welfare families in their study into linguistic *deficiencies.*" For example, they described direct requests by parents to children as having a "'prevailing negative tone'" (Hart & Risley, 1995, p. 177), but they "offer no evidence that the children and parents in the welfare families shared this interpretation of directives in their homes." It was never taken into consideration that the families might have taken a different perspective of these directives, possibly viewing them as "mainly positive, business-like, honest, or highly involved" (Dudley-Marling & Lucas, 2009, p. 365).

The study disregards the impact that the presence of the observers in the homes could have on the observations. It also does not take into account the kind of activities that the families engaged in during the monthly observations. It is possible that the "professional parents chose to be observed during activities that were richer in language opportunities than when poor families chose to be observed" (Dudley-Marling & Lucas, 2009, p. 365).

Dudley-Marling and Lucas state that Hart & Risley's study is based on the assumption "that there is a *culture of poverty* that limits the academic and vocational success of poor people." But there is no "...reason to believe that Hart & Risley's welfare families—or other people living in poverty in the United States—share a "culture of poverty." The study presumes that the six families studied from Kansas City, Kansas are all alike and are like all other poor families. But no convincing evidence is given to support the idea that the poor families they studied have much in common with each other or with poor people from other locations. The only commonalities among the 6 welfare families in the study were "income, a willingness to participate in the study, race (all the welfare families were Black), and geography (all lived in the Kansas City area)." The study does not acknowledge that families who live in poverty are "ethnically, linguistically, and racially diverse" (U.S. Census Bureau, 2003) in (Dudley-Marling & Lucas, 2009, p. 364).

Liberman adds that "it's not clear how to reconcile this picture of monetary poverty engendering linguistic poverty because of the central role that 'lower SES' people have always played in American linguistic creativity" (Liberman, 2006, p. 5). One example of this creativity comes from researchers Miller, Cho, and Bracey, who found that lower SES working class families valued storytelling more highly and produced far more stories then the middle-class counterparts (Miller, Cho, & Bracey, 2005). The adults in these families are described as participating "prolifically, avidly, and artfully in personal storytelling, in their homes and communities and that they brought children into this valued activity from an early age." The children's home environments were "saturated with stories..." The researchers conclude that "by the time they were 3 years old, it is likely that telling stories of personal experience had become second nature to them" (Miller, Cho, & Bracey, 2005, p. 125).[6]

Hart and Risley also did not take into account that children have the ability to discover and generate their own understandings of language. They also failed to acknowledge that children learn not only from their parents, but from their siblings, peers, and environment as well. For example, researchers Alonzo Anderson and Shelley Stokes observed Anglo American, African American and Mexican American families to determine the average frequency of literacy events per hour of observation. From this research, they identified nine "domains of literacy activity," including (1) religion, (2) daily living, (3) entertainment, (4) school-related activity, (5) general information, (6) work, (7) literacy techniques and skills adult-initiated, child-initiated, (8) interpersonal communication, and (9) story-book time (Anderson

& Stokes, 1984, pp. 28–30). Contrary to the belief that many minority students do not begin school with rich literacy backgrounds, Anderson and Stokes found that the children in their study had a variety of literacy experiences in these domains of literacy activity. Entertainment (30.2%) and religion (26.5%) were the most prominent (Anderson & Stokes, 1984, p. 33).

Furthermore, as *Strong Foundations: Early Childhood Care and Education* states, "Qualitative anthropological fieldwork underscores the fact that significant differences in parenting practices exist across and within countries."

> For example, young Kenyan children are often present as non-participants in situations dominated by adult interaction; they are not necessarily the focus of attention of the adults, but they are rarely if ever left alone. In contrast, young children in North America and Western Europe experience a sharp disjuncture between long periods when they are left alone and moments when they interact with their parents and receive much attention and stimulation. (UNESCO, 2006, p. 155)

In other cultures, silence is valued as a form of respectful "talk." As metaphysician Dorothy M. Neddermeyer, Ph.D. explains:

> Native American languages hold silence as part of the meaning. They believe the silence is more informative, than, words and that unless silence is included, it is impossible to achieve full meaning. Silence gives the speaker and listener time to reflect on the meaning and to refine, revise or let it stand. (Neddermeyer)

In some places, children learn more from intermediaries than from their parents. *Strong Foundations: Early Childhood Care and Education* states, "In societies where preschool children spend most of their time with siblings, parental responsiveness is more limited" (UNESCO, 2006, p. 154).

As researchers Edelsky, Altwerger, and Flores explain:

> In some cultures, it is the parents, caretakers, or other adults who are the baby's primary talk partners. In others, it is older siblings or other children in the community. Sometimes, adults (having higher status) speak to toddlers only through intermediaries. But no matter who does it, the same phenomenon is occurring: someone assumes that the youngster is a meaning maker and, by assuming, creates the condition for the assumption to be borne out. (Edelsky, Altwater, & Flores, 1991, p. 15)[7]

For example, very early in life, Samoan children learn to interact, not with a single family member, but with many family members who are their caregivers and talk partners (Ochs, 1982).

Researcher Elinor Ochs points out, "...in using language a particular way, caregivers are acting on certain assumptions concerning the capacities of human infants and young children, and concerning the nature of the caregiver role, the behaviors of those providing care." The caregiver is conveying those "assumptions to the child as well," thereby providing both "linguistic" and "cultural input" to the child. Ochs adds that the purpose of uncovering differences in parenting practices is to bring about "understanding the *cultural sources* of these behaviors" (Ochs, 1982, p. 79).[8]

Dudley-Marling and Lucas (Dudley-Marling & Lucas, 2009, p. 367) cite researchers who describe "a re-emergence of deficit-based explanations for disproportionate school failure among poor Black and Hispanic youth" (Foley, 1997; Ladson-Billings, 1999). Unfortunately both school personnel and policy makers "have been persuaded to view poor students as culturally and linguistically deficient" (Dudley-Marling & Lucas, 2009, p. 362). They draw on Dudley-Marling's past work and that of Foley to argue that the "uncritical acceptance of Hart and Risley's findings is emblematic of a trend among some educators, educational policy makers, and educational researchers to readily embrace a deficit stance that pathologizes the language and culture of poor students and their families" (Dudley-Marling, 2007; Foley, 1997).

People who take this perspective see the glass as being nearly empty instead of filling up, and they often see the water in the glass as polluted. They place blame for academic failure on "parents who pass on to their children inadequate language and flawed culture" (Dudley-Marling & Lucas, 2009, p. 369). They believe these perceived "*deficiencies* must be overcome—or 'fixed'—before children can succeed academically" (Dudley-Marling & Lucas, 2009, p. 362).

FOLLOW-UP STUDIES

Studies similar to that of Hart and Risley continue. In 2012, a study entitled *SES Differences in Language Processing Skill and Vocabulary are Evident at 18 Months* was conducted by Anne Fernald, Virginia A. Marchman, and Adriana Weisleder from Stanford University. The study found that a language gap between children from low-income and higher-income homes becomes evident even earlier than Hart and Risley thought (Fernald, Marchman, & Weisleder, 2012).[9]

These researchers report that, by 18 months, children from higher-income homes could identify pictures of simple words they knew—'*shoe*' or '*kitty*'—much more quickly than children from low-income families. Additionally, they found that at age 2, the children from the lower-income homes were demonstrating the same level of performance as children from higher-income homes who were only 18 months of age (Fernald, Marchman, & Weisleder, 2012). Forty-eight children participated in the study. The children who were higher-income children came from communities where the median income per capita was $69,000. The children who were low-income came from communities with a median income per capita of $23,900.

An additional study conducted by Weisleder and Fernald took place in 2013. Only low-income children who spoke Spanish as their first language participated in this study (Fernald, Marchman, & Weisleder, 2012). Twenty-nine infants were subjects. They were tested at the ages of 19 and 24 months. The child's parents recorded the child during a typical day at home. The duration of the recordings averaged 11 hours over the course of 1–6 days. Families kept logs of the locations of the recordings. They documented who was present, the activities the child engaged in, and whether anything out of the ordinary happened. Additionally, the picture identification task that was administered in the study described above was also given to the children in this study (Weisleder & Fernald, 2013).[10]

As a result of this study, the researchers found that there was "striking variability in the total amount of speech accessible to the infant." Over the course of ten hours, adults in one family spoke fewer than 2,000 words to an infant, while in another family, adults spoke 29,000 words during the same time period. During the course of a day, an infant from one family heard 670 words, while an infant in another family heard 12,000 words (Weisleder & Fernald, 2013, p. 2146). This difference amounts to a disparity of 11,330 words per day. Over the course of a year, this number could increase to a difference of over four million words. The researchers were surprised to find "differences in the amount of child-directed speech between families that were almost as large as those differences reported in the landmark study by Hart and Risley (1995)" (Weisleder & Fernald, 2013, p. 2150). The families compared in this study were all low-income. Those compared in the Hart and Risley study were from a much broader demographic range.

The results of this study led Dr. Fernald to report:

> A central message of this research is the SES does not determine the quality of children's language experience...Despite the challenges associated with living in poverty, some of these mom's really engaged with their children, and their kids were more advanced in processing efficiency and vocabulary. (Fernald, 2013)

Therefore, considering that the differences in the amount of speech directed to children in this study were similar to the differences in the Hart and Risley study, and considering that children's interactions with their mothers affected their processing efficiency and vocabulary, SES alone cannot be considered as the sole determiner of the quality of children's language experience.

Like Dudley-Marling and Lucas, I take exception to the characterization of the children in terms of linguistic or cultural deficiencies. Like these researchers, I believe that the language differences that Hart and Risley identified are exactly that—"*differences*." Furthermore, I believe, "All children come to school with extraordinary linguistic, cultural, and intellectual resources" (Dudley-Marling & Lucas, 2009, p. 369). But not all of these resources are the same. Some children have larger vocabularies than others. As described later in this book, vocabulary development is extremely important. Word count, however, is not the only issue.

View from a Small Place

> On October 7, 2011, Leymah Gbowee of Liberia was one of three women rights pioneers awarded the Nobel Peace Prize. She received the prize for mobilizing women to bring about the end of the war in Liberia. The women came from diverse religious and ethnic groups. Part of their mission was to secure their participation in elections. (Norweign Nobel Committee, 2011)
>
> In 1996, Leymah was displaced by the war, and forced to live in the household of the father of the child she was expecting. He was abusive. He hit her. Women in the household would not talk to her. His mother would not speak her name and called her "You." Leymah had no job and was always short of money. One day she was so hungry, she ate the leftover yams from the dinner of another woman in the household. Leymah was suffering from depression. She had few resources. She had graduated from high school. She could read and write. She knew that she had to improve her situation. She knew she had to educate her three young children.
>
> Despite her circumstances, she began to do so.
>
> She read to and sang with her young children. Leymah listened to their stories and participated in their play. In her small place and in these simple ways, she supported her children's education and literacy. Thereby, she was supporting their human rights. Soon, she began to see that her mission went beyond improving just her own life and that of her own children. (Gbowee & Mithers, 2011)

Across the world, teachers, caregivers, and community members need to be able to identify, value, and build upon the children's initial language resources. When the "quantity" of language is the focus of research reports, the richness of the language that children possess is often lost or not considered valuable enough for school. When these things happen, children's personal histories of language and literacy are eradicated, and their instructional programs consist of imposed practices that are devoid of connections to their language, culture, and understandings.

NOTES

[1] From Literacy learning and pedagogical purpose in Vivian Paley's 'storytelling curriculum': by Patricia M. Copper, in Journal of Early Childhood Literacy, Vol. 5(3), pp. 229–251. Copyright © 2005 by SAGE Publications. Reprinted by Permission of SAGE Publications.

[2] From A is for Avatar: Young children in literacy 2.0 worlds and literacy 1.0 schools *in Language Arts*, Volume 88, Number 2, November 2010. Usage determined by the National Council of Teachers of English.

[3] From the EFA 2007 GLOBAL MONITORING REPORT, STRONG FOUNDATIONS: EARLY CHILDHOOD CARE AND EDUCATION. UNESCO. Copyright © 2006 United Nations. Reprinted with permission of the United Nations.

[4] From Pathologizing the Language and Culture of Poor Children by Curt Dudley-Marling and Krista Lucas in *Language Arts*, Volume 86, Number 5, May 2009. Usage determined by the National Council of Teachers of English.

[5] From DISCOURSE ANALYSIS & THE STUDY OF CLASSROOM LANGUAGE AND LITERACY EVENTS: A MICROETHNOGRAPHIC PERSPECTIVE by David Bloome. Stephanie Power Carter, Beth Morton Christian, Sheila Otto, Nora Shuart-Farris. Copyright © 2005. Reproduced with permission of Lawrence Erlbaum Associates via Copyright Clearance Center.

[6] From Working-Class Children's Experience through the Prism of Personal Storytelling, by Peggy J. Miller, Grace E. Cho, and Jeana R. Bracey, in Human Development, Vol. 48 (3), pp. 115–135. Copyright © 2005 by Karger Publications. Reprinted by Permission of Karger Publishers, Basel, Switzerland.

[7] From WHOLE LANGUAGE WHAT'S THE DIFFERENCE by Carole Edelsky, Bess Altweger, and Barbara Flores. Copyright ©1991. Published by Heinemann, Portsmouth, NH. Reprinted with permission of the publisher. All rights reserved.

[8] From Talking to Children in Western Samoa by Elinor Ochs in Language and society by Cambridge University Press. Copyright © 1982. Reproduced by permission of CAMBRIDGE UNIVERSITY PRESS in the format reprint in a book/ebook/anthology via Copyright Clearance Center.

[9] From SES Differences in language processing skill and vocabulary are evident at 18 months by Anne Fernald, Virginia A. Marchman, and Adriana Weisleder in Developmental Science. Copyright © 2012 Reproduced with permission of BLACKWELL PUBLISHING LTD.

[10] From Talking to Children Matters: Early Language Experience Strengthens Processing and Builds Vocabulary, by Adriana Weisleder and Anne Fernald, in Psychological Science, Vol. 24 (11), pp. 182–190. Copyright © 2013 by SAGE Publications. Reprinted by Permission of SAGE Publications.

PART 3

RESEARCH THAT BUILDS ON STRENGTHS AND LEADS TO THE REALIZATION OF LITERACY AS A HUMAN RIGHT

CHAPTER 6

CRITICAL PEDAGOGY: TAKING CONCERTED ACTION

Education takes place on a 24/7 basis and everyone has an obligation to participate in the education of all citizens.
—Joan Kagan, president and CEO of Springfield Massachusetts Square One early-education and after-school programs

CONCERTED ACTION

As we saw in the first part of this book, the United Nations is working with leaders on the world stage to address education and literacy issues, particularly in places that have been disrupted by global issues of debt, economic stagnation and decline, the trauma of war, occupation, or civil strife. Taking on all of these factors is clearly beyond the scope of this book. This book can, however, contribute to the conversation about connecting the responsibilities and concerted actions of ordinary citizens to the realization of literacy as a human right.

Eleanor Roosevelt believed that change requires popular movements of activism and persuasion. According to historian and author Blanche Wisen Cook, Roosevelt contended that people "cannot depend on politicians," but they "must organize door to door, block by block, community by community" (Roosevelt, 2001, p. xiii). She placed the destiny of human rights "in the hands of all of our citizens in all our communities" and called for "concerted citizen action" to uphold human rights in the "small places close to home" (Roosevelt, 1958a). She realized that the work would be arduous and would require continuity. Eleanor Roosevelt witnessed the power of building relationships within small places. She helped design the Declaration, a rights document based on dignitarian principles. She advocated for citizens in all communities to come together to uphold their rights in ways that worked for them within their individual worlds. In this account, she describes one change that she witnessed:

> Some years ago, I studied a snapshot which I have never forgotten. It was a picture showing two men standing outside a primitive grass hut in the Philippines. One of the men was naked except for a loincloth. He had wild bushy hair. In either hand he held a skull. He was a headhunter from the bush.
>
> The young man beside him wore a white suit and glasses. In his hand he carried a small professional bag. He was a trained physician, working in the field of public health. He was the headhunters son!

> The transition, from headhunter to scientist, was not even the work of one generation; it was the work of perhaps fifteen years at the outside. What had been required to change human nature and make the leap from the Stone Age to the present? Opportunity, education, recognition of his human potentialities, and a chance to be trained for a job in the field for which he was best suited. (Black A., 1999, p. 305)[1]

Eleanor Roosevelt stated, "Now the only way we can judge human nature is by human behavior, and behavior is modified and changed and developed and transformed by training and surroundings, by social customs and economic pressures" (Black A., 1999, p. 305). She saw that in turn, the citizens who learn the new skills can then support the transformation of others in their communities.

Eleanor Roosevelt had exceptional political skills and ideas, however, she did not have a specific theory that underpinned beliefs about literacy and learning. A reader of one of her columns once asked her opinion about ways of teaching young children to read. She responded that her children learned to read in various ways. She added, "I think no matter how children learn to read, the stress should be on acquiring the habit of reading. It is this habit which makes for fluency and rapid reading" (Roosevelt, 1946, p. 79).

Paulo Freire's literacy work, however, has influenced both the work of the UN and "literacy and liberation movements throughout the world" (Nieto & Bode, 2008, p. 56). Based on the work of Freire, Shor describes the "participatory" classroom that "invites all expressions from all students." I would add, regardless of their age. "Participatory learning also opens the possibility of transforming the students' powers of thought." Shor notes that these classes go beyond merely repeating what we know or what we have been taught. Rather, they allow us to "reflect on reality and on our received values, words, and interpretations in ways the illuminate meanings that we hadn't perceived before." Furthermore, the "refection can transform our thought and behavior, which in turn have the power to alter reality itself if enough people reconstruct their knowledge and take action" (Shor, 1992, p. 22).

Freire is perhaps the most well-known adult literacy educator whose work integrated notions of active learning within socio-cultural settings (UNESCO, 2005). Freire viewed this "process of connecting reflection and action in the pursuit of knowledge and social change" as "praxis" (Nieto, 2000, p. 384). Embedded in the concept of praxis is the idea that "all good education connects theory with reflection and action" (Nieto & Bode, 2008, p. 51).

As *Literacy for Life* describes:

> Freire emphasized the importance of bringing the learners socio-cultural realities into the learning process itself and then using the learning process to challenge these social processes. Central to his pedagogy is the notion of critical literacy, a goal to be attained in part through engaging with books and other written texts, but, more profoundly, through reading (i.e. interpreting,

reflecting on, interrogating, theorizing, investigating, exploring, probing and questioning) and writing (acting on and dialogically transforming) the social world.

Freires ideas have been used as pedagogical tools to support learners who have been oppressed, excluded or disadvantaged, due to gender, ethnicity or socio-economic status. (UNESCO, 2005, p. 152)

Brian Street identifies features that are related to curricula and New Literacy Studies. He believes that they are "well established in theory, but need careful work for application and practice" (Street, 1997). Several aspects of these features are explored in this book. Street puts forth the following list:

- Literacy is more complex than current curricula and assessments allow;
- Curricula and assessments that reduce literacy to a few simple and mechanistic skills fail to do justice to the richness and complexity of actual literacy practices in people's lives;
- If we want learners to develop and enhance the richness and complexity of literacy practices evident in society at large, then we need curricula and assessments that are themselves rich and complex and based upon research into actual literacy practices;
- In order to develop rich and complex curricula and assessments for literacy, we need models of literacy and of pedagogy that capture the richness and complexity of actual literacy practices;
- In order to build upon the richness and complexity of learners' prior knowledge, we need to treat "home background" not as a deficit but as affecting deep levels of identity and epistemology, and thereby the stance that learners take with respect to the "new" literacy practices of the educational setting (Street, 2005, p. 420).[2]

CRITICAL PEDAGOGY IN SMALL PLACES

As noted in Chapter 4, "critical pedagogy begins with the experiences and viewpoints of students..." (Nieto & Bode, 2008, p. 56), rather than on an imposed culture. This concept can apply to even very young children.

As Nieto and Bode write:

Even before Freire, critical pedagogy was being practiced in other parts of the world. Almost half a century ago, Sylvia Ashton-Warner, teaching Maori children in New Zealand, found that curriculum, materials, viewpoint, and pedagogy that had been used in educating them were all borrowed from the dominant culture. Because Maori children had been failed dismally by New Zealand schools, Ashton-Warner decided to develop a strategy for literacy based on childrens experiences and interests...Because Ashton-Warner's approach was based on what children knew and wanted to know, it was extraordinarily successful. (Nieto & Bode, 2008, pp. 56–57)

We often look for the next new trend in research, but sometimes the most effective research synthesizes ideas from the past with those from the present. Innovations are not recognized right away. Innovators are defined by their success over time, the longevity of their ideas, and the ways in which they change the world. Later in this book, there will be more about Ashton-Warner's teaching and that other educators and researchers who worked from similar critical perspectives that were child-centered and respected children's knowledge.

As stated in *Strong Foundations: Early Childhood Care and Education*, "The relationship between language and power is not easy to address, but early childhood is an important place to start" (UNESCO, 2006, p. 159). It is also important to note, as stated in that report, "First, early childhood programmes need to be rooted in the young children's cultural environment and care must be taken not simply to import models from abroad without appropriate adaptation" (UNESCO, 2006, p. 265).

Researcher Sue Booth (Booth, 2005), drawing on the work of others, notes that children acquire literacy skills in social situations—through interactions with parents, other adults, teachers, and peers. Therefore, their sociocultural background influences children's understandings of literacy practices (Pullen & Justice, 2003; Speaker, Taylor, & Kamen, 2003). School literacy can be taught by adding to, not replacing the literacy practices already occurring at home. It is necessary for teachers to be patient and value what they see and hear, rather than what they think they should see or hear.

Street adds, "Good educational practice today requires facilitators to build upon what learners bring to class, to listen, not just to deliver, and to respond to local articulations of 'need' as well as make their own 'outsider' judgements of it" (Street, 1996, p. 6).

Shirley Brice Heath's longitudinal study of families in the Piedmont Region of the Carolinas made it clear that various styles of language interaction and uses of language and literacies across communities are differences, not deficits (Heath S., 1983). Heath found that in the community she called "Trackton," the families' ways of asking questions differed from the school's ways. The parents' questions were "linguistically complex." The answers to the parents' questions typically "involved telling a story or describing a situation." There was no one right answer to these questions. The questions that the teachers asked, however, typically had a single answer (Nieto, 2000, p. 233).[3]

As Nieto reports, once teachers who were working with Heath in a research project became aware that families questioning rituals differed from those of the schools, they began to study the kinds of questions that the adults in the community asked. Teachers then used "these kinds of questions as a basis for asking more traditional 'school' questions, to which children also needed to become accustomed if they were to be successful in school." The results of changing the questioning style were "dramatic." Children, who had been viewed by teachers as "deficient in language or unintelligent," turned out to be "active and enthusiastic participants in these lessons" (Nieto, 2000, p. 233).

Julia Lopez-Robertson and her colleagues from the University of South Carolina documented the visits of 225 teachers to students' homes to understand more about children's home languages, ways that family and community members value and support each other, what was important to them, and the many literacies in their lives. When teachers visited homes that they had previously described as lacking in literacy, they found that reading and writing were used everywhere. Among the places they discovered literacies were "church programs, hymnals, memorization of Bible verses, song lyrics, wall posters, DVD covers, juice labels, and signs on familiar institutions (apartment complexes, fast food restaurants, stores)" (Lopez-Robertson, Long, & Turner-Nash, 2010, p. 100).

In the following example, Liezl Malan, who studied the literacy practices of everyday life in Bellville South, South Africa, describes the displays of print within the neighborhoods of that community. She also explains how and why these practices were "hidden" or invisible within the community.

View from a Small Place

> There was a public display of writing and reading all over Bellville South. Children wrote letters to each other on the wall of the flats, youth gangs spray-painted shop walls with their symbols, men occasionally sat on the stairways of flats reading a newspaper or pamphlet. Between the shacks in people's backyards lay piles of discarded magazines and newspapers. Even so, teachers and headmasters of schools in Bellville South said that hardly any reading happened in the area (apart from religious and bureaucratic practices). It seemed that the literacy practices of the neighbourhood were hidden to the gaze which relates literacy to the linguistic codes and formats associated with schooled literacy. (Malan, 1996, pp. 142–143)[4]

Malan further explains that these literacy practices were also 'hidden' to the people themselves. She proposes that the reason is that literacy, particularly reading, was not valued in the neighborhood. Reading was done mostly by women at home who read romance novels and magazines. Reading was regarded "as a trivial feminine pursuit." One woman who was interviewed by Malan "emphasised the educational qualities of the books." She stated, "Articles in popular magazines…helped her with the education of her children" (Malan, 1996, p. 143).

Betty Murray, an educator from Thursday Island in the Torres Straight north of Australia, wrote about Louise Carothers, a teacher from that island. She taught children who did not speak English to become confident speakers of English. Carothers states, "What it really comes down to is that we must have respect for the children themselves. Intellect and interest are not tied to their ability to communicate in English" (or any language). She continues, "With respect comes confidence. With confidence comes a willingness to take risks. With risk taking comes learning" (Murray, 1991, p. 66).[5] The following *View from Small Place* is adapted from the comment from Carothers that is published in a chapter written by Betty Murray. I believe the ideas apply to speakers who are learning both first and additional languages.

View from a Small Place

> It is essential that the classroom becomes a talking place.
>
> Unfortunately, we can often underestimate what kids will say. I have been astounded many times at what they came out with. They transferred language we used in one situation to others with incredible ease. Because the language was used in understandable contexts they learnt its meaning without real any effort. They actually talked their way to understanding.
>
> Although all children are free to speak and are encouraged to do so, it is important not to force them to talk before they are ready. When they do speak, it is important to listen to their meanings. I remember the following exchange between Jack and a teacher.
>
> We went to Nagi on Saturday, Sir.
>
> How far away is Nagi, Jack?
>
> Four drums, Sir. (Murray, 1991, p. 66)

"Four drums" is Jack's way of explaining the distance of this journey in a dinghy powered by an outboard motor. It is a distance that would require the use of four drums of petrol. It was necessary for the teacher to listen beyond the literal meaning of the words to hear Jack's meaning.

Once teachers begin to see children's capabilities, they view differences as a resource on which further teaching and learning can be built. In the words of Australian educator and researcher John Dwyer:

> ...our teaching response will be to seek to extend the skills that the children already have. We will see ourselves as helping the children to further successful learning, rather than as attempting to remediate past failure. If they fail to learn, we will question our strategies rather than blame their weakness. We will acknowledge past success and build in expectations for future successes. (Dwyer, 1991b, p. 56)[6]

Furthermore, we will protect both their education and literacy as human rights.

As noted in the introduction to this book, in his second inaugural address, President Obama spoke of "a little girl born into the bleakest poverty who knows she has the same chance to succeed as anyone else..." But this little girl cannot succeed on her own. Since learning begins at birth, having access to information about what young children learn both before and after they enter early care programs or schools is important. The adults surrounding her need to support and advocate for her, and they need knowledge in order to provide that support.

View from a Small Place

> In 2009 and 2010, Save the Children implemented the Literacy Boost programme in Zomba district of Malawi. Teachers in government schools received eight training sessions on teaching core reading skills; on using regular, classroom-based assessment to develop these skills; and on supporting second-language acquisition. Sessions were linked to the national curriculum and teachers were given model lessons and other resources. The programme also provided villages with book banks, trained community members to manage these and other resources, and ran workshops for parents on how to support their childrens reading. Communities and parents adopted a variety of strategies to support literacy: events to promote reading, reading with children at home, telling folk stories and preparing reading materials from local resources. Literacy Boost communities also increased the frequency and variety of initiatives to support orphaned and other vulnerable children.
>
> An evaluation found that the programme had improved grade 2 pupils literacy. In 2009, the vast majority of second graders in both Literacy Boost and comparison schools could not read a single word in their local language. After one year, the share unable to read fell to 65% in Literacy Boost schools, but hardly changed in comparison schools, remaining at 91%. Grade 2 pupils whose parents had attended Literacy Boost workshops made greater vocabulary gains than those who had not, and the gains were greatest for children of parents with little or no literacy skills. Grade 2 pupils who borrowed and read books from book banks also demonstrated significantly greater vocabulary gains than peers. (UNESCO, 2013, p. 286)

Especially in times of economic downturn, it is more difficult than ever for ordinary citizens to imagine the realities of "freedom, solidarity, and peace" (UN General Assembly, 1948). For many people, the realizing education, and thereby literacy as a human right, appears to be nearly impossible. But we live in an ever-shrinking world. In the 21st century, information about learning is available and we have the capability to communicate that information worldwide. Teachers, parents, caregivers, day care providers, policy makers and others can take that information into their own hands. The time is right to become involved and thoughtful.

Children throughout the world have thoughts, words, and memories. They also have ways of putting words together and ways of using language within their communities. We now have new tools that help us learn about children's learning, value it, document it, and build upon it. As members of a world-wide community of learners, people everywhere can access new understandings about the development of the brain, language and literacy, and knowledge of the potential of new technologies and new literacies. Using this information can enable all of us to take down the invisible barriers that prevent the realization of literacy as a human right. These practices come to life in small settings in small places throughout the world. It is, indeed, within these small places that literacy as a human right begins. They can become part of the fabric of evolving literate societies where the individual and the community are bound together in reciprocity. When parents, caregivers, educators, day care providers, and others in the community understand and value what children know before going to early care or school, they can advocate for the child as a learner in these settings and throughout the children's lives.

Research about how the brain develops, conditions under which children learn, how language, early writing, and reading are acquired are explored in upcoming chapters of this book. Ways that people within their own communities support the development of language and literacy at little or no cost are described.

NOTES

[1] From COURAGE IN A DANGEROUS WORLD: THE POLITICAL WRITINGS OF ELEANOR ROOSEVELT by Allida Black. Copyright © 1999 Columbia University Press. Reprinted with permission of the publisher.

[2] From At Last: Recent applications of New Literacy Studies in educational contexts in *Research in the Teaching of English* Volume 39, Number4, May 2005. Usage determination of the National Council of Teachers of English.

[3] From NIETO, SONIA; AFFIRMING DIVERSITY: THE SOCIOPOLITICAL CONTEXT OF MULTICULTURAL EDUCATION, 3rd, ©2000. Printed and Electronically reproduced by permission of Pearson Education, Inc., Upper Saddle River, New Jersey.

[4] From Literacy mediation and social identity in Newtown, Eastern Cape by Liezl Malan in THE SOCIAL USES OF LITERACY (1996) Mastin Prinsloo and Mignonne Breier, (Eds.). Copyright © 1996 by Sached Books and John Benjamins Publishing Company. Reprinted by permission of John Benjamins Publishing Company.

[5] From Talking when English is a Foreign Language, by Betty Murray, in A SEA OF TALK, (1989). Primary English Teaching Association Australia (PETAA), Sydney. Reproduced with permission from PETAA—Primary English Teaching Association Australia.

[6] From Talking in Class, by John Dwyer, in A SEA OF TALK, (1989). Primary English Teaching Association Australia (PETAA), Sydney. Reproduced with permission from PETAA—Primary English Teaching Association Australia.

CHAPTER 7

LEARNING ABOUT THE BRAIN

To look closely at child mind is to take it seriously. Children are small; their minds are not. Child mind is human mind. —Glenda Bissex, "The Child as Teacher" in *Awakening to Literacy*, p. 100

LEARNING ABOUT THE BRAIN THROUGH NEW TECHNOLOGIES

Within recent decades, we have acquired more knowledge about the workings of the brain than we did in previous centuries. "Neurobiology and other brain research fields have been especially influential in recent decades, as they have highlighted the role of the early years in the formation of the human brain" (Center for Early Education and Brain Development, 2002; Mustard, 2002; Mustard, 2005) in (UNESCO, 2006, p. 109). Furthermore, understandings about how the brain is formed, structured, and how the parts function together are no longer the domain of only neuroscientists. This information is a topic of interest and study for educators, parents and the general public. It can also contribute to the realization of education and literacy as human rights.

View from a Small Place

A young woman I know who was in the early stages of pregnancy complained to her physician that she was tired. The doctor told her that of course she was tired because her body was going through the work of growing a baby! In the early weeks of pregnancy, much of that growth centers on the baby's brain.

Author David Sousa identifies two categories of technology have been developed to study the brain: technology that provides images of the structure of the brain, and technology that looks at how the brain actually works (Sousa D. A., 2005, p. 2).[1] The diagnostic tools that produce computer images of the brain structure are computerized axial tomography (CAT) and magnetic resonance imaging (MRI). According to brain researcher David Sousa, additional tools that isolate and identify the areas of the brain where distinct levels of activity are occurring include: Electroencephalography (EEG), Magnetoencephalography (MEG), Positron Emission Tomography (PET), functional Magnetic Resonance Imaging (fMRI), and Functional Magnetic Resonance Spectroscopy (fMRS) (Sousa D. A., 2005).

The following are kinds of brain scans:

- Electroencephalography (EEG) and Magnetoencephalography (MEG) measure the electric fields in the brain and assist in determining the speed at which something occurs in the brain (Sousa D. A., 2005, p. 2). These techniques utilize large arrays of sensors or electrodes that are placed on the scalp. The sensors are harmless. Almost instantaneously, they record the firing of brain cells (The next generation of brain scans, 2013).
- Positron Emission Tomography (PET) allows scientists not only to observe brain structure in great detail, but also to record and measure with precision the activity levels of various parts of the brain (GMR, 2006). This technology "involves injecting the subject with a radioactive solution that circulates to the brain. Brain regions of higher activity accumulate more of the radiation, which is picked up by a ring of detectors around the subject's head." PET scans, however, are "invasive" since they use an injection. They also present a risk to the subject since they use radioactive materials. PET scans are "not used with normal children because the radioactive risk is too high." PET scans are being replaced with functional Magnetic Resonance Imaging (fMRI), a newer technology that is "painless, non-invasive, and does not use radiation" (Sousa D. A., 2005, p. 3).
- Functional Magnetic Resonance Imaging (fMRI) locates "areas of greater and lesser activity" in the brain (Sousa D. A., 2005, p. 3), offering new insights into how the brain works. Magnetic Resonance Imaging has given neuroscientists a far more detailed view of the brain than was previously possible. Functional MRI offers new insights into how the brain works.
- Functional Magnetic Resonance Spectroscopy (fMRS) uses "the same equipment as the fMRI but uses different computer software to record levels of various chemicals in the brain while the subject is thinking" (Sousa D. A., 2005, p. 3).
- Molecular Imaging Techniques use a variety of molecular and cellular imaging techniques to study parts of the brain and examine how neurons connect at the microscopic level in real time. This technology also enables scientists to see how the signal is passed from one neuron to the next across the synapse (Stamm, 2007).[2]
- Diffusion Tensor Imaging (DTI) is a method for analyzing the structure of neural areas in the brain. DTI measures white matter tracts made up of axons that connect different neurons in the brain. These axons are covered with white myelin sheaths. These tracts are "information highways" in the brain (Hruby & Goswami, 2011).[3]
- New technologies are also being introduced to the rapidly growing field of neuroscience. These include transcranial magnetic stimulation (TMS), and optical imaging techniques, such as near-infrared spectroscopy (NIRS) in (Stamm, 2007).

The early years are a time of extraordinary brain development that sets the foundation for later learning. The brain is the only organ in the body that is incomplete at birth. The distinct areas of the brain are in place, but much growth will still occur. New technologies now provide us with ways of viewing the brain both before and after birth. Through the use of these technologies, researchers now know that by the 17th week of pregnancy, the fetus already has 1 billion brain cells more than the adult brain (Ngala Family Services, 2009). The "growth happens simultaneously: from Back to Front, from Inside Out, and from Bottom Up" (Stamm, 2007, p. 22). The inner layer of the brain is "a subcortical area called the limbic system" (Sprenger, 2008, p. 11).[4] According to Jill Stamm, Cofounder of the New Directions Institute for Infant Brain Development, this "system is critical for learning, motivation, memory, and emotion…" (Stamm, 2007, p. 291).

The limbic system includes the following structures:

- The amygdala is an "almond-shaped complex of related nuclei" (Jensen E., 1998, p. 115).[5] It "receives a great deal of sensory information" and is "a key link between experiences and emotional reactions to them" (Nolte, 2010, p. 183).[6]
- The hippocampus is the part of the brain involved with learning memory, specifically converting temporary memories into long-term memories that can be stored within the brain and retrieved later. As the hippocampus develops and neural networks become more complex, a single word can trigger the brain to call up an entire *neural net* of associated ideas (Stamm, 2007).
- The thalamus is in the center of the brain. It relays incoming information from the senses to different areas of the cortex. It regulates a person's level of awareness and level of activity (Stamm, 2007). When a learner is involved at a level that entails personal meaning, the information will encode through the thalamus and will be relayed to and stored as long-term memory in the hippocampus (Sousa D., 2011).
- The hypothalamus is involved with drive-related behavior and informing as well as controlling functions of the "automatic nervous system" (Nolte, 2010, p. 2), such as "blood pressure and body temperature" (Nolte, 2010, p. 179).
- Base ganglia are "clusters of nuclei deep within the *cerebrum* and the upper parts of the brain stem that play an important part in producing smooth, continuous muscular action in stopping and starting movement" (Jensen E., 1998, p. 116).

Educator and author Merilee Sprenger explains that the "outer layer of the brain that we sometimes call our gray matter" is the neocortex, or cerebral cortex. It "makes up about 80% of the brain's volume" (Sprenger, 2008, p. 11). It's considerable size is necessary because information coming in to the brain is processed and stored here (Stamm, 2007). In addition to the cortexes, the brain has two hemispheres. The hemispheres work together, but each has some separate functions. The corpus callosum is a "white matter bundle of 200–300 million nerve fibers that connect the left and right hemispheres" of the brain and allows them to communicate" (Jensen E., 1998, p. 116). The hemispheres have parts called lobes that have the following specific functions:

- The occipital lobe is located in the "rear of the *cerebrum*…this lobe processes our vision" (Jensen E., 1998, p. 117).

- The parietal lobe is the "top of our upper brain…" It "plays a part in reading, writing, language, and calculation" (Jensen E., 1998, p. 117). The parietal lobe also becomes active during "problem solving." It is involved in the brain receiving "sensory information" (Sprenger, 2008, p. 13).
- Wernicke's area, is located in the parietal-temporal lobe "above the left ear and is about the size of a silver dollar" (Sousa D. A., 2005, p. 13). This area is "responsible for receptive language" (Sprenger, 2008, p. 13).
- The temporal lobe is positioned in the "middle of our upper brain, near our ears." This is an area that is involved with "hearing, senses, listening, language, learning, and memory storage" (Jensen E., 1998, p. 118). This lobe contains the hippocampus that plays a major role in storing long-term, conscious memories. "Between the ages of two and three years, connections between the hippocampus, neocortex, and limbic system become stronger" (Herschkowitz & Herschkowitz, 2002). This would indicate "that the brain is beginning to be able to store long-term semantic memories" (Sprenger, 2008, p. 35). Memories may be stored from an earlier age, but since the hippocampus is not developed until this time, expression of these memories is not likely.

We now know that brain function depends upon the rapid, efficient passage of signals from one part of the brain to another. To function efficiently, the brain needs a well-organized network. The building blocks of this network are brain cells. There are two types of cells, neurons and glial cells. Neurons do most of the communicating in the brain that we associate with learning. Glial cells are "support cells" that "remove unneeded debris" (Sprenger, 2008, p. 10). Some of these cells encase the extension of the neuron known as the axon, forming a "fatty, white shield" called the "myelin" (Jensen E., 1998, p. 117). It is these shields, or "myelin sheaths that allow axons to conduct action potentials more rapidly" (Nolte, 2010, p. 5). Further, "The more myelin sheaths the axon, the faster the neuron can conduct its charge" (Wolf, 2007, p. 94).[7] Neurons also have dendrites, "receptor sites for *axons*" (Jensen E., 1998, p. 116). They receive messages that have been sent from other axons. Brain chemicals called neurotransmitters carry messages between neurons. The following neurotransmitters will cause changes in the brain that will indicate growth and development:

- Acetylcholine is involved in the formation of long-term memories (Jensen E., 1998).
- Dopamine is a "powerful and common *neurotransmitter*" that helps produce positive moods and feelings (Jensen E., 1998, p. 116).
- Norepinephrine "responds to novelty and aids in memory formation" (Sprenger, 2008, p. 14).
- Serotonin "helps control impulsivity, calms the brain, aids in reflective behaviors" (Sprenger, 2008, p. 14).

The neurotransmitters are released into a space called the synapse, "the junction communication point where *neurons* interact" (Jensen E., 1998, p. 118). In summary, synapses are critical to healthy development and learning. They connect up to form neural pathways. As new synapses take shape, others that are not necessary are pruned away. The brain is designed to find and generate patterns. The brain changes as an outcome of experience. Learners create a personal understanding of the environment through a process of interaction, reflection and action. The brain requires external stimulation in order to learn. As a person interacts with the environment, reacts to stimuli, takes in information, processes or stores it, new signals race along these neural pathways. New brain cells are formed daily, linking new information to prior experiences. A number of areas of the brain are stimulated simultaneously when a child is engaged in a learning experience (Rushton, Eitelgeorge, & Zickafoose, 2003). The more stimulation the brain receives, the more diverse the branching of the dendrites and the greater the number of synaptic connections are made.

> For very specific aspects of brain development, certain 'critical periods' exist before age 3, during which adequate stimulation must be received or development is impaired, in some cases permanently. For instance the absence of a reasonable amount of light in the first weeks after birth alters the development of the visual system (e.g. development of binocularity is not possible). Similarly, a child who never hears language, or who receives extremely poor care (as in some orphanages), will likely suffer developmental deficits. (UNESCO, 2006, p. 109)

NEUROPLASTICITY

Such effects have led some to view the first years of life as an extended critical period that ends by age three. Researchers still have much to learn about the persistence of these effects and the ability of the brain to overcome them (UNESCO, 2006). One focus of this research is neuroplasticity, the capacity of the brain to change and adapt in response to stimuli, cognitive demands, injury and new learning. Plasticity allows the brain to create new neural pathways and connections. Kurt Fischer, education professor and director of the Mind, Brain, and Education Program at Harvard University, states, "There are a few broad principles that we can state come out of neuroscience." The number one broad principle, however, is "The brain is remarkably plastic…Even in middle or old age, it's still adapting very actively to its environment." The concept of neuroplasticity does away with the idea that intelligence is fixed at birth. Instead, intelligence continues to form and develop throughout life (Bernard, 2010).[8] Neuroplasticity challenges the notion of absolute critical periods for learning. Therefore, the idea of a window of opportunity closing by age three is difficult to support.

As explained in *Strong Foundations: Early Childhood Care and Education* (UNESCO, 2006, p. 109), "although some critical periods do exist, the concept of 'sensitive periods' is more relevant to understanding early childhood" (Bailey D., 2002; Horton, 2001).

> Sensitive periods are times in development when the absence of some kind of stimulus results in development going awry. Sensitive periods are generally longer than critical periods and are characterized by more flexibility in the timing of input or experience to the brain and in the brain's ability to learn and develop over time. Thus, it may never be too late to acquire a skill (as the notion of a critical period implies), but acquiring it early is preferable. For example, adults are certainly able to learn a second language, but it is less intuitive for them than for young children, and they typically do not learn it as well. (UNESCO, 2006, p. 109)

Some researchers use the term 'windows of opportunity' for the periods that are the "ideal time to provide the input that these active brain areas require." These time periods involve more growth of dendrites in a specific area that provide more "receivers of information." Increased synaptic density in a specific area can allow "more space for connections between neurons." More myelination of a specific area accommodating "faster and easier transmission of messages" and increased "brain wave activity" also occur at these times (Sprenger, 2008, p. 15). Sprenger writes that "most windows never completely close" (Sprenger, 2008, p. 17).

THE BRAIN, LANGUAGE, AND MEMORY

Between the ages of two and three years, connections between the hippocampus, neocortex, and limbic system strengthen and the brain starts to store long-term memories. During the first three years of life, blood flow is heavier in the right hemisphere of the brain. Sprenger draws on the work of researchers who explain that around the age of three, blood flows more heavily in the left hemisphere (Herschkowitz & Herschkowitz, 2006). The left hemisphere is associated with the "production and understanding of language." Therefore, the increase in blood flow "may be a sign of great strides in speech and language development" (Sprenger, 2008, p. 35). The synaptic density in the connections between Broca's and Wernicke's areas, which are involved with language and reading, also increase at this time (Sousa D. A., 2006). Increased blood flow to these areas means that these language structures are getting more energy. They need this additional energy "to create and increase connectivity" (Sprenger, 2008, p. 35). As a result, the growth of speech and vocabulary increase.

Additionally, episodic memories begin to form. Episodic memory is type of long-term memory that centers on recalling of specific events, situations and experiences. Examples of these recollections include one's first day of school, attending a birthday party, and going to the beach for the first time. Closely related to episodic memories are autobiographical memory, or one's memories of personal life history. Episodic and autobiographical memories play an important role in self-identity (Cherry). "This memory system which is associated with events and locations, allows three-year-olds to make sense of occurrences and makes them better able to tell and retell stories and events in their lives" (Sprenger, 2008, p. 35).

At age four, language abilities continue to grow as there is increased growth of dendrites in Broca's area resulting in improved syntax (Eliot, 1999).[9] Myelin continues to grow in the cerebellum and the frontal and parietal lobes continue to develop. These areas also continue to connect. These connections bring about dramatic gains in motor coordination from gross movements, like throwing a ball to finer movements like printing letters. These connections also support cognition (Berk L., 2006). "After the fourth birthday," neurons appear that produce "acetylcholine" (Kagan & Herschkowitz, 2005, p. 210). This "neurotransmitter aids in long-term memory" (Sprenger, 2008, p. 47). "By age four, the hippocampus is developed and is forming impersonal memories." Impersonal memories are also called semantic memories. Semantic memory is the type of long term memory that is concerned with ideas, meanings, and concepts which are not related to personal experiences (What is semantic memory, 2013). Both personal and impersonal memories help children learn.

Kagan and Herschkowitz (Kagan & Herschkowitz, 2005, p. 210)[10] draw on research showing that between the ages of three and six, myelination of the axons of the anterior corpus-callosum, that connects the frontal lobes of the two hemispheres, accelerates (Young, Fox, & Zahn-Waxler, 1999). Further, Sprenger cites findings revealing that growth of this "white matter structure in children correlates with increased development of motor skills and reading ability and increased cognitive function" (Casey, 2000; Paus, 2001; Schmithorst, Wilke, Dardzinski, & Holland, 2002). With experience, vocabulary continues to expand and children comprehend more through dialogue. As Sprenger describes, "A small increase in the short-term memory system called *immediate or conscious memory* may be seen." The "hippocampus and amygdala are creating greater connections to each other and to other areas of the brain." Therefore, "memories should become clearer as both the emotional aspect of the memory and the factual aspect can be connected" (Sprenger, 2008, p. 61). Coherence is the degree to which different brain regions work together, or show "synchronized neuronal activity" (Kagan & Herschkowitz, 2005, p. 211). The coherence between the frontal lobes of the brain, and the occipital and temporal areas increases between 3–6 years (Ornitz, 2002; Thatcher, 1992) in (Kagan & Herschkowitz, 2005, p. 211). This "enhanced coherence should aid the brain's ability to integrate past with present" (Kagan & Herschkowitz, 2005, p. 211).

NOTES

[4] From THE DEVELOPING BRAIN: BIRTH TO AGE EIGHT by Marilee B. Sprenger. Copyright © 2008. Reproduced with permission of SAGE PUBLICATIONS INC.

[5] From TEACHING WITH THE BRAIN IN MIND by Eric Jensen. Copyright ©1998. Reprinted by permission of the Association for Supervision and Curriculum Development. All rights reserved.

[6] From THE ESSENTIALS OF THE HUMAN BRAIN by John Nolte. Copyright © 2010 by Mosby, Inc., an affiliate of Elsevier Inc. Reprinted with permission of Elsevier, Inc.

[7] Excerpts from PROUST AND THE SQUID by MARYANNE WOLF. Copyright © 2007 by Maryanne Wolf. Reprinted by Permission of HarperCollins Publishers. Also Reprinted by Permission of Icon Books, London.

[8] Quote from Kurt Fischer in Neuroplasticity: Learning Physically Changes the Brain, by Sara Bernard, in *edutopia*. Copyright © 2010 by *edutopia*. Reprinted by permission of *edutopia*.

[9] Excerpts from: WHAT'S GOING ON IN THERE? HOW THE BRAIN AND MIND DEVELOP IN THE FIRST FIVE YEARS OF LIFE by Lise Eliot, copyright © 1999 by Lise Eliot. Used by permission of Bantam Books, an imprint of Random House, a division of Random House LLC. All rights reserved. Any third party use of this material, outside of this publication, is prohibited. Interested parties must apply directly to Random House LLC for permission.

[10] A young mind in a growing brain by Jerome Kagan and Norbert Herschkowitz. Copyright © 2005. Reproduced with permission of LAWRENCE ERLBAUM ASSOCIATES INC in the format Educational/Instructional Program via Copyright Clearance Center.

CHAPTER 8

TALK: THE GREAT BRAIN BOOSTER

The time has come
The walrus said
To talk of many things:
Of shoes- and ships-
And sealing wax-
Of cabbages and kings-
And why the sea is boiling hot-
And whether pigs have wings.

— Lewis Carroll, from *The Walrus and the Carpenter* (Carroll, The Walrus and the Carpenter, 1865)

ACQUIRING TALK

In the introduction of this book, I told of the Irish who starved because they did not take up fishing, a practice that could have provided a readily available food source. In relation to the development of a child's brain and language, there is a valuable resource that is right in front of us. As Jill Stamm states:

> Everybody's searching for the next great brain booster. Well, scientists have found it—and it's accessible to every family, guaranteed to improve intellectual development and prevent certain kinds of learning problems later in life. And to reap its benefits, you don't have to buy a thing—or even learn any special new technique. In fact, it's free. And it's right under our noses (literally!): Talk. (Stamm, 2007, p. 217)

In 1979, Don Holdaway noted:

> Since time before history, regardless of race, class, or educational background, families have succeeded in transmitting their native language to their infants—or their infants have succeeded in learning the language within a natural environment of language use. (Holdaway D., 1979, p. 19)

Lise Eliot, neuroscientist and author of *What's Going On in There? How the Mind and Brain Develop in the First Five Years of Life,* notes, "Whether carried as 'papooses,' in slings, or in high-tech infant seats, all healthy babies manage to walk, talk, and throw food in much the same way, at much the same age, give or take a few weeks"

(Eliot, 1999, p. 8). She further states, "The fact that all children learn language in a very similar way and on a very similar schedule shows just how deeply rooted it is in our biological makeup." Even though "there are a few notable differences between languages, kids throughout the world follow remarkably similar paths on their rapid journey to fluency." A healthy infant is capable of learning any of the 3,000 languages spoken throughout the world. Eliot adds, "We are born with a brain primed for language-learning. As long as it is exposed at the right time, a child's linguistic skills will inevitably flower on schedule" (Eliot, 1999, p. 376).

Furthermore, "Through social interaction and cultural support, an infant's neurological network is formed and cultivated for the particular language to which the child is exposed." When "a child is exposed and immersed in more than one language, especially during the formative years (1 to 5), the developing cell weight and expansion of dendrites is increased" (Rushton, Eitelgeorge, & Zickafoose, 2003, p. 13). If use of one of the languages does not continue, however, neural pruning takes place, and over time the perception of the sounds of that language no longer exists (Thompson, 2001).

Professor Judith Lindfors describes language acquisition as an interactive process through which a child comes to understand how language is organized and used. This process takes place when the child actively participates in actual communication events. Lindfors (Lindfors J., 1985, p. 55) notes that British educator James Britton calls this "practice." But he is not referring to the rehearsal type of practice that a juggler does alone to get ready for a show. He means the kind of practice that lawyers and doctors engage in when they "practice" law or medicine (Britton, 1973, p. 130). This kind of "practice" requires the presence of another person. The process of language acquisition is "*continuous, dynamic*" and "*evolving*" (Lindfors J., 1985, p. 54). Talking and listening are tightly interwoven. As Holdaway states, "In spoken-language learning no-one would consider separating listening from speaking…" (Holdaway D., 1979, p. 24).

The best situation for stimulating language development is one of responsiveness to and acceptance of the child's communicative attempts. In *Developmentally Appropriate and Culturally Responsive Education,* Dr. Rebecca Novick states, "By responding to infant's babbles, coos, and smiles as if they are meaningful and including children in conversations long before they say their first words, parents help children to become confident and competent language learners" (Novick, 1996, p. 18). As members of a world of learners who strive to assure children's rights to education and literacy, we need to be willing to undertake study to learn what children know. Communication through language is one of the primary areas of learning in which the brain engages early in life.

Valuing the language that children acquire early in life requires understanding what they have acquired. New technologies and brain research allow us to study how language develops, even before a child is born. We need far more specific information than vocabulary word count to understand what children know about language and literacy, and to determine how we can build upon their knowledge. We cannot say that children learn beginning at birth, and then deny what some children have learned by the age of six.

During the first six years, the brain sets up the circuits needed to understand and reproduce complex language. "Learning to talk is not a matter of being formally instructed in nouns, verbs, and vocabulary words; it's a matter of hearing natural conversation directed at you, over and over and over" (Stamm, 2007, p. 224). Talk and listening go together. Rather than engaging in formal instruction, caregivers of children who are confident oral language learners understand that their children's attempts to communicate are meaningful. They expand on the children's utterances, and regard the children "as competent conversationalists, long before children say their first recognizable words" (Novick, 1996, p. 8). Caregivers "provide a language-rich environment, where 'meaningful spoken language washes over and surrounds children' (Cambourne B., 1987), from birth and (as the DeCasper research demonstrates) even before" in (Novick, 1996, p. 9).

Furthermore, Novick (Novick, 1996, p. 9), drawing on the work of psychologist Jerome Bruner, explains:

> Rather than serving as reinforcer and corrector, adults act as "providers, expanders, and idealizers" of language. Because children are motivated to learn by "doing something with words in the real world" (Bruner J., 1983), grammar is learned, not as an isolated skill, but in a meaningful conversational context.

John Dwyer's work focused on the importance of talk. He worked with Aboriginal children in the Torres Strait Islands. Drawing on James Britton's (1983) words, "Reading and writing float on a sea of talk." Dwyer explains language development this way:

> Children set sail on this 'sea' from a variety of starting points. While some have better navigational aids and more supportive pilots than others, all must plot their own course. Along the way they may meet many shoals and often capsize. As they struggle to right themselves, they progressively construct their own chart of the sea—a chart which, over time, more and more closely matches the general chart used by the people in their world. (Dwyer, 1991a, p. 2)

Dwyer describes talk as "our prime means of communication." He adds:

> We talk in response to events and in preparation for action. We talk to define ourselves to ourselves and to others. We talk to define the situation and our place in it. We talk to establish, strengthen or end personal relationships. We receive and develop ideas and explore our understandings initially through talk. (Dwyer, 1991a, p. 3)

Dwyer describes many purposes for talk, including the need to "…persuade, explain, instruct, entertain, narrate, speculate, argue a case, report, describe, find out, express feelings, clarify or explore an issue, solve a problem, interpret, summarise, evaluate, reflect, announce, criticise and deal with a criticism." Each situation requires a different style of language, presenting new challenges and providing opportunities to develop new strengths. He promotes classrooms "where children learn to talk; learn through talk; and learn about talk." He states, "Children should be encouraged to develop speaking and listening skills both 'in-role' (as themselves) and 'out-of-role' (through role play and drama)" (Dwyer, 1991a, p. 3). These kinds of settings help children become aware of the features and conventions necessary to participate in conversations. These abilities to think about, play with, analyze, talk about and make judgments about correct forms of talk are called metalinguistic skills (Snow, Burns, & Griffin, 1998, p. 48).

TALK STIMULATES A BABY'S BRAIN

Since language is fundamental to most of the rest of cognitive development, the acts of talking and listening to a child are among the best ways to make the most of their early years of brain development (Early experiences matter, 2012). Language development begins before a child is born. In utero, the fetus hears the cadence, pitch, intonation—melody of the mother's voice. To some degree, the voice of the father and others, as well as environmental sounds, like music, are also heard. A baby is born physically equipped to hear distinct language sounds of all languages. Babies learn according to what they are exposed to (Stamm, 2007). Infants are born interested in listening to human voices and so have the tendency to produce babbling sounds. Their sounds imitate the rhythms and tones of the speech of the adults around them. Whatever language a baby hears every day—French, or Afrikaans, or English, "those word sounds and grammatical patterns are what his brain gets practice hearing and will eventually reproduce." Furthermore, "healthy babies everywhere start out with brains that have the exact same language potential." These babies "have the ability to detect sounds from any language, all those intricate stresses and pronunciation nuances that make native tongues so distinct" (Stamm, 2007, p. 208).

Stamm states, "Sorting out and becoming attuned to these intricate language sounds (phonemes) happens with repeated exposure. The structures within your baby's brain that process language are literally shaped by what he hears." When those around the baby talk, the baby's "brain listens…and learns… and *physically changes and grows.*" By one year of age, "a child loses the ability to hear sounds that are not found in his native language and, in turn, to easily pronounce them" (Stamm, 2007, p. 209). "Hearing more than one language early in life will not stunt your child's ability to be proficient in either, or both languages" (Stamm, 2007, p. 226).

Parent-infant educator, Lucia Quiñonez Sumner cites extensive research that explains the size of the vocabularies of bilingual children.[1] She states:

> …it is not uncommon for "preschool bilingual children to know fewer words in each language than monolingual children when each language is examined separately" (Genesee F., 2012). In fact, good evidence exists that bilingual

> children and young adults have smaller vocabularies in each of their languages than do monolingual children of the same age (Pearson B. Z., 1993 v15; Pearson, Fernandez, Lewedeg, & Oller, 1997; Hoff & Elledge, 2003) as cited in (Hoff & McKay, 2005). Nevertheless, if we count the total number of words a child has in both languages, "Bilingual children have vocabularies that are the same size or larger than those of monolingual children" (Pearson, Fernandez, Lewedeg, & Oller, 1997), as cited in (Hoff E. & McKay J., 2005). This discrepancy in vocabulary size may exist, "Because bilingual children must share their limited memory with two languages, they can store fewer words in each language than monolingual children—but the same number, or more words, when you consider both languages." (Genesee F., 2012) in (Quiñonez Sumner L., 2014, p. 4)

Quiñonez Sumner continues:

> Another explanation of bilingual children's smaller vocabularies in each language is related to the learning environment. Many bilingual children do not have totally equivalent vocabularies in both languages, because they often learn each language from different people and/or in different settings (Genesee, 2007). "The current view is that this difference reflects differences in the amount of input in each language that children receive." (Pearson, Fernandez, Lewedeg, & Oller, 1997) as cited by (Quiñonez Sumner L., 2014, p. 4)

View from a Small Place

A child in my family is bilingual. Her father is American and her mother is Russian. Since the time she was born, she has spent approximately half of the year in New York and half in Moscow. Since that time, she has been spoken to, read to, sung songs, and told stories in both English and Russian. In addition to being read a bedtime story, she requests that her father to tell her a story every night before she goes to sleep. She also watches children's videos and educational shows in both languages. She speaks both languages. When she is in the U.S. with speakers of English, she speaks English. When she is in Moscow, with speakers of Russian, she speaks Russian. By the age of three, she was able to alternate between languages with ease. She changes languages when she flies to the U.S. or Russia, because she converses in the language spoken in the locality. When she is in the U.S. and the phone rings, if the caller speaks Russian, she will immediately begin talking to the caller in Russian. If her American grandmother speaks to her in English during the call from Russia, she will speak English for the side conversation. When she is in Russia, if a caller speaks English, she will hold side conversations with her Russian family in Russian. Occasionally, when she is speaking English in the U.S, she will "borrow" a Russian word. She is making use of all of the words in her

> bilingual lexicon to communicate. In this instance, it is also possible that she knows the word in both languages, but uses the Russian word to draw attention to and emphasis her point.

In her writings, Quiñonez Sumner explains, "Borrowing is 'the introduction of single words or short, frozen, idiomatic phrases from one variety into another'" (Gumperz, 1982), as cited by (Cal & Turnbull, n.d.). She cites research (Milroy & Muysken, 1995) who define code-switching as "the alternative used by bilinguals of two or more languages in the same conversation." She adds, "Children as young as 2 are able to code-switch in socially appropriate ways" (Lanza, 1992), as cited by (King & Fogle, 2006). Code-switching is sometimes viewed by adults as a sign of confusion. It is not. Rather, "the ability to switch back and forth between languages is a sign of mastery of two linguistic systems, not a sign of language confusion" (Lanza, 1992) as cited by (King & Fogle, 2006; Quiñonez Sumner L., 2014, p. 5).

BEGINNING TO TALK

Babies learn about speech and sounds as they babble, coo and cry. In the first few months of life, children begin to experiment with language. Early on, babies recognize facial expressions and gestures. Young babies make sounds that imitate the tones and rhythms of talk that surrounds them in their speech communities. They begin to grasp the meaning of words that are part of their daily lives (Berk L., 2012).

At 3 months, the brain has the potential to distinguish several hundred spoken sounds. Babies babble when they are with other people and when they are alone (Anderson B., 1998). A six-month-old can recognize vowel sounds that are the basic building blocks of speech. In the coming months, the brain organizes itself to recognize hundreds of sounds (Porter, 2007). Sprenger (Sprenger, 2008, p. 23) quotes researchers Bergen and Coscia who state, "By eight months there is notable increase in activity in the frontal lobes, indicating higher cognitive functioning" (Bergen & Coscia, 2001).

By one year of age, "English-speaking babies can produce most of the vowels and about half of all the consonant sounds in the language. It can take many more years, however, before they finally master the most difficult consonant sounds" (Eliot, 1999, p. 370). The babbling of the youngest babies generally sound similar, but "cross-cultural studies" of children who speak "English, French, Chinese, or Arabic" found that "ten-month-olds babble in distinctive ways, reflecting the dominant language of their country of origin…" The evolution of babies' talk is affected by the maturing of the vocal machinery, but also by adult interactions. The amount of attention that adults give to babbling impacts the amount of babbling in which the infant engages. When given response or imitated, the number of a child's vocalizations will increase. Ignoring a child's utterances can result in "potentially long-lasting ramifications" (Eliot, 1999, p. 371).

LANGUAGE PLAY

Psychologist Jerome Bruner states, "...children's language use (during acquisition) is most daring and most advanced when it is used in a playful setting" (Bruner J., 1984, p. 196).

David Crystal, author of *Language Play,* points out that this play begins in the first months of life when, along with talking, "parents chant or sing to their children." These adults "sometimes use nonsense syllables with no particular tune, and sometimes using real words in a traditional tune, such as lullabies and nursery rhymes. By six months of age, most children have heard several rhymes and have begun to develop 'favourites'." Parents and caregivers who engage in language play may also invent special words or words may be altered so their sounds are repeated and therefore easier to learn. Examples of these words are: "*woof-woof, nana* ('banana')...and choo-*choo* ('train')" (Crystal, 1998, p. 162).[2]

Language play is central to interactions between parents and babies. What Crystal calls "baby talk" takes place from the time a child is born and is a "highly distinctive way of speaking, in which normal sounds, grammar, vocabulary, and patterns of discourse are altered, in varying degrees, so as to foster a communicative rapport with the child" (Crystal, 1998, p. 159). When talking in this manner, speakers "simplify" formal speech. Other features of speech are also changed. "Sentences become simpler and shorter, and structures are frequently repeated" (Crystal, 1998, p. 160).

Stamm draws a distinction between parentese and baby talk. As she describes, parentese is "*regular* speech modified to match the processing capabilities of what your baby hears." Baby talk on the other hand is comprised of "nonsense sounds" like "Ga ga ga gaga goo goo." Baby talk is appropriate for occasional language play, but the brain is seeking patterns and "baby talk doesn't teach the pattern-seeking brain about how actual language works" (Stamm, 2007, p. 228).

Throughout the world, many parents engage in "parentese," this form of language play that manipulates the rules of language, and as Sprenger (Sprenger, 2008, p. 24) describes, stretches out "syllables and sounds in a singsong fashion." Drawing on Tallal, she explains that talk slows down as the adult a deliberately accentuates the phonemes that will become part of the child's world (Tallal, 2007). Vowels, particularly long vowels, are elongated. Parentese is spoken at a higher pitch than everyday speech. It is "exactly the tone, pitch, and speed a baby's brain can hear!" Parentese also "perfectly matches the auditory processing speed that a very young infant can hear" and is used "naturally in response to careful observation of what a baby seems to pay attention to the most" (Stamm, 2007, pp. 227–228).

This talk is not the language of formal, adult speech and some adults are not comfortable speaking it. Some adults will not engage in this kind of talk. Some "scrupulously avoid" it, "believing that they will interfere with the child's learning of normal vocabulary." But adults who do this "underestimate the immense language learning capability of young children, who are able to assimilate without any difficulty several language varieties (or, for that matter, languages), including the distinction between playful and serious uses" (Crystal, 1998, p. 162). In order to play with language, the speaker takes a known word or phrase and will "manipulate it" by "bending and breaking the rules" of the way it is typically used and "make it do things it does not normally do" (Crystal, 1998, p. 1). Crystal notes that remarkably, by the third year of life, children use this kind of talk themselves when they play at being parents with their dolls and teddies. Or as in the following example from a friend of mine, a new baby sister!

View from a Small Place

> When a friend of mine gave birth to her baby and brought her home, the baby's six-year-old sister went up to the infant several times a day, leaned in and said in parentese, "Ooooooohh! Do youuuu neeeeed you're big siseeeeee?"

Later language play, particularly rhyming, supports language growth and development. Many aspects of spoken language, including acquisition and "all levels of phonological awareness," can be fostered through "fun, engaging oral language activities" (Opitz M., 2000, p. 16). Phonemic awareness in particular can be improved through rhyme recognition and phoneme manipulation (Widdowson, 2001).

VOCABULARY DEVELOPMENT

As early as "nine or ten months of age," babies "bridge the gap between sounds and meaning" as they go beyond mere sound play and link sounds with the world around them: objects, people, actions, and concepts. First words are often the "names of family members and pets, the meaning of *no!* and perhaps a few general labels like *shoe* and *cookie*" (Eliot, 1999, p. 372).

Stamm points out that it is the "direct interaction between child and adult that seems to be the crux of language learning." She describes how "Across the world… babies and toddlers ask parents or caregivers to label objects in their environment through such means as pointing and grunting. ('*Dat? Dat?*') Typically most adults (or older siblings) oblige." Stamm continues, "Psychologists call this human event *shared visual attention,…* and it appears to be necessary for vocabulary development" (Stamm, 2007, p. 244).

At first children accompany their gestures with a single word. The child takes in the meaning and eventually begins to use new words. According to Lindfors, a "child can use the names of people, objects, actions, locations, and properties of objects to bring a partner to her focus of attention and, thus, start a conversation." A child who holds up a toy dog and says "Doggie" may be naming the toy or asking if the name is correct. Other language users in the child's world engage in the conversation and help interpret and expand the child's meaning by saying, "Yes, that's your doggie, isn't it. What does the doggie say?" or by confirming, "Yes, it's a dog" –adapted from (Lindfors J., 2008, p. 11).

Then children begin to use speech as the major way of expressing meaning. Eliot explains, "There's typically about a five-month lag between the time a toddler can understand a certain number of words and when he can actually speak that many." She continues, "The median number of words spoken by a one-year-old is six, but many say none at all, and a few speak up to fifty." Between twelve and eighteen months, the number of words builds up slowly. Then the child starts saying new words every day. All of a sudden, when a child can say about fifty words, vocabulary "hits a critical mass" and "vocabulary explodes." On a daily basis, children add up to three new words to their speech, "and their receptive vocabulary—the number of words a child understands—grows even more quickly" (Eliot, 1999, pp. 372–373).

The "vocabulary explosion is associated with a spurt in brain development." Eliot explains that "all normal toddlers enter this explosive phase of vocabulary growth sometime during the second year, a period when synapse formation and metabolic activity are at their all-time high in the cerebral cortex." Between the ages of two and six, "children are estimated to learn the meaning of a staggering eight words a day." Learning results in "more than one new word every two hours they are awake, and they continue at this rate into the elementary school years." By the age of six, it is estimated that children understand "some 13,000 words," although they do not "speak nearly that many" (Eliot, 1999, pp. 373–374).

Within a few months of the vocabulary explosion, a grammar explosion also occurs as the child rapidly acquires all the basic rules of syntax. As they continue to speak, children begin to use a progression of parts of speech that make their sentences sound more complete to those around them. "There are really just two basic tricks of grammar used by all languages of the world. You can create meaning either by adjusting the order of words or by changing the little pieces (known as inflections) that are tacked onto the ends of words (or beginnings in some languages)." Children "appreciate the meaning embedded in word order at a very young age," and use that understanding "when they begin speaking in two-word phrases themselves, usually between eighteen to twenty-four months" (Eliot, 1999, p. 374).

By early in the third year, children put together longer strings of words. At first these sentences "lack most of the inflections" and "function words—*of, to, the, am, do, in...*" But they soon begin to add additional "bits of grammar." They do not do this "by trial and error; they are figuring out the actual *rules* for how classes of words are combined." They intuitively understand "the distinctions between different parts of speech—nouns, verbs, adjectives." They also figure out how to "adjust and assemble these various parts of speech to produce the precise meaning they intend" (Eliot, 1999, p. 375). As they continue to speak, children begin to use a progression of parts of speech that make their utterances "sound smoother and more complete to the adult's ear" (Lindfors J., 1991, p. 123).[3] By four years of life, the child has the "ability to say virtually anything" his or her "mind can think of" (Eliot, 1999, p. 374).

As children's language develops, their first sentences express one idea, but they move on to "progressively longer" sentences. They also come to say ones that express a combination of ideas. At first, they acquire and use regular patterns in their speech and then learn irregular patterns. Over time, children develop negatives and patterns of questioning. Eventually, their language productions come to match those of the adults in their speech communities more closely (Lindfors J., 1985, pp. 44–45).

SOCIOCULTURAL CONSIDERATIONS

In addition to learning how to speak the words of a language, young children also learn how language is used in various situations to shape the social relationships in their community. Children gain understanding of "rules for opening and closing a conversation," how to take turns during a conversation, and "how to tell a story or joke." How differential power relations are revealed through language, and how cultural values and norms of politeness, respect, and status affect conversations are also learned. For example, "Addressing a person as 'Mrs.', 'Ms.', or by a first name is not really about simple vocabulary choice but about the relationship and social position of the speaker and addressee" (Wolfram, 2005).[4] Children also come to understand the kinds of language and behaviors that are appropriate for formal and informal settings. For instance, the words and actions of a church service are different from those of a conversation during play with friends. Not just speech is learned, but body language too. Examples include culturally appropriate uses of eye contact and gestures during conversations.

Typically, within a country there is a wide range of cultures and dialects. Speakers "from one geographical region will speak differently from people from another region" (Lindfors J., 1991, p. 395). These differences are known as geographic, or regional, dialects. Some differences occur in the pronunciation of words, others in words and word combinations used. Less obvious differences are also conveyed through dialects including: tone of voice, pitch and rhythm, how fast one talks, and when to begin and stop talking. What to talk about, when and to whom, the "point" one is likely to make, and how to get it across are also features of dialects (Tannen, 1981; Lindfors J., 1991).

In addition to geographic, dialects, there are social dialects. Dudley-Marley and Lucas (Dudley-Marling & Lucas, 2009, p. 366) state, "There is an alternative tradition in linguistic research informed by a sociocultural theory of language." Researcher Sarah Michaels contends that this theory respects the linguistic and sociocultural strengths of members of non-dominant communities. When these strengths are recognized, they can influence schools and the reception and achievement of non-mainstream children within them (Michaels, 2005).

Linguists have "demonstrated the richness, complexity, and rule-governed nature of the language practices of non-dominant groups" (Labov, 1970; Michaels, 1981; Heath S., 1983; Gee J., 1996; Gonzalez, Moll, & Amanti, 2005) in (Dudley-Marling & Lucas, 2009, p. 366). Lindfors points out, "Typically that dialect used by the more powerful social group in an area is the most prestigious." However, "a more socially prestigious dialect is not more expressive, or more cognitively powerful, or more abstract, or more anything else." Often, speakers of a less socially prestigious dialect are not heard as using valid, rule-governed variety, but rather will be viewed as making flawed attempts at "standard" dialect. "Different dialects are simply different expression systems for conveying meaning. No dialect is inherently better or worse than any other" (Lindfors J., 1991, p. 397). Furthermore, Gorski (Gorski P., 2008, p. 34) makes the point that "linguists have known for decades that language varieties are highly structured with complex grammatical rules" (Gee J. P., 2004; Hess, 1974; Miller, Cho, & Bracey, 2005).

As Lindfors explains:

> Each dialect serves the intellectual and social purposes of it speakers with full adequacy and effectiveness. But dialects spoken by social groups that hold less of the power and prestige within a society tend to be looked upon by the mainstream group (and often the speakers themselves) as inferior ways of speaking. In fact, these less prestigious dialects are often considered not as intact systems (which they are), but as error-ridden or garbled, inadequate attempts of a group of people to use a regional standard dialect (which they are not). (Lindfors J., 1991, p. 397)

When language differences are perceived as errors, they can have a devastating effect on children. In many situations outside the home, children's speech may not be acknowledged or may be regarded as flawed. In schools, "Often as the year progresses, the task of educating students disintegrates into a struggle to impose 'correct' or mainstream forms upon children who may be confused and uncomfortable with such forms" (Kiefer & De Stefano, 1985, p. 159).

Lisa Delpit presents an example of a preschool teacher from Mississippi who has been drilling the three- and four-year-old children in her care to respond to the greeting, "Good morning, how are you?" with "I'm fine, thank you." (Delpit, 2006, p. 51). One four-year-old answers his teacher's greeting in his home dialect. He becomes uncomfortable when she persists in requiring him to say the response in the way that she expects. Delpit describes the interchange in the following way:

View from a Small Place

TEACHER:	Good morning, Tony, how are you?
TONY:	I be's fine.
TEACHER:	Tony, I said, How are you?
TONY:	(with raised voice) I be's fine.

TEACHER: No, Tony, I said how are you?
TONY: (angrily) I done told you I be's fine and I ain't telling you no more! (Delpit, 2006, p. 51).[5]

Delpit (Delpit, 2006, p. 51), drawing on Krashen (Krashen, 1982), adds that Tony will not be predisposed to "identify with" this teacher or "unconsciously" acquire her "language form." Language is "deeply personal" and "direct attacks on their speech ('for improvement') can be perplexing and often devastating to children." Language develops "in the caring supportive environment of the home, language is 'part and parcel' of all one knows and *is*. A frontal attack on one's speech touches the innermost self" (King M., 1985, p. 27). Even more harmful, denying the existence of a child's language, as I once did, suppresses the very existence of the child.

Gloria Anzuldúa, author of *Borderlands, La Frontera: The New Mestiza*, addresses the issue in this way: "So, if you want to really hurt me, talk badly about my language. Ethnic identity is a twin skin to linguistic identity—I am my language. Until I can take pride in my language, I cannot take pride in myself" (Anzuldúa, 2007, p. 81).[6]

Edwards, Thompson McMillon, and Turner state, "Most teachers of those African American children who have been least well served by education systems believe that their students' life chances will be further hampered if they do not learn Standard English." They continue, "In the stratified society in which we live, they are absolutely correct. While having access to the politically mandated language form will not by any means guarantee economic success, not having access almost certainly will guarantee failure" (Edwards, Thompson McMillon, & Turner, 2008, pp. 73–74).

It is important to consider, however, that teachers must carry out Standard English instruction in a manner that encourages, not disheartens, students who speak African American Vernacular English (AAVE) (Brock, McMillon, Pennington, Townsend, & Lapp, 2009). The approach should acknowledge that different language varieties are used for various purposes in various situations.

No matter what language, dialect, or kind of verbal interaction is taking place, respect for the child should be our most important concern. Author and activist, bell hooks proposes that some African American learners resist learning Standard English, although they are fully capable of learning it. These learners do not take up Standard English because they view it as "the language of conquest and domination" (hooks, 1994, p. 168). Therefore, it is incumbent upon teachers of African American students to balance their ability to hear the authentic voices of students and recognize their resistance, while helping the students understand the purposes of learning Standard English. Brock and her colleagues (Brock, McMillon, Pennington, Townsend, & Lapp, 2009) refer to the work of Hollie who employed successful instructional approaches to strike this balance. These approaches employ culturally relevant literature, active learning, role playing and performance (Hollie, 2001).

Through the lens of deficit thinking, linguistic differences among poor people and children are transformed into deficiencies that are seen as the cause of high levels of academic failure among poor children. This failure results in the loss of their human rights of education and literacy.

In 1989, Dwyer described the issue in the following way:

> If, as teachers, we see these differences as a 'problem', then our teaching response will be to remediate and compensate, to try to stamp out and replace undesirable language…
>
> …if we operate from a remediation/compensation position, we operate from a belief in the child's past failure; we build in an expectation of future failure; and at the same time we build in a cop-out for ourselves. 'I taught them, but they wouldn't (or couldn't) learn'. (Dwyer, 1991b, p. 56)

Educators Pamela Mason and Emily Phillips Galloway add:

> When seen from a strength-based perspective, these children are competent communicators in their families and in their communities where language is the medium to form social connections and to communicate, needs, wants, and hopes. They may have mastered an oral and/or written language that is different from English. They may have mastered an oral dialect. They know which language or dialect to use with different members of their families and communities to accomplish goals. Nevertheless, they may not exhibit these language competencies in the classroom if they perceive that the skills are not relevant or valued in this setting. (Mason & Galloway, 2012, p. 29)

LISTENING TO STORIES

In addition to engaging in talk, when children listen to storytellers, they respond by creating images in their minds of the characters and places portrayed by the words. This "process of developing internal images and meaning in response to words is the basis of imagination." Researchers who study the brain and the development of behavior view imagination as the "essence of creativity" and as the source of "higher order thinking." Imagination allows learners "to understand symbols, create solutions, and find meaning in ideas." These abilities, along with imagination, facilitate "mastering language, writing, mathematics, and other learnings that are grounded in the use of symbols" (Fredericks, 1997, p. 2).

Children who become familiar with stories can refer to them to understand what living in the world is all about. Stories help them learn about their own culture and the culture of others. Daniel Willingham, author of *Why Don't Students Like School?,* states, "The human mind seems exquisitely tuned to understand and remember stories—so much so that psychologists sometimes refer to stories as 'psychologically privileged,' meaning that they are treated differently in memory than other types of material" (Willingham, 2009, pp. 66–67).[7] Most children love to share personal information about themselves. These conversations allow the child to engage in multiple exchanges with others. The use of storytelling with young children enhances children's oral language (Speaker K. & Kamen, 2004). Storytelling is also a passageway to literacy because it improves listening skills and increases the child's ability to organize their thoughts.

Researchers Miller, Cho and Bracey studied personal storytelling as practiced by working-class children and their families. They wanted to find out which realities the families personal stories allowed them to see. They found that the "high frequency, positive valuing, exceptional level of normative competence," and open access that "characterize storytelling in many working-class communities constitute a version of the genre that privileges the individual's right to have a voice, to celebrate his or her own unique experiences and perspectives on the world" (Miller, Cho, & Bracey, 2005, p. 125).

These researchers state:

> This version allows people to see that each person—however humble his or her resources, status, and place in the world—has had many story worthy experiences; that each person has the right to tell these experiences from his or her own perspective; that it is fun, entertaining, and enlightening to tell and listen to such stories; and that while some people are especially talented narrators, almost everyone can become a competent storyteller. (Miller, Cho, & Bracey, 2005, p. 125)

These researchers note that the storytellers they studied used "dramatic language... rhythm and nonverbal enactment" to "heighten the significance of their experiences." These devices "allowed the listeners to appreciate the experiences more fully" and to enter into them vicariously. They add that through these tellings, ordinary experiences become "a little more vivid—funnier, scarier, more infuriating, more surprising." They conclude, "Selves become a little more substantial, a bit larger than life when people seize the stage as narrators and actors in their own multi-modal dramas" (Miller, Cho, & Bracey, 2005, p. 128).

Storytelling can also be especially valuable for bilingual learners. As *Strong foundations: Early childhood care and education* states:

> Speaking and listening activities, especially bilingual storytelling and reading, can be used in a variety of linguistic environments to give children the opportunity to develop literacy skills, which can be transferred from one language to another. Books and learning materials in other languages or dual-language books (even home-made ones) are important to promote bilingualism and tolerance of linguistic and cultural minorities as well as to raise the status of the languages spoken by children and their families. (UNESCO, 2006, p. 160)

Listening to stories enables children to experience vocabulary that is richer than that of daily conversations, hear grammar and sentences that are complex and unique. Hearing stories helps children develop a sense of story. Children who listen to storytellers often become storytellers themselves. Storytelling also provides opportunities for listeners to make inferences and understand causes and outcomes. When children read a familiar story that was previously told, such as *The Gingerbread Man*, their knowledge of the story facilitates their reading. They can predict what will happen in the story, as well as familiar lines and words.

Researchers Miller, Cho and Bracey cite work that shows how the richness of storytelling, however, can diminish in school. For example, opportunities for kindergarten children to engage in oral narrative in school were "extremely limited" and most personal stories told by both children and teachers were not as "complex as those told in homes" (Miller & Mehler, 1994). Furthermore, the narrative practices of middle-class teachers and children can conflict with those of working-class children (Heath S., 1983; Michaels, 1991). Therefore, although narrative development of these children gets "off to a very strong start," there is a risk that "their fluent participation in personal storytelling will not necessarily be recognized for the strength that it is when they venture beyond home and community" (Miller, Cho, & Bracey, 2005, p. 133).

MUSICAL ARTS

In addition to talk and storytelling, "chant, song, dance are linguistic rituals that are among the most powerful forms of human learnings, … satisfying, deeply memorable, and globally meaningful" *(adapted from Holdaway).* The power of music extends across all cultures. Musical arts activate many areas of the brain, and has many positive effects on the mind. Engagement in musical arts, such as listening to music, saying rhymes, singing songs, and playing musical instruments, nurtures "…our integrated sensory, attentional, cognitive, emotional, and motor capacity processes…" These systems are "the driving force behind all other learning" (Jensen E., 2000, p. 3).

Music and rhythm facilitate the memory of words even if the song is not especially melodic (Willingham, 2009). Singing helps children memorize and attend to language. Music assists memory "because the beat, melody, and harmony serve as 'carriers' for the semantic content. The language in songs is produced in a manner that flows without extended pauses between words. This is why it's easier to recall the words of a song than the words of a conversation" (Jensen E., 2000, p. 73). Furthermore, "music making seems to activate and synchronize neural firing patterns that orchestrate and connect multiple cognitive brain sites" (Jensen E., 2000, p. 30). Musical activities also help develop a child's physical coordination and timing (Stamm, 2007).

Music has other benefits as well. Music provides opportunities to play with sounds and discriminate sounds in words. It allows children to engage in word play such as rhyming, repeating words, and saying a succession of words that begin with the same sound. The words in songs are often unique words that are not typically part of everyday conversations. Examples of such words include *merrily*, *rise*, and *harmonies*. Furthermore, music provides opportunities for children to communicate ideas, feelings, and stories and express their imagination and emotions. Through music, children learn about their culture and the culture of others. Children who hear and engage in music are likely to appreciate and enjoy music throughout their lives.

This chapter has explored some concepts about the development of the brain. Talk, storytelling, and music—resources that are right in front of us—have also been considered. The next chapter explores ways in which written language develops.

NOTES

1 From Language Acquisition for the Bilingual Child: A Perspective on Raising Children in the United States by Lucia Quiñonez Sumner in The NCHAM eBook: A RESOURCE GUIDE FOR EARLY HEARING DETECTION, Les R. Schmeltz, (Ed.). Copyright ©2013 The National Center for Hearing Assessment and Management. Reprinted with permission from The National Center for Hearing and Assessment Management.

2 From LANGUAGE PLAY by David Crystal. Copyright © David Crystal 1998. Reproduced with permission of David Crystal. Website edition of LANGUAGE PLAY is available at http://www.davidcrystal.com.

3 From LINDFORS, JUDITH WELLS, CHILDREN'S LANGUAGE AND LEARNING, 2nd, © 1987. Printed and Electronically reproduced with permission of Pearson Education, Inc., Upper Saddle River, New Jersey.

4 Quotes from Walt Wolfram are from DO YOU SPEAK AMERICAN (2006), WNET, New York Public Media. Permission for use granted by THIRTEEN PRODUCTIONS LLC.

5 From LANGUAGE DIVERSITY AND LEARNING by Lisa Delpit in *Perspectives on Talk and Learning*, Susan Hynds and Donald L. Rubin, eds. Copyright ©1990 by the National Council of Teachers of English. Reprinted with permission.

6 From BORDERLANDS/LA FRONTERA: THE NEW MESTIZA. Copyright © 1987, 1999, 2007, 2012 by Gloria Anzaldúa. Reprinted by permission of Aunt Lute Books. *www.auntlute.com*

7 Republished with permission of John Wiley and Sons, from WHY DON'T STUDENTS LIKE SCHOOL?: A COGNITIVE SCIENTIST ANSWERS QUESTIONS ABOUT HOW THE MIND WORKS AND WHAT IT MEANS FOR THE CLASSROOM by Daniel Willingham. Copyright © 2012 by John Wiley and Sons, permission conveyed through Copyright Clearance Center, Inc.

CHAPTER 9

THE DEVELOPMENT OF WRITTEN LANGUAGE

If one is to write, one must believe—in the truth and worth of the scrawl, in the ability of the reader to receive and decode the message. —William Strunk and E.B.White (Strunk & White, 1979, p. 84)[1]

THE IMPORTANCE OF UNDERSTANDING CHILDREN'S WRITTEN LANGUAGE

Australian researcher Marie Clay notes that parents and teachers of young children attribute great importance to reading experiences during the preschool years, but understand very little about the value of preschool writing experiences (Clay M., 2001). Don Holdaway remarks that "the major written output of very young children in natural or developmental ways" has generally been seen as having "little value or significance in traditional schooling." He proposes that a child's attempts at written language need to be "better understood," and "compared from week to week for significant growth." He also asserts that these attempts at written language should be "as strongly rewarded" as a child's first attempts at spoken language. If these changes happen, a "quite new perspective" on children's "early production of written language" would come to light (Holdaway D., 1979, p. 36).

In their studies, Holdaway and his colleagues recognized a "natural and continuous progression from scribble-like forms of play-writing, through a very complex series of approximations and experiments each displaying the mastery of some new convention." They believed that children were working "towards goals which imply an understanding of the conventions of print rather than simply the ability to form acceptable letter shapes" (Holdaway D., 1979, p. 34).

Some adults view "scribble" as careless writing in which children do not attend to the shape and legibility of letters, and disregard the accuracy of spelling or grammar. Many researchers, however, believe that the term "scribble" is not an appropriate one to use to describe children's early writing. They see scribble as an "extremely functional" strategy that "allows language users to search for, find, and placehold text" (Harste, Woodward, & Burke, 1984, p. 142). They find that early writings are organized and include systematic reflections of decisions the child has made about how written language and artistic systems are organized.

Frequently adults view children's early writing as erroneous, disorganized, or lacking meaning, or cute. Educator John Holt points out that when we view youngsters "as being 'cute' we become incapable of perceiving their behavior accurately or taking its significance with due seriousness" (Holt, 1975). Similarly, researcher Kate Foley Cusumano (Foley Cusumano, 2008, p. 11)[2] notes David Yaden's statement that it is important to understand,"…every mark a child makes on a paper is made for a purpose" (Yaden, 2008).

Understanding and supporting language learners so that they can realize the human rights of education and literacy require a shift in emphasis. Adults need to turn their attention from a focus on the form of language to a focus on the child. They need to consider the child's interests, level of maturity, natural language, learning activities and the meaning the child is attempting to make. Learners need confidence to take risks, to make mistakes and readjust, and to ask for help. Risk taking can result in learning new skills, concepts, and knowledge about written language. Learners also need to be willing to share and engage with others. In a world of learners, not only teachers, but parents, grandparents, other caregivers—adults in general—need to understand and value what the child is writing. By studying a piece of writing, it is possible to find out many things about the child's knowledge of the world and the child's knowledge of written language. We see how children use their current understandings of written language to generate new understandings.

All too often, the significance of their written words goes unnoticed. That was not the case in my household, however, when I put a protest in writing as a young child.

View from a Small Place

> My first realization of the power of writing occurred when I was four-years-old. It was the Friday before Easter, and the members of my Roman Catholic family were observing a three-hour period of silence on the afternoon of Good Friday, a ritual that commemorates the period of time during which Christ hung on the cross. My father was cooking the noontime meal. Because it was Good Friday, my family abstained from eating meat, and he was cooking fish. I did not like fish and absolutely refused to eat it. Usually, I would just voice my resistance to having fish for lunch. But no one was talking because of the Good Friday rule of silence. As the fish continued to cook, my anxiety rose. I would not eat the fish. In desperation, I found a small piece of paper and wrote the word "no" and drew the outline of a fish. I marched to the stove and handed the message to my father without speaking. My father's reaction taught me the power of written symbols. The silence of the Good Friday ritual was immediately shattered as he called my mother, and I was chastised by both of my parents for refusing to eat the fish that my father was preparing. I cannot remember if I reluctantly ate a bit of fish that day, but I have never forgotten the power of putting my protest in writing.

THE BEGINNINGS OF WRITING

From the time they are born, children gesture as a way of communicating their intentions. Children babble when they begin to speak. Likewise, when they begin to grasp writing implements, they engage in what could be called, babbling on paper.

Howard Gardner describes the transition from these early markings to the child's recognition that markings have meanings and are of importance.

> To be sure, in these early markings [the child] has yet to discover the full potentials of his behavior… his activity is limited to just what it is called—sheer scribbling. Yet, something of a moment has already occurred. For in the transition from infant who is not cognizant of the product of his pen to the child who cares deeply whether a mark has been made, a crucial realization has come about: the awareness that, by the action of his own hand, he can create something—something that lasts, something that has importance for him, and (judging by their responses) something that has significance for those about him. (Gardner, 1980, p. 24)

Gardener further states:

> The potential to create a product that matters—a mark that can stand on its own—is one of the first indications to the child of his own efficacy, his nascent capacity to use a tool to create a product with it. At this time when the child is gradually breaking away from his caretakers and attempting to establish autonomy, this evidence (as clear as a black line against a white backdrop) that he can himself produce something assumes critical developmental importance. (Gardner, 1980, p. 24)

Writing researcher Liliana Tolchinsky concurs. She states that the child does not produce the marks "for the sake of the activity, nor as a mere exercise, but for the traces." She describes a study by Gibson and Levin (Gibson & Levin, 1980) who gave children, age fifteen to thirty-eight months, paper attached to a board and one of two tools. The tools looked "identical except that one left a trace whereas, the other did not." The researchers found that "elimination of the trace significantly reduced the graphic activity." The children rejected the non-tracing tools. During and after making the marks, "the infants pointed and named the products, but this behavior disappeared when no traces were left" (Tolchinsky, 2006, p. 84).

Russian psychologist, Lev Vygotsky noted that until the early 1900's psychology had conceived of writing as a complicated motor skill. In reference to psychology, he writes, "It has paid remarkably little attention to the question of the acquisition of written language as such, that is, a particular system of symbols and signs whose mastery heralds a turning point in the entire cultural development of the child." He also states, "It seems clear that mastery of such a complex sign system cannot be accomplished in a purely mechanical and external manner; rather it is the culmination of a long process of development of complex behavioral functions in the child" (Vygotsky, 1978, p. 106).[3]

Gardner adds:

> The contriving of certain geometric forms –circles, crosses, rectangles, triangles—coupled with an increasing proclivity to combine these marks into

> more intricate patterns, is a fundamental development of the third and fourth years of life. The child is establishing a vocabulary of lines and forms—the basic building blocks of graphic language—which, like the sounds of language, eventually combine into meaningful, referential units. (Gardner, 1980, p. 11)[4]

Edelsky and her colleagues state, "Like reading, writing is a dynamic process as writers discover new meanings. Just as readers do in the course of their reading, writers in the course of their writing continuously revise their own thoughts, meanings, and linguistic expressions as they read their own texts" (Edelsky, Altwater, & Flores, 1991, p. 20). Holdaway explains that oral language tends to occur in, and be supported by, the senses and social situation in which it takes place. Ambiguities can be clarified within that situation—and by voice intonation, facial expression and gesture. Written language lacks the support found within the immediate situation of talk, and therefore conventions are necessary to avoid ambiguity. These conventions are so distinctive that they make written language a separate dialect (Holdaway D., 1979, p. 54). Written language is a language and therefore it cannot be reduced to a series of skills. It is not learned from doing activities or exercises.

Mayer (Mayer, 2007, p. 35), drawing on the work of several researchers, notes that children gain knowledge about how to write through their observations and interactions with more advanced writers (Teale, 1995; Chapman, 1996; McGee & Purcell-Gates, 1997; Morrow & Sharkey, 1993; Schickedanz, 1999). Like speech, written language develops over time. Both drawing and writing convey meaning. Therefore, children do not initially distinguish the two (Schickedanz & Casbergue, 2004; Mayer, 2007). Understandings of written language are not gained in an all-or-none fashion. Concepts build up slowly and generalizations emerge from words that are familiar to the child (Taylor, 1986). At first, children take in generalities and gradually gain understanding of the specifics. For this reason, children's writing does not look like that of adults. Children manipulate and extend what they already know to create increasingly complex texts.

The period from ages 3–6 is seen as "a period of phenomenal literacy growth for all children" (Harste, Woodward, & Burke, 1984, p. 45). Like acquiring oral language, a great deal of this learning occurs through a child's involvement with people and things in the environment. Harste and his colleagues describe this involvement as "inclusion," in daily events like cooking, going shopping, going to the courthouse, or going on trips. Their research shows that children who are "underfoot," and therefore naturally part of these events have an advantage for acquiring literacy (Harste, Woodward, & Burke, 1984). Drawing on the work of several researchers, Mayer (Mayer, 2007) also explains that when acquiring literacy, children interact with others and the things that surround them (Teale, 1995; Chapman, 1996; McGee & Purcell-Gates, 1997; Schickedanz, 1999). When learning to write in any language, learners need to witness many demonstrations of how written symbols work. Demonstrations need to be meaningful and relevant to a child's life, not just abstract concepts beyond the child's grasp. Children require numerous examples of how the markings relate to their world as they interact with others through notes, lists, bible passages, web pages, books, maps and other text. "This process of attending to and orchestrating available demonstrations is never-ending… There is no sequence to the order in which demonstrations are inherently learned" (Harste, Woodward, & Burke, 1984, p. 195). Citing the work of Dyson, Mayer (Mayer, 2007, p. 35) points out, "…children learn about writing by constructing texts with one another and expressing their ideas in other unbounded ways" (Dyson A., 1997; Dyson A., 2003). As children interact with one another, they explore and gain an understanding of the process and purposes of writing (Mayer, 2007).

Young children show interest in the print around them on signs, labels, advertisements, television and electronic devices, and often imitate these forms. In its earliest forms, even though the child's writing does not look like that of the more experienced writers around him, the child has become a written-language user. Universally, written language users assume that written marks are signs that have the power to make meaning. This assumption holds true even before children can report what the marks that they've made signify, or have a purpose. Frequently, young children make marks on paper and ask an adult or older child, "What does this say?" The question itself indicates that the child believes that the markings have meaning. Clay refers to the point at which the child comes to realize that the marks signify meaning the sign concept. The next step she identifies is when the child realizes that a whole message can be written down (Clay M., 1982). The assumption that written marks are intentional is a force that provides access to literacy and moves literacy learning forward. The endeavor to make meaning controls any written-language user's very first markings as well as her present ones. The assumption holds true for both reading and writing (Wilson, 1988).

When children first write, they treat writing as speech. They draw to supply background for their subject, run words together, spell words the way they sound, allow words to run around the page, talk out loud as they write, blacken in letters, use capital letters and exclamation points liberally (Graves, 1979). But writing is not a direct representation of speech, and the entire writing task is not limited to what's on the page. Young children surround their written marks with meaning by talking about them as they write. This talk helps them organize their writing. The presence of "speech during writing almost always reflects the presence of a plan, either in being abandoned or in operation" (Harste, Woodward, & Burke, 1984, p. 37). Drawing on the work of several researchers, Johnson and Sulzby (Johnson & Sulzby, 1999, p. 2) explain that children often 'read' their printed messages using language and a style that sounds like reading (Clay M., 1982; McGee & Richgels, 1996; Sulzby, 1985). Children who read print in this way have internalized the difference between the sound of written and oral language.

Children who are writing explore the ways in which messages are organized on the page. This organization is something that they learn by noticing print, by observing others as they write, and by attempting to write themselves. By observing children as they write, adults can come to understand the knowledge that children have gained through interactions with other learners, what they know about stories and other genre, and how they connect speech and sounds to print. First letters are often capital letters that children mimic from signs. Capital letters are more distinctive than lower case letters, and many, such as the letters T and W, retain their identity even if reversed (Goodman & Goodman, 1983). Organizational decisions are strongly influenced by the written form of a child's name. As children learn to write their names, they also explore how to create letters and letter-like symbols with a variety of writing devices. Children who make recognizable objects in their drawings also make recognizable letters (Brittain, 1979).

Children's first written letters appear in the midst of drawn objects—these letters represent significant aspects of the environment. As linguist Carol Chomsky states, "Much of the early the writing looks unkempt, until inexperienced fingers develop the control to make it more readable" (Chomsky, 1976, p. 19). As children continue to write, they continue to explore the ways in which words and messages are generated from a finite group of twenty-six symbols. "Using recurring letters and words helps develop fluency and habitual responses, and likely makes [the child] feel more capable" (Foley Cusumano, 2008, p. 13).

View from a Small Place

> When my son, Noah was four years old, I was collecting writing samples for a graduate class. I asked him to write on a plain piece of paper. At first, all I saw were a few squiggles. Noah had written three small circular symbols at the top, and three larger circular figures in the middle of the page. When I asked him what this said, he told me that the figures at the top of the page were leaves and a wheel. He then pointed to the larger figures and named three items: the ambliance (sic), the man inside, and the big thing. He became annoyed and did not give me further information when I asked for the specific name of the "big thing." I believe that this was the stretcher inside the ambulance. I then asked him what the paper was "for" and he said, "It's for Santa." I understood immediately.
>
> The previous day, we had been in the toy aisle at a local store and Noah found an ambulance with a stretcher and small figures inside that he wanted for Christmas. Now, using his own symbols in a way that held meaning for him, he was writing a message to Santa. The day after he wrote the message, I took the paper out again and asked Noah what it said. He put his hands on his hips—annoyed this time by my lack of recall—and in a loud voice, informed me that as he had told me yesterday, the figures were leaves and a wheel, the ambliance (sic), the man inside, and the big thing.

Although his writing would certainly be described by some as just scribble, and it would be probably be difficult to determine what language he spoke from his markings, Noah understood that his markings served the function of conveying his message to Santa. At the time he wrote this letter, he was able to print his name, a few other words, and some letters. This text, however, required words that he had not yet acquired orally or was not yet able to write in conventional or invented spelling. Therefore, he reverted to representing them with circular-style markings. Several researchers have noted that the more complex the task, the more emergent the form of writing used by the child. As Mayer (Mayer, 2007, p. 35) notes from other researchers, even when young children are aware that letters represent sounds, "they may still produce writing samples characteristic of lower levels of development in order to preserve a message they are trying to convey" (Barnhart, 1986; Fox & Saracho, 1990; Strickland & Morrow, 1991; Burns & Casbergue, 1992; Greer & Lockman, 1998; Bus, Both-de Vries, de Jong, Sulzby, de Jong, & de Jong, 2001).

Noah's writing stemmed from demonstrations of a purpose for writing in our community and household. He had seen me write and receive letters and knew that sending messages through the mail is common practice. He also understood that children write letters to a man named Santa and ask him to bring them presents for Christmas. Each symbol on his paper represented an individual item. Although the words were not arranged in a linear manner, his letter was actually a list of the items that he wanted. A list is the conventional way of organizing a letter to Santa. Noah had a purpose for his writing and a particular reader in mind. He saw his markings as fixed symbols that had meaning and retain meaning over time—from one day to the next, from the day he wrote them until Christmas. He also understood that through his markings he could convey a message that would reach someone in a distant place. Noah's message came from his oral language. He could read it both when he wrote it and the next day. He was able to retrieve the content of the message since he had composed it himself. The writing stemmed from an interest of his and served a need. If he had gone to visit Santa in person, he would have told him what he wanted, but it was two months before Christmas, and oral language would not suffice. He needed to preserve the information in written form. As seen in Noah's example, writing does not wait for oral language to develop completely. He could not fully pronounce each word yet, and he did not know the name for the "stretcher," so he used the general term "big thing." Although his oral language was still in the process of developing, he plunged in and took the risk of attempting written language, and, of course, the result was that he received the "ambliance" for Christmas!

In both Noah's example and my story about Good Friday from my childhood, oral language was not sufficient. As writers, both of us were driven by more than interest. We were not just making marks on paper; we were compelled to use writing to get something that we wanted—or in my case did not want. We were learning at very young ages that writing has agency, allowing us to take responsibility and advocate for ourselves. The examples I present are rooted in our cultural practices, situated within our specific contexts. My written note with the fish symbol would not have been needed within my household on another day or even at a time outside the three-hour period of silence on Good Friday. People from different places and cultures engage in different practices and events, but the use of symbols to represent meaning and the act of writing about what is compelling, necessary, and sought after, are the same.

THE WORK OF HARSTE WOODWARD AND BURKE

Researchers Jerome Harste, Virginia Woodward, and Carolyn Burke from the University of Indiana conducted a 10-year longitudinal study examining what children ages 3–6 knew about reading and writing prior to going to school. Black and White boys and girls were included in the study. They were from high, middle and low income families and lived in both small towns and urban neighborhoods. The study resulted in the publication of *Language Stories & Literacy Lessons* in 1984 (Harste, Woodward, & Burke, 1984).

These researchers state, "In use, language is an open system which permits the maintenance and generation of meaning" (Harste, Woodward, & Burke, 1984, p. 118). They continue, "…engagement and reengagement in the language process increases the opportunities language users have to discover for themselves the generativeness and self-educative aspects of language in use" (Harste, Woodward, & Burke, 1984, p. 119). They explain that "access to the process" of constructing written language "can only be gained through involvement in the process." This engagement has to take place on the language user's terms. Therefore, it is necessary for language users to "set aside" constraints that are either "perceived or real" and take risks to try out new forms of expression (Harste, Woodward, & Burke, 1984, p. 130).

Several studies document that children learn to write before beginning school (Ferreiro & Teberosky, 1982; McGee & Purcell-Gates, 1997; Harste, Woodward, & Burke, 1984; Freeman & Sanders, 1989). Long before formal instruction, the young child is making sense of the world, including the world of print. Harste, Woodward, and Burke caution that age is a "dangerous criterion" by which to measure language development because "it does not consistently covary with the operational factor of experience" (Harste, Woodward, & Burke, 1984, p. 23). However, their studies led them to conclude that "by the age of 3, children demonstrate a personal as well as a social history of literacy" (Harste, Woodward, & Burke, 1984, p. 146). They state:

> The single act of putting pen to paper when requested to write, repeated as it was across sixty-eight children in our Bloomington and Indianapolis studies… tells any observer—including a hypothetical man from Mars—that the children being observed came from a culture in which making marks on paper is an accepted and important form of social behavior. (Harste, Woodward, & Burke, 1984, pp. 146–147)

Harste, Woodward, and Burke also find:

> Many middle- and upper-class homes…were far from ideal literacy environments. Because both parents worked, many children in these homes were left with baby-sitters or involved in preschool programs that had little

> or no interest in literacy. While the homes were supposedly better literacy environments, little of this benefit automatically shifted down to the children in any directly observable way. (Harste, Woodward, & Burke, 1984, p. 42)

They did not find major distinctions between lower-, middle-, and upper-class homes. They note "Some homes whether upper- or lower-class, were rather sterile literacy environments, while others were filled with ongoing written language events and were seemingly hard places in which to avoid print involvement" (Harste, Woodward, & Burke, 1984, p. 42).

Harste, Woodward and Burke contend:

> The most salient home factor relating to literacy learning is one we have termed the "availability and opportunity to engage in written language events." Homes where books were out and readily available, where paper, pens, pencils, crayons, magic markers, and other instruments were handy, where children seemed quite naturally to be included and involved, seemed to provide the key conditions for children to go exploring and for parents to involve themselves in using and encouraging reading and writing, whether they "technically" reported that they knew what they were doing or not. (Harste, Woodward, & Burke, 1984, pp. 42–43)

These researchers further propose that the "quantity of literacy materials (number of books, for example) does not seem to be the key element but rather, that what materials there are, are highly accessible, so that both parents and children have to be more or less constantly tripping over them." They find, "When paper and books were in the way, children used them, often coming up with quite creative uses (writing out a menu for supper, writing traffic tickets, writing notes, posting signs on doors, labeling their toys during play). When there were books in the family room, children were read to, an activity which seemed to be equally initiated by both parents and children." They also note, "Some homes stored quantities of little-used literacy materials. Others made creative and concentrated use of more minimal quantities of readily accessible materials" (Harste, Woodward, & Burke, 1984, p. 43).

DIFFERENT CONTEXTS: DIFFERENT DISPLAYS OF WRITTEN LANGUAGE CAPABILITIES

Argentinean researchers, Emilia Ferreiro and Ana Teberosky, studied the literacy behaviors of four-, five-, and six-year-olds in the urban areas of Buenos Aires. They believe that children learn by constructing "their own categories of thought while organizing their world." They state that, "It is absurd to imagine that four-or five-year-old children growing up in an urban environment that displays print everywhere (on toys, on billboards and road signs, on their clothes, on TV) do not develop any ideas about this cultural object until they find themselves sitting before a teacher at the age of six." Ferreiro and Teberosky view urban children as empowered language and literacy learners who are not waiting "for someone to transmit knowledge to them in an act of benevolence" (Ferreiro & Teberosky, 1982, p. 12).

African American reading scholar, Dorothy Strickland drawing on the work of Donaldson, (Donaldson, 1978) Smith, (Smith F., 1982) and Wells (Wells, 1986), makes a similar case for African American children. She states:

> African American children deserve literacy programs that stress the construction of meaning right from the start. As with every other aspect of their learning, these young children are attempting to make sense of the world around them. Print is simply one of the many curiosities in the world about which they are eager to learn. (Strickland D., 2005, p. 153)[5]

Additionally, researcher Carole Edelsky points out that when looking at one's child's writing under different circumstances, it is possible to see that different contexts elicit different displays of what a child knows (Edelsky, 1985, p. 66).

After studying the work of other researchers, I conducted a study of my own that documented the understandings of written language of fifty African American, White, and Latino first-grade participants from within the same city (Wilson, 1988). In the study, I attempted to tap different displays of what a child knows (Edelsky, 1985) by framing different contexts for writing. I wanted to get beyond limitations and find out as much as possible about what they knew. I theorized that the writers would produce connected text within certain tasks.

I worked individually with each writer, presenting three tasks adapted from Harste, Woodward, and Burke's work (Harste, Woodward, & Burke, 1984). First, the children were asked to write anything of their choice that they could write or pretend to write. Second, they were asked to write a known text they knew, like a story, poem, song, rhyme, or jingle or part thereof that they held in their head. Third, they were asked to write a story about themselves. I attempted to discover whether requesting these writers to produce texts within in different contexts revealed different understandings that the writer had of written language. I hypothesized that within different contexts, children would reveal what they knew about writing connected text.

The second task differed from the other two tasks because I tried to get at a text that was so meaningful or familiar that the child had committed it to memory. I was trying to snag a thread of the tapestry of language within the child's personal storehouse of language, beyond the conversational level. Within a context where children were generally not viewed as writers, I wanted to find out what they could write. The children reread and self-corrected as they wrote, therefore I saw that they were using their knowledge of the text, words, letters and sounds. They were not writing strictly from memory, but because they held the text in memory, they could refer to it as they wrote it on the page.

The writings were not exact transcriptions from memory—rather, they were written re-enactments that merged the child's knowledge of syntax, knowledge of how print works, vocabulary, and their interest in print. Although the writing came about in a school setting, the children drew upon modes of language common outside of school, including songs, stories from their daily lives, and language play. In all, I collected and analyzed 150 writing samples. Many of the texts were ones that they had encountered in the domains described earlier in this book by Anderson and Stokes (Anderson & Stokes, 1984), including religion, daily living, entertainment and school-related events. In the third task, children wrote stories about themselves.

As the children wrote, I focused on helping them recall text that was meaningful to them. I removed constraints by encouraging children to spell as best they could or put down as much as they knew. I encouraged the children to spell words by saying them slowly and putting down the letters that they heard, so they would try out texts that would go beyond the limits of conventional spelling.

This study shows that there were variations among the responses of the writers to the three writing tasks. These variations occurred in the writers' processes and in the genre, organization, spelling and length of their products. It is important to note that by the time they completed the third task of the study, forty-six of the fifty writers, or ninety-three percent wrote at least a single line of connected text. Six writers wrote no words or only a few words in the first task, and therefore appeared to reveal limited knowledge of written English. Major changes took place when these writers were able to write down a text that they held in their head or a story about themselves. They wrote lengthier responses in other tasks and revealed more extensive knowledge of written language when the tasks were framed within a different context. The writers showed greater evidence of organizational patterns, revealed a sense of story, and employed other organizational strategies when writing out pieces of familiar oral language. These pieces also helped establish a connection between oral and written language.

As the chart that follows indicates, only 14% of the African American writers and 28% of the Hispanic writers wrote connected texts in the first task. When the context changed, 86% of these African American and 56% of the Hispanic writers wrote connected text. In the third task, the 86% of the African American writers continued to write connected text. The percentage of Hispanic writers doing so increased to 58%.

Percentage of Writers Who Wrote Connected Text Across Three Tasks

	TASK I	*TASK II*	*TASK III*
African American Writers	14%	86%	86%
Hispanic Writers	28%	56%	58%

(Wilson, 1988)

This chart includes the percentages of African American and Hispanic writers who wrote connected text for each of the three tasks in the study. The differences in percentages among the tasks show that writers who had not produced connected text initially were able to do so when the context changed.

THE GROWTH OF WRITTEN LANGUAGE

In cultures where book reading takes place, infants participate in book-reading activities. "Book reading is, however, a cultural practice that is not democratically distributed." Therefore, children who grow up in "communities with no experience with book reading practices, develop a representation of writing before developing a meaning for reading" (Tolchinsky, 2006, p. 84).

Tolchinsky cites research that shows across many languages, children's writing languages displays common characteristics of form. These characteristics include: linearity, directionality, distinct units, and recurrent placement of blanks (Gibson & Levin, 1980). She reports on the findings of several additional studies (Tolchinsky, 2006, pp. 87–88) that show, "By the age of 4, children's writing already appears as a linearly arranged string of distinctive marks separated by regular spacing." Again, these results are "supported by numerous studies carried out in a variety of languages…" They are consistent regardless of "socioeconomic status or microcultural milieu" (Bissex, 1980; Clay M., 1982; Chan, 1998; Gibson & Levin, 1980; Goodman Y., 1982; Harste, Woodward, & Burke, 1984).

Further, Tolchinsky notes that Emilia Ferreiro identified criteria of *distinctive features* that graphic displays must have in order to be readable. First, the number of forms in a string must be limited. Secondly, there has to be a variety of forms. Even before children know how to write conventionally they understand these criteria for readable graphic displays. These two constraints also influence children's writing, and they appear "to hold true across languages and scripts" (Tolchinsky, 2006, p. 88). Children eventually come to write using the symbols, directionality, and conventions that are employed within their culture. For example, children writing English orient the letters from left to right and use capital letters and punctuation. Children progress from writing letter-like forms, to writing the letters of the alphabet, to writing strings of symbols, to eventually spelling words. However, even when children are capable of writing a number of letters, they may use a number of strategies to create messages.

Names are reference points for learning about print (Dyson A., 1984). The first conventionally written words are often names (Clay, 1977; Durkin, 1966; Stine, 1980; Dyson A., 1984). Tolchinsky finds, "In all studies in the different languages explored, whenever a child is required to write his or her name along with other words or sentences, the child's name always shows the higher level of development in any of the features being considered" (Tolchinsky, 2006, p. 89). The studies to which she refers were conducted in Hebrew, Spanish, and Chinese.

Novick explains, "Like infants and toddlers who can speak a number of clearly enunciated words but who use a mixture of jargon and words to approximate sentences, young children may use a mixture of scribbling and writing when they write long messages" (Novick, 1996, pp. 11–12). As young writers add new forms to their repertoires, they continue to employ older forms, but less frequently (Fox & Saracho, 1990; Burns & Casbergue, 1992; Greer & Lockman, 1998; Bus, Both-de Vries, de Jong, Sulzby, de Jong, & de Jong, 2001) in (Mayer, 2007).

SPELLING DEVELOPMENT

Judith Schickedanz, professor and author of *More than ABC's*, explains that following "much exploration" and "much exposure to print, children discover that letters represent phonemes, and not some larger unit of speech, such as a syllable or a word." Schickedanz views this as a "very important discovery" (Schikedanz, 1986, p. 87). She also notes that children's first attempts at spellings are not conventional form. For example, some may include only the initial and final sound, like "kr" for car, and "bl" for ball. However, they are systematic, and they provide evidence of children's ability to distinguish similarities and differences in the production of sounds.

Many adults view these spellings as erroneous. They fail to see the child's systematic way of producing the words. They also fail to understand the level of phonemic awareness and systematic knowledge of phonics that the child has internalized. When observing a child who is writing, we begin to understand what the child knows about spelling. In this developmental view, invented spelling is seen, not as a sign of incompetence, but as an important component of writing. We can also come to understand the child's message and what the child understands about directional rules, the concept of a word, the alphabet, and letter names.

View from a Small Place

> The concerns of many adults focus on spelling. One teacher asked me about a child in her room who was copying messages from the board and various other print sources in the classroom. As long as she was copying, her spelling remained conventional, and her paper was neat, then the teacher was satisfied. Correct spelling and neatness fit her expectations. When the child began writing on her own with temporary spellings, however, relying on her understandings of the rules of spelling, the teacher became upset. She feared that she was encouraging the child to develop immature habits. To her eyes, the child's work was erroneous and of lower quality than the work she had copied. The teacher did not understand that the child was using her own knowledge of the letters and sounds. The teacher did not understand that children acquire knowledge about language by working with language. When children simply copy, they are working at the surface level of language. They are not actually constructing the meaning themselves.

Teacher-researcher Kate Foley Cusumano states, "A successful young writer uses symbols to communicate a message while testing out rules for making and combining those symbols" (Foley Cusumano, 2008, p. 10). What is important is that adults look for and value the message that the child is composing without cleaning up the conventions at this point in their growth.

Foley Cusumano documents the reaction of one parent to what she perceived as spelling errors.

View from a Small Place—Kate Foley Cusuamo's Classroom

> Bryan's mother, a volunteer in my first-grade classroom, had tears in her eyes when she turned to me one day. She asked if I have ever seen Bryan's eyes rolling or flickering as if he were having mini-seizures. I assured her I had never observed that.
>
> "Well, "she continued, "I've asked the doctor for a CAT scan. I'm convinced he's having seizures during writing workshop time."
>
> Stunned, I asked, "What makes you think that?"
>
> "Just look at his paper today. He spelled 'like' wrong and he spelled 'want' two different ways, neither of them right. I know he knows how to spell those words because I give him weekly spelling tests at home. He must be having seizures while he's writing."
>
> Bryan's mother is not alone in expecting adult conventions out of 6-year-old children. Regardless of the education or socioeconomic level of the children's families, all of them care about their children's progress in writing, and they may have concerns, expressed and unexpressed, about their child's progress. My encounters with students' families and other community members over the years have led me to believe that teachers need to take a proactive role in educating them on this matter. (Foley Cusumano, 2008, pp. 9–10)

Carol Chomsky explains that once children use invented spellings, using some letters from the conventional spellings of words, "The message can usually be retrieved, and the children are deriving the satisfaction of self-expression." She adds, "By age five or earlier many children's ability to analyze words phonetically will already be well developed" (Chomsky, 1976, pp. 18–19). Young children are also able to "recognize words that begin with the same sound, and words that rhyme." If they cannot do these things, they "will need practice in this sort of analysis before they can be expected to spell (cf Liberman, 1973)." Chomsky notes, however, "It is surprising how much phonetic information is available to introspection at this age, and how readily this knowledge can be raised to the level of awareness through word play, questioning and talk about sounds." She emphasizes that "in order to get started with spelling only the simplest phonetic awareness is needed." For example, "Children who know that *man* begins with a [m] sound are ready. If they know letter names or sounds, they are prepared to find the letters that they need to spell their first word." This does not mean that children need to be drilled in learning all letter names and sounds before they are allowed to begin to write. Chomsky adds, "Just the letters needed for the particular word are enough" (Chomsky, 1976, pp. 18–19).

Researchers Johnson and Sulzby note that even when children begin to employ phonetic knowledge to create invented spellings, they do not immediately employ phonetic cues to read what they write (Johnson & Sulzby, 1999, p. 2). These researchers cite studies showing that in place of using letter-sound cues, children will try to recall what they have written or will rely on a picture that they have drawn to convey the message of text (Snow, Burns, & Griffin, 1998; Kamberelis & Sulzby, 1988). Chomsky explains that an additional aspect that contributes to the greater accessibility of writing is that when writing, the writer already knows the words and messages, but in reading, the words must be identified (Chomsky, 1976). She also states, "Although much of the same background information may be required in translating from pronunciation to print and from print to pronunciation, the need to identify the word, which reading involves, is a considerable extra step that is not required in learning to write" (Chomsky, 1976, p. 8).

ENGAGEMENT IN OTHER WRITTEN LANGUAGE SYSTEMS

So far in this chapter, the writing that has been considered uses an alphabetic writing system. Writers from various countries, however, parts of the world use different writing systems, direct symbols differently and employ them in different ways. As Gunther Kress, professor of semiotics and education at the University of London states, "It's a hugely important thing." He explains that in some areas of the world, direction of symbols "tends not to be linear as in the West; it tends to be much more centering." He cautions that this is where the "danger is" (Harste J., 2012, p. 209).[6]

Kress continues:

> The moment there is something that resembles a grammar-like concept, then people are glad to have it and apply it as if it were the same everywhere…I would want to join the people who are saying, "No, no. We need to understand how those from the Indian subcontinent or from Southeast Asia or from China or from a Middle Eastern country use semiotic means." (Harste J., 2012, p. 209)

Researcher Benedetta Basetti states, "The main language feature investigated in many studies originates from the alphabetic system, English." She explains other kinds of writing systems as well:

> However, there are different types of writing systems depending on what linguistic units are represented by their graphemes: phonemic (or alphabetic) writing systems represent phonemes (e.g. English, Greek); consonantal writing systems represent consonants (e.g. Hebrew, Arabic); syllabic writing systems represent syllables (e.g. Thai, Tibetan); morphemic writing systems represent morphemes (e.g. Chinese, Japanese). (Bassetti, 2008)[7]
>
> A writing system represents a language by segmenting it into a sequence of small discrete units, each represented by a *grapheme* (the smallest identifiable unit of a writing system). For instance, the English writing system segments

> language into phonemes, represented by letters or letter combinations (<b> represents /b/, <sh> represents / ʃ /). The Chinese writing system segments language into monosyllabic morphemes represented by 'hanzi', or 'Chinese characters' (东 represents the morpheme 'East', pronounced /tuŋ/; 冬 represents 'winter', also pronounced /tuŋ/). Japanese kana mostly represent syllables (か represents /ka/, き represents /ki/); Arabic and Hebrew graphemes represent consonants. (Bassetti, 2008)

The following are examples of studies of written language that were conducted in languages systems other than the alphabetic system. They address both the reading and writing of these systems. Many brain imaging studies have focused on handwriting, rather than on meaning-making processes, development, or sociocultural aspects of learning to write. Others have focused mainly on transcription rather than text generation. Most imaging studies have been done on adults who speak English, Japanese, Italian, German, or Finnish. More research is needed to evaluate if the findings about adults apply to children (Berninger & Winn, 2006). Some of the studies described here compare the writing of bilingual writers who are using two different writing systems.

Researchers Sylvia Scribner and Michael Cole conducted five years of research on the written language of the Vai people of Liberia. The Vai have a writing system that is of their own invention. It is used for commercial and personal affairs. The Vai script is generally learned by young men who are in their late teens or twenties. It is taught at home rather than in schools. It is almost always learned by an individual from another person. The average lesson lasts for about 45 minutes. Usually, the learner is provided with a letter written in Vai. He learns the content of the letter and how to identify each character. Once the first letter is learned, others are studied. After a few letters, the learner writes one of his own. A person who is able to read Vai is considered to be fully literate in the language, although people who read it report that they are able to write it as well. (Scribner & Cole, 1981). As a result of their study, Scribner and Cole approach literacy as "a set of socially organized practices which make use of a symbol system technology for producing and disseminating it." They also state, "Literacy is not simply knowing how to read and write a particular script but applying this knowledge for specific purposes in specific purposes in specific contexts of use" (Scribner & Cole, 1981, p. 236).[8]

Another study described the writing of a third-grade Japanese bilingual child who lives in both Japan and the U.S. and writes in both Japanese and English. Eiko Kato-Otani, the researcher, found that the child was able to acquire both writing systems simultaneously and successfully. The child also used code- switching to effectively support her writing. When she was writing, and did not know a word in English, she would put in the word in Japanese. The study showed that being schooled in both Japanese and English supported the child's writing in both languages (Kato-Otani, 2008).

View from a Small Place

> By the age of three, the Russian American child in our family, who was introduced in the previous chapter, was able to differentiate between books written in the English and those written in Russian. When she was looking through a Russian picture book, her grandfather would play a game with her and tell her that the book was written in English. She would staunchly protest, saying, "No, R-r-r-ussian, R-r-r-ussian!"

Researcher Charmian Kenner takes a multimodal approach to the production of written symbols. She believes that this process is not just a mechanical or lower-level skill. Rather, it has the equivalent cognitive value of other aspects of learning to write. She worked with bilingual children who spoke Chinese and English, Arabic and English, and Spanish and English. She studied the children's understandings of the act of writing. Kenner found that the children understood the differences between their two writing systems, but they looked for ways to connect them to transform meaning across the languages. Kenner also saw that even though the time that children committed to English was greater than the limited time committed to Chinese, Arabic, and Spanish, they still understood the key concepts of their two writing systems. Kenner concludes that young biliterate writers acquire "embodied knowledges" of the production of written symbols, spatiality, and directionality. These knowledges position these writers to both design and understand multimodal texts, particularly texts on the screen that are non-linear and have varied arrangements and directionality (Kenner, 2003).

This chapter has focused on the production of written language. The next chapter focuses on how children come to understand writing produced by others.

NOTES

[1] From Strunk, ELEMENTS OF STYLE, 3rd, ©1979. Printed and Electronically reproduced by permission of Pearson Education, Inc., Upper Saddle River, New Jersey.

[2] Every mark on the page: Educating family and community members about young children's writing by Kate Foley Cusumano in *Language Arts*, Volume 86, Number 1, September, 2008. Usage determined by the National Council of Teachers of English.

[3] Reprinted by permission of the publisher from MIND IN SOCIETY: DEVELOPMENT OF HIGHER PSYCHOLOGICAL PROCESSES by L. S. Vygotsky, edited by Michael Cole, Vera John-Steiner, Sylvia Scribner, and Ellen Souberman, p.106,Cambridge, Mass.: Harvard University Press, Copyright © 1978 by the President and Fellows of Harvard College.

[4] From ARTFUL SCRIBBLES: THE SIGNIFICANCE OF CHILDREN'S DRAWINGS. Copyright ©1980 by Howard Gardner. Reprinted by permission of the Perseus Books Group.

[5] From Educating African American Learners at Risk: Finding a Better way in TEACHING AFRICAN AMERICAN LEARNERS TO READ. Copyright © 2005 International Reading Association. Reprinted with permission of John Wiley & Sons Ltd.

[6] From Image, Identity, and Insights into Language by Jerome Harste and Gunther Kress, in *Language Arts*, Volume 89 Number 3, January 2012. Usage determined by the National Council of Teachers of English.

[7] From Learning Second Language Writing Systems by Dr. Benedetta Bassetti. Reprinted with permission of LLAS Centre for languages, linguistics & area studies, University of Southampton, UK. https://www.llas.ac.uk//resources/gpg/2662.

[8] Reprinted by permission of the publisher from THE PSYCHOLOGY OF LITERACY by Sylvia Scribner and Michael Cole, p. 236, Cambridge Mass.: Harvard University Press, Copyright © 1981 by the President and Fellows of Harvard College.

CHAPTER 10

READING: MAKING SENSE OF THE WORLD OF PRINT

> *Family literacy, like all forms of reading, will never lend itself to being fast, easy, or efficient. Reading together calls for real time committed and unattached to a specific goal or tangible reward. Intangible are the rewards that reading together gives: social intimacy, laughter, fulfillment of curiosity, and contemplation of the wonders of real and imagined worlds.* —Shirley Bruce Heath (Heath S. B., 2010)

THE BRAIN AND READING

Researcher David Sousa states that humans have been using language for tens of thousands of years. "During this time, genetic changes have favored the brain's ability to acquire and process spoken language, even setting aside specialized areas of the brain to accomplish these tasks." Although the brain is designed to learn language naturally, it is not specialized for reading in the same way. Reading did not develop over thousands of years as a survival skill. Reading is a "relatively new phenomenon." Sousa continues that by the time children begin school "they have a well-developed language system consisting of an active vocabulary of about 3,000 words and a mental lexicon of over 5,000 words." He adds, "At some point, the child's brain encounters the written words and wonders, 'What are those symbols? What do they mean?'" (Sousa D. A., 2005, pp. 31–32).

Educational psychologist Gerald Coles, explains:

> While language areas of the brain, such as those related to aspects of reading, are important in processing particular functions, all are intertwined in extensive networks (a polyphony) of brain areas that are simultaneously and interactively communicating and constructing and reconstructing particular areas within the whole. Yes, the brain has fundamental mechanisms for beginning to learn written language but it does not begin with a 'fixed pattern of connectivity.' Instead, the 'connectivity pattern is set by experience' with 'countless interconnection points, or synapses, which connect neurons to one another in various patterns' (Donald, 2001). In other words, learning and experience create and shape the brain's circuits and how they are used in learning to read; the circuits are not predetermined. (Coles, 2004, p. 349)[1]

Coles contends that research on the brain and reading must be "informed by the complexity of reading acquisition." He argues for reading and brain research approaches that are "grounded in an understanding of the unified interrelationships of the brain, active child, and learning environment" (Coles, 2004, p. 351).

The circuits described above are created as the brain perceives and formulates patterns. Researchers Caine and Caine state:

> Designed to perceive and generate patterns, the brain resists having meaningless patterns imposed on it. By meaningless we mean isolated pieces of information that are unrelated to what makes sense to a particular student ...concentrating too heavily on the storage and recall of unconnected facts is a very inefficient use of the brain. (Caine & Caine, 1990, pp. 67–68)

Stamm adds, "Nothing in neuroscience suggests that it's useful to hook a one-year-old on phonics or run alphabet skill drills with a two-year-old" (Stamm, 2007, p. 240). Cole explains that from a connectivity pattern model, the areas of the brain that are involved in grasping sound/symbol correspondence do "not have to be primed before other areas of the pattern can become effectively operable." Furthermore, "the creation and function of these areas depends on connections within the entire pattern." This "pattern of connectivity is not innately fixed." Therefore, if instruction stimulates certain areas of the brain "more than others a particular connectivity pattern would occur." That pattern, however, might not be the only pattern that leads to reading success and "it might not be superior to other connectivity patterns." Richer written language learning could result in the emergence of a more complex connectivity pattern (Coles, 2004, p. 350).

In her book, *Proust and the Squid*, neuroscientist Maryanne Wolf identifies three large areas of the brain that are activated when a young child reads. She states, "The principle job for the young reader's brain is to connect these parts." The first area covers the occipital lobes and the fusiform gyrus. The occipital lobes are visual and visual association areas. The fusiform gyrus is an "evolutionary important area" deep within these lobes. Activity involving these areas takes place in both hemishperes of the brain. The second area of reading activity involves the "temporal and parietal lobes." This area is "also bihemispheric." The "angular gyrus and supramarginal gyrus, two important structures for integrating phonological processes with visual, orthographic (spelling) and semantic (meaning-making) processes," are located in this area. Parts of Wernicke's area, "an essential language comprehension region," are also located in the temporal lobes. The third area is made up of "portions of the frontal lobes" and "Broca's area" that is located in the left hemisphere and is important to speech (Wolf, 2007, pp. 124–126).

Wolf points out "...in every domain of learning...children develop along a continuum of knowledge, moving from a partial concept to an established concept" (Wolf, 2007, p. 116). When first learning to read, the young reader's brain expends a great deal of effort. The greater the effort, the more the brain is activated, and generally in more expanded areas. With experience, however, less effort needs to be expanded because the regions begin to interact with increasing speed. Wolf lays out a history of a child's reading development during which the areas of the young reading brain become increasingly connected and processing speed increases. She makes clear, "Not all children, however, progress in the same way" (Wolf, 2007, pp. 115–116).

Wolf presents five kinds of readers. Here is a brief overview of each here, although the remainder of this chapter focuses mainly on the first two kinds of readers.

- The emerging pre-reader who "samples and learns from the full range of multiple sounds, words, concepts, images, stories, exposure to print, literacy materials, and just plain talk during the first five years of life" (Wolf, Proust and the squid, 2007, p. 115).
- The novice reader begins to figure out, or decode, the print and understand the meaning of what is printed on the page. As Wolf explains, "...most children come to reading.with a notion that the words on the page mean something." Novice readers come to understand that "letters connect to the sounds of the language"(Wolf, 2007, pp. 116–117). They also learn "all the most common letter patterns in their own language" and "many of the most frequently written words that don't necessarily follow the phonological rules" (Wolf, 2007, p. 120). Examples of these words are "said" and "who."
- The decoding reader is a more confident reader on the verge of becoming fluent. These readers are learning variations in the sounds of letter patterns. They begin to see the "chunks" in words like *be-love-ed,* as they learn prefixes and suffixes. Their knowledge of vocabulary and grammar moves them from basic decoding to fluent reading. Wolf sees fluency as "not a matter of speed," but "a matter of being able to utilize all the special knowledge a child has about a word—its letters, letter patterns, meanings, grammatical functions, roots, and endings—fast enough to have time to think and comprehend." Working memory affords children "temporary space for holding information about letters and words, just long enough so that the brain can connect it to the children's increasingly sophisticated conceptual information" (Wolf, 2007, pp. 130–131). Emotional engagement is also important at this point, and the reader "who is moving from decoding well to decoding fluently" frequently requires "heartfelt encouragement" (Wolf, 2007, p. 132) from adults in order to make an attempt at more difficult reading material.
- The fluent comprehending reader develops "an increased capacity to apply an understanding of the varied uses of words—irony, voice, metaphor, and point of view." These skills allow the reader "to go below the surface of the text" (Wolf, 2007, p. 137). These readers employ a variety of strategies for comprehending. This part of a reader's history can last untill young adulthood. The readers task is "to use reading for life," both within and outside of the classroom (Wolf, 2007, p. 140).
- The expert reader can read almost any word in one-half second. This event is described by Wolf as "the almost instantaneous fusion of cognitive, linguistic,

and affective processes; multiple brain regions; and billions of neurons that are the sum of all that goes into reading" (Wolf, 2007, p. 145).

In her book, Wolf provides details of the expert reader reading a word in half a second. The description clearly makes evident the complexity of the moment—as it takes up nearly eleven pages!

ENVIRONMENTAL PRINT

We now know that long before formal instruction, young children are making sense of the world, including the world of print. Young readers bring a range of background knowledge, experiences, and feelings to text. Acknowledging the child's knowledge, experiences, and feelings are the seeds of securing the human rights of education and literacy.

Some children write before they read, and their writing supports them as they begin to read texts written by others. As Carol Chomsky describes:

> …children who have been writing for months are in a very favorable position when they undertake learning to read. They have at their command considerable phonetic information about English, practice in phonemic segmentation, and experience with alphabetic representation. These are some of the technical abilities that they need to get started. They have in addition an expectation of going ahead on their own. They are prepared to make sense of the print by figuring it out or by asking questions. They expect it to make sense, their purpose is to derive a message from print, not just to pronounce the words.
>
> …Their approach from the start is 'What does it say?' rather than 'How is it pronounced?' (Chomsky, 1976, pp. 14–15)

Thirty years later, Wolf notes that children who engage in invented spelling want to read what they have written. She also notes that these spellings allow children to learn individual sounds in words. She concludes that children's motivation to write along with "learning the individual sounds in words" through "'invented spelling,' makes children's early writing an extremely useful precursor of learning to read, and a wonderful complement to the actual reading process" (Wolf, 2007, p. 98).

The question, "What does that say?" often first emerges when children see print in their environment. Children often read the print on boxes or other print in the environment sooner and more conventionally than they read books. Environmental print is less complex than continuous text, and it is highly familiar to children because it surrounds them every day. Even in the first few years of life, children come into contact with print in the form of signs, labels, text on television, and electronic text. The presentation of print, within the setting in which it occurs, plays an important role in developing young children's awareness of print, like the letter 'P' in the sign in a pizza shop. When attempting to read environmental print, children may not always come up with the exact word on the label, but even young children come up with a meaningful one. Exposure to environmental print helps young children "mentally substitute a symbol for the 'real' thing," engaging in what is called "representational thinking" (Stamm, 2007, p. 248). Learning to read is dependent upon the brain's ability to perform these mental substitutions.

Views from Small Places

> Researcher Glenda Bissex describes her son Paul's reading development in her book Gyns at Wrk (Bissex, 1980). She reports that at age five, books were not Paul's basic reading materials. At first, Paul most likely recognized a words by using its total configuration and the context. For example, he knew that some large green Turnpike signs said "Exit." Then his own writings became his reading material. When he had a book, his attention centered on captions and signs that were embedded in the illustrations. He also read print in his environment, including titles, and labels and other writing on packaging—especially cereal boxes.
>
> Among my son Noah's first reading materials were large decals that extended across the windshields of sport utility vehicles. On the way to preschool, he'd see several makes and models of these vehicles. He'd ask me if the word on the truck was "Chevrolet", "Bronco," or "Blazer." He quickly began reading these words himself.
>
> Researcher Margaret Phinney explains the understandings of three children ages 2, 4, and 6 who saw a sign at a Sunoco gas station and read it in ways that correspond to their experiences. The two-year-old saw the sign and yelled 'Gas! Gas!' He associated the purpose of the sign with the print and the symbolic shape and colors of the sign that surround the print. The four-year-old questioned if the sign said, "Gulf station." Her response was categorical. She knew that the sign identified a particular brand of gas, but she had not had enough experience with the names of stations and the details of print to identify it precisely. The six-year-old gave a specified response. She said that the sign said "Sunoco." She relied on her memory and background knowledge of previous trips to the station. Additionally, she had developed an awareness of letter-sound relationships and word length that she used as clues, and she recognized the word "sun" by sight. These pieces of understanding helped her confirm the accuracy of her reading. (Phinney, 1987, p. 79)

READING ALOUD

Reading aloud has been called the single most important activity for building the knowledge required for eventual success in reading. Success in reading is a major aspect of securing literacy as a human right. Reading to children can begin very early in life, even before a child is born!

View from a Small Place

> I first became interested in finding out about what infants hear in-utero many years ago when I taught with a teacher who was pregnant. We read the children the book "Chicka Chicka Boom Boom" regularly (Martin, Archambault, & Ehlert, 1989). When her son was born at the end of the school year, my colleague told me that of all the books that she read to him, he would always respond most enthusiastically whenever she read him that particular book. We were convinced that he had been hearing "Chicka Chicka Boom Boom" before he was born!

In 1986, two researchers, Anthony DeCasper and Melanie Spense, studied mothers reading to their children in the later stages of pregnancy (7.5 months) (Saxton, 2010). They asked expectant mothers to read one of three stories aloud twice a day. Just three days after giving birth, the newborns were tested and showed a clear preference for the specific story they had heard in the womb. The researchers monitored the rates at which the infants sucked. "Infant interest was measured via their sucking behaviour on a nipple, with high rates of sucking being taken as a sign of increased attention...Modulations in pitch, up and down, during the course of an utterance provide speech with its melody. It turns out that the unborn child can perceive and later recall very specific information from the intonation contours produced in the telling of each story" (Saxton, 2010, p. 6).

Several researchers have shown that parents assist in their children's literacy development with sensitivity to culturally specific routines in book reading (Snow, Burns, & Griffin, 1998, p. 58). Adults who read to young children demonstrate that book reading is enjoyable, meaningful, and important. Children who hear stories use them to understand what living in the world is all about. They associate hearing stories with positive experiences with adults. Book reading should be a personal, meaningful, nurturing experience for children and adults. It should be an experience that both children and adults anticipate—an experience of great joy.

Holdaway describes the satisfaction that parents get from reading to their children. He states that parents (or other adults) "who engage in it" derive "deep satisfaction and pleasure" from reading to children. The adults do not see the reading as a "duty" or means of achieving "specific educational advantages for the child." Rather, "it is a simple giving and taking of pleasure." The adult does not make "demands on the child, but is deeply gratified by the lively responses and questions that normally arise" (Holdaway D., 1979, p. 39). The pleasure gained from the reading times inspires the adults to continue to read to the child.

From the child's perspective, Holdaway believes that being read to is among the "happiest and most secure" of experiences. He describes the stories themselves as "enriching and deeply satisfying." But he adds that there is also an "emancipating" feature of the experience that "transcends normal time and space." Further, "The nature of the relationship with the parent is very special to the situation," since the child has the parent's complete attention, "and there is a feeling of security and special worth arising from the quality of the attention." Holdaway concludes, "*Thus the child develops strongly positive associations with the flow of story language and with the physical characteristics of the books*" (Holdaway D., 1979, pp. 39–40).

Thirty-five years later, in the era of electronic global communication, Maryanne Wolf writes:

> One of the single best aspects of the earliest reading experience is this connection between affect—if you will, love—and the reading life. It's one of the most precious aspects of early childhood and early parenting. I worry that this is being threatened. So many parents simply do not read to their children because they believe they're doing their child a favor by providing this panopoly of technological gadgets, especially in the first two to three years.
>
> Little is more beautiful than having a parent and child reading together. Why would we ever want to lose that when we know how important it is socially and emotionally and when it starts out a reading life in the best possible way? Bringing together the richness of a caretaker's love of reading and the caretaker's love of the child through the human voice, that's just a wonderful thing. Why would we ever want to replace that? (Wolf, 2014, p. 18)[2]

When a child is read to, the brain constructs a "storehouse" in which patterns for words, stories and poems and sentences and words are kept. These patterns are available for reading, writing, and speaking throughout a lifetime for reading, writing, and speaking. Therefore, a strong reader is able to see a page of print and begin calling up these patterns that are available in this linguistic reserve (Martin & Brogan, 1975).

In the initial months of life, as Stamm explains, the goal of reading to a child is to expose the child to words and sounds—so it doesn't matter much what is read. As Stamm describes:

> By six months, a baby's brain has already created permanent neural networks that recognize the subtle sounds and rhythmic patterns of his/her native language(s). By about 12 months, however, babies usually recognize and have cognitive meaning for words that are frequently used in their home. Their receptive or listening vocabulary has grown rapidly and they're ready to delight in storybooks made for children. (Stamm, 2007, p. 241)

Holdaway states:

> Infants are not born with the ability to understand and use cognitive structures and logical processes—these must be learned. Written language is distinctive in using a wider range of such structures, more rigorously developed, more crucial to understanding, and more sophisticated in their refinements, than occurs anywhere in conversational language. Lack of experience with these encompassing structures of logical arrangement, temporal sequence, cause and effect, plot, and so on, can present tremendous impediments in learning to read. (Holdaway D., 1979, p. 54)

However, as Holdaway continues, children who are read to experience "three to four years of unpressured learning" during which they work persistently at "understanding complex cognitive structures." This learning occurs because the "stories they love abound in examples of the most central structures involved in early cognitive development." These structures include "opposites, hierarchies (small, middle-sized, big), structures of logical relationship or consequence (because, if…,then…, however…)." By the time they enter school, these children are accustomed to "all the important cognitive structures which give stories their shape and meaning" (Holdaway D., 1979, p. 54).

Additionally, Harste, Woodward, and Burke explain several things that readers demonstrate when reading to children. Readers show children how to hold the book and turn the pages. They demonstrate "what a story is, how authors put stories together, how pictures and print work together to form a surface text, and how you package the whole thing" (Harste, Woodward, & Burke, 1984, p. 184). Reading aloud provides opportunities for children to observe as the reader constructs the story of text from the print on the page. They see what language looks like when it is put together and formatted. When readers turn the pages, they show how the story moves forward (Harste, Woodward, & Burke, 1984). In their quest to make sense, children consider and talk about what is happening and what is likely to happen next. Children are learning that a book is a special way of telling a story and that readers can re-visit, as often as they like. With repeated readings, they come to understand that the words remain the same.

During reading aloud, powerful strategies of reading are being demonstrated, including "how one reads, how one corrects in reading, and how the speaking voice changes" while reading to convey meaning (Harste, Woodward, & Burke, 1984, p. 184). As children listen to stories and other texts, their attention span increases. They create images in their minds and begin to make inferences. They become aware of the links between causes and consequences. Not all of these demonstrations are attended to in a single reading event, so children need to revisit favorite books. Children should be introduced to many different kinds of books, including picture storybooks, nonfiction books and poetry. Repeated reading of favorite books and playing with literary language builds familiarity, increasing the likelihood that the children will attempt to read these books alone.

Research shows that during read aloud times, there is far more happening than just "reading" the words in a book (Booth, 2005). Hansen (Hansen, 2004) refers to the work of Rosemary and Roskos (Rosemary & Roskos, 2002) who suggest that meaningful conversation may be the most important part of the reading time. Conversations about stories and other texts support and encourage literacy development. In order to make connections between meaning and print, there needs to be time to talk together about the book. Talking about the story and raising questions help children make connections to ideas and concepts they already know. These literacy events also provide opportunities for children to explore and talk about ideas, feelings, topics, and reactions that extend beyond their personal experiences

(Booth, 2005). Further, these conversations help develop vocabulary and expressive language. Talk, therefore, is an essential part of the reading event.

A 2012 study found that there are long-term benefits when adults bring the child's attention to print while reading aloud. Researchers Piasta, Justice, McGinty, and Kadervak conducted this study of shared-book readings in 85 preschool classrooms. In experimental classrooms, teachers talked about and pointed out the print. In comparison classrooms, books were read in the teacher's typical book reading style. The results showed that for two years following the conclusion of the study, the references to print had "significant impacts" on reading, spelling and comprehension (Piasta, Justice, McGinty, & Kadervak, 2012, p. 810).

Researchers Parish-Morris Mahajan, Hirsh-Pasek, Golinkoff, and Collins describe "dialogic reading" that occurs when adults do the following: "(1) use techniques (such as questioning or prompting) to encourage a child to actively participate in telling a story; (2) offer children expansions on the story, recast the story if it is unclear to the child, and offer positive commentary on the story, and; (3) progressively raise the bar for the child's current independent level of story comprehension and reading skill (Arnold & Whitehurst, 1994; Zevenbergen, Whitehurst, & Zevenbergen, 2003)." They also describe *distancing prompts*. These are utterances "encouraging the child to relate story contents to the child's own emotional experiences...make inferences about characters or events, and draw parallels between the story and the child's life outside the book" (Parish-Morris, Mahajan, Hirsh-Pasek, Golinkoff, & Collins, 2013, p. 201).[3]

There are many benefits of dialogic reading. Over a dozen intervention studies have found that "engaging with an adult in dialogic reading results in children using more words, speaking in longer sentences, scoring higher on vocabulary tests, and demonstrating improvement in expressive language skills" (Parish-Morris, Mahajan, Hirsh-Pasek, Golinkoff, & Collins, 2013, pp. 201–202). Furthermore, the dialogic style has been "shown to be predictive of improved later literacy skills" (Parish-Morris, Mahajan, Hirsh-Pasek, Golinkoff, & Collins, 2013, p. 208).

Elizabeth Nel (Nel, 2000) cautions that forcing young children into formal reading instruction can lead to emotional instability and possible psychological damage. It appears that the reason for these problems is that children are usually not interested in the instruction and only participate for the sake of pleasing their parents. On the other hand, it is critical that children participate in informal literacy events, during which they acquire important prerequisites to reading, such as print awareness, and knowledge of the structure of oral and written language (Justice & Kadervak, 2002; Justice L., 2004).

THE LANGUAGE OF BOOKS

In addition to understanding cognitive structures and logical processes, Holdaway explains the importance of the language that is found in books. From his perspective, the language of books used by parents (and other adults) "even with infants below the age of two years" is "remarkably rich in comparison with the caption books and early readers used in the first years of school." Holdaway acknowledges that "adults are usually willing to explain meanings and answer questions" but that they are not usually concerned about assuring that babies "understand every last word or have direct sensory experience of every new concept." The adults usually let the stories "carry growing understanding from an initial grasp of their central meanings." Holdaway compares the development of the language of books to the development of speech. He describes speech as developing in an "environment which is immensely richer than the immediate needs of an infant." He emphasizes that "*orientation to book language develops in an environment of rich exposure beyond immediate needs*." In learning language from speech and books, "*the infant selects appropriate significant items to learn from an immensely rich range*" (Holdaway D., 1979, p. 40).

Researcher David Corson identifies a barrier called the "lexical bar" (Corson, 1985) that exists between the words of everyday conversations and the words of academic, literate language. In order to be successful in academic settings, learners need to be able to cross the lexical bar and get meaning from the words in written text. Children who can derive meaning from text can then build meaning of other words using the vocabulary of written language (Beck, McKeown, & Kucan, 2008).

Even young children benefit from the vocabulary they meet in written text. Researchers Donald Hayes and Margaret Ahrens, examined children's books to identify the numbers of rare words, that is, words beyond the most frequent 10,000 words in the language. These words are beyond the lexical bar. According to their findings, children's books had about 30 rare words per thousand. Adult conversation, however, even that of college educated adults, has only 17 rare words per thousand (Hayes & Ahrens, 1988, p. 401).

As noted in the previous chapter, the conventions of written language are "so distinctive" that written language becomes a "special dialect" that is different from any spoken dialect. Further, "conversational language tends to deal with the trivial and ordinary and usually lacks memorable content." In contrast, written language "... normally records memorable matters in as memorable a way as possible" (Holdaway D., 1979, p. 29). Stamm adds, "Reading *to* a child...expands the total number of words your child hears, processes, and knows, which we now know to be critical to overall intelligence" (Stamm, 2007, p. 241).

BOOKS IN THE HANDS OF CHILDREN

So far in this chapter, reading to children and reading with them has been considered. Young children take the first steps to reading by themselves as well. Very early on, children take books into their own hands and engage with them in ways that generally reflect their age and experience. As educational psychologist Catherine Snow describes:

> Infants between 8 and 12 months who are read to by their parents typically show monthly progress from grabbing and mouthing books, to 'hinging' the covers, to turning the pages. Much of this reading-like behavior is accompanied by babbling. (Snow, Burns, & Griffin, 1998, p. 57)

Beginning readers of books explore them in a global fashion. When children first begin to read books, they may prefer to focus on the pictures because they do not realize that the story is told in the print on the page. Just as children do not speak in complete sentences or write full sentences or spell words in conventional form in the beginning, they do not read in the conventional manner from the start either. They may read books from back to front or from top to bottom. Children are still coming to understand the organization of pages in a book and the layout of words on a page.

Holdaway states, "From the very beginning the infant is involved in the selection of those books which will deeply preoccupy him." He sees the child's persistent request "to 'read it again'" as coming from "a natural and important developmental demand." The child who plays "at 'being a reader'" quickly engages in "practise and experiment with a selection from the material made available through repeated readings." Holdaway emphasizes that similar to "the mastery of other developmental tasks, *self-selection rather than adult direction characterizes the specific tasks which will be intensely practised by the infant*" (Holdaway D., 1979, p. 40).

Holdaway also emphasizes that literacy orientation does not wait for oral language to be accomplished. He explains that the infant starts "to experiment with book language…while still using baby grammar and struggling with the phonology of speech." He adds that the earlier engagement with books takes place, "the more likely it is that book handling and experimental writing will become an important part of the infant's daily preoccupation" (Holdaway D., 1979, p. 40).

Researcher Caitlin McMunn Dooley points out that young children's construction of meaning "begins at birth via experience with primary caregivers and other important adults" (McMunn Dooley, 2010, p. 121).[4]

When children are read to, they often begin to read along *with* someone who is reading to them. Researcher David Doake described ways in which young children engage in reading along. He has identified four categories of this kind of mentored reading. They are as follows:

- Mumble reading—The child mumbles in an attempt to read along with the reader. Key words, mainly nouns or verbs, emerge from the mumbling as the story is reread.
- Cooperative reading—The reading becomes a shared between the child and the more experienced reader. Sometimes the words are read in unison, sometimes, one voice proceeds the other slightly, and sometimes, with one voice reads alone.
- Completion reading—The reader pauses and the child completes the sentence.
- Echo reading—The child repeats a phrase or sentence without delay after it is read. (Doake, 1985)

Literacy researcher, Elizabeth Sulzby, found that around age 2, children talk about story, but their talk sounds more like speech than book language. At age 3, the use of oral language increases as children narrate the book. After that, their narrations sound more like written language and include more actual wording from stories. Sulzby also found that by age 5 most children viewed the book as a whole unit rather than focusing on each page as a separate entity (Sulzby E., 1985; Sulzby E., 1991).[5,6]

These reading behaviors, however, may not be viewed by some adults as "actual reading," just as early talking is considered by some to be just "babbling" and early markings are frequently seen only as "scribbles." One term that used to be applied to this early reading was "pretend" reading. However, these readers are using the mannerisms and intonations they have heard from more experienced readers, therefore, they are not simply pretending (Barron, 1990). When children turn the pages and recite their way through a book, adults may also describe this kind of reading as memorizing the book. Holdaway, however, found that the children had not memorized the text, but rather were using their language skills to reconstruct the story. He called this kind of reading-like behavior *re-enactment.* He states, "A superficial assumption about this reading-like behaviour would be that it is a form of rote learning, based on repetitive patterning without deep comprehension or emotional response—that it would produce attempts at mere surface verbal recall" (Holdaway D., 1979, p. 42).

Holdaway describes a four-year-old child who is reading *Where the Wild Things Are* by Maurice Sendak (Sendak, 1963). He argues that her reading "clearly refutes" the idea that she is reading solely from memory. He notes, "…at the very least, some of the parts she doesn't remember are filled from her own verbal inventory in an encoding activity springing from deep understanding." Holdaway also states that the reader understands that "the message comes from the print and not from the picture." She also knows "where to begin the book, and turns pages with unfailing precision" (Holdaway D., 1979, pp. 41–42).

View from a Small Place

> When working with kindergarten children, I found that they engaged in the same kind of re-enactment as the children who worked with Holdaway in New Zealand. One African American boy was reading a Dr. Seuss book. He relied on his general knowledge of the world, on his knowledge of text, his memory of this text, and his knowledge of print. Although he was not actually matching his voice to each word of the text, his words matched the meaning of the text for each page. All of his reading made sense. His use of specific language from the story showed that he drew upon the story as he constructed meaning. He swept his finger from left to right, and proceeded down the page. This behavior showed that he was developing an understanding of the directionality of text.

Later, when I typed the transcript of the boy's reading, I realized that I could not capture the story on the page in exactly the way he had read it. He had put so much enthusiasm into the reading that it was far more animated than I could represent on the page. He read in a highly expressive narrative, or story voice. He repeated phrases in the same way in which they were repeated in the story. He used his knowledge of how a story sounds as he brought print into spoken form. Like the child in Holdaway's study, he was not simply reciting the story strictly from memory. He was energetically re-enacting Seuss's text.

Generally, adults read a book and young children echo the words in the way that Doake (Doake, 1985) describes. But young readers continually influence each other as well. The boy described in the vignette above was reading alone at first. A little while later, another boy sat down next to him. As the first child read, the second boy echoed his words. The first child was actually taking the second child on as his apprentice. Although he may not have realized it, he was providing a demonstration about how to read. He was introducing the other child to what it is like to become a reader. He was not only taking responsibility for his own learning, but that of the other boy as well.

Holdaway studied children who had been read to at an early age. These children began to read before they entered school. They showed evidence of a "formidable range of early skills and attitudes." He called this range of skills a 'literacy set.' He determined that children who have acquired a strong literacy set address print "immediately and automatically in appropriate ways" (Holdaway D., 1979, p. 49). Although he identified these factors over thirty years ago, many of these competencies parallel those identified by Parish-Morris and her colleagues as benefits of dialogic reading. The competencies are also similar to the three categories of outcomes that constitute a balanced reading program currently described by Opitz, Ford, and Ereksen and noted in Chapter 4 of this book. Holdaway defines four kinds of these literacy skills and attitudes that make up the literacy set: Motivational Factors, Linguistic Factors, Operational Factors, and Orthographic Factors. Below are descriptions of each factor:

Motivational factors (High expectations of print). Children who have deeply rewarding, positive, joyful experiences with print expect print to be meaningful. These children gradually acquire "unshakably positive expectations of print, and powerful motives to learn how to interpret it for themselves" (Holdaway D., 1979, p. 52). They seek experiences with books, go to books independently, are curious about all kinds of print, and they experiment with written language. They are interested in print and motivated to figure it out for themselves. They are impelled to engage with print in ways that are similar to the ways that they practiced spoken language when they were toddlers. Their intrinsic motivation enables them to approximate text, self-correct, and engage in repetitive practice (Adapted from Holdaway, pp. 52 and 62).

Operational factors (Essential Strategies for handling written language). When adults and others read to children, a great deal of learning takes place. The children learn to monitor what they are reading. They self-correct when something does not make sense. They also slow down and check the text to confirm that what they are saying matches the text on the page. They can "follow plot" and understand "temporal and causal sequences and logical arrangements." These children are able to "'use the context'" of a sentence to predict meaningful words "to fill particular language slots." They are able to "understand language without the help of immediate sensory context," and they can "create images" that have "not been experienced" (Adapted from Holdaway, p. 62).

Orthographic factors (Knowledge of conventions of print). Children who are read to come to understand how print works. They realize that the story comes from the print, not the pictures. They know the "front of the book," and that "the story begins where the print begins," that in English the "left-hand page comes before the right-hand page." These children discover that "print moves from the top to the bottom" and from "left along line to the right" and then sweeps back to left for the beginning of the next line (Holdaway D., 1979, p. 62). If the book is written in language that is oriented on the page following a different directional pattern, the child would discover that pattern. Children begin to recognize where words begin and end. They perceive the spaces in between words, and they can locate individual letters. These children also generalize letter forms, recognizing that the same letter can be written in upper and lower case forms and can appear in different styles of print. They begin to understand punctuation. They figure out that letters are related to the sounds of speech, and that the same word always has a consistent spelling (Adapted from Holdway, p. 62).

Linguistic factors (Familiarity with dialect in oral form). Children who have heard many stories understand the language of books. They are familiar with written dialect in oral form, and they understand the special features of written dialect. These features include grammatical structures, such as forms of contractions and patterns that imply consequences like "If…then…" When they substitute words, they choose highly appropriate substitutions. They also include the vocabulary of books, words that are not normally used in daily conversation. According to Holdaway, examples of these words would be "however", "dine", "ogre." In addition to single words, the children also hear complex grammar. They understand idiomatic expressions that do not follow normal rules of meaning and syntax. They are able to understand the appropriate intonations for literary or non-conversational English. Holdaway gives the examples of "Fat, indeed!" and "The very idea of it (Holdaway D., 1979, p. 62)." As he describes, "the tunes of language ring in their ears and sing in their voices" (Holdaway D., 1979, p. 53).

THE SHARED BOOK EXPERIENCE

Holdaway developed the Shared Book Experience in the 1970's in response to New Zealand educators' concerns that populations of Native Polynesian and Maori children were not succeeding in traditional reading and language programs (Hirst & Slavik, 2012, p. 5).

Two major goals for instruction were established:

1. Children would not be segregated by ability.
2. Children of different cultural backgrounds would experience success (Hirst & Slavik, 2012, p. 5).

The Shared Book Experience is modeled upon the "framework for the natural acquisition of oral language" (Holdaway, 1982). "Young children learn to speak in a supportive social context in which they endeavor to convey meaning." Their goals are "to be understood and to have their needs met." Holdaway endeavors to "replicate these dimensions in his literacy program" (Hirst & Slavik, 2012, p. 5).

Lois Hirst and Christy Slavin of Native American Language Issues describe the components of the Shared Book Experience in the following way:

> Texts used in the approach are selections from quality children's literature and are to be shared and enjoyed. These selections have been enlarged so that they can be shared with large groups and are called Big Books. The teacher's role is to induce rather than to directly teach a process. As the class enjoys books, active participation is encouraged as together, children respond in unison, discuss, and become involved in extension activities. The lessons are presented to involve children in using their visual, auditory, and kinesthetic senses. In these contexts, social and cooperative skills are promoted and developed. Each child's progress is monitored individually and there is no competition among peers. (Hirst & Slavik, 2012, p. 5)

The Shared Book Experience fosters cooperative and social skills. It has been used throughout the world. Hirst and Slavik advocate its use with Native American Learners. They report:

> The success of this approach has been thoroughly documented and the model has been adapted internationally (Holdaway D., 1982). Children from diverse backgrounds perform at levels equal to or above their peers. In addition, all children seem to develop very positive attitudes about reading. Thus, children who participate in this program which emphasizes cooperative and social skills seem to become communities of readers as described by literacy experts such as Yetta Goodman and Frank Smith. They also are involved in opportunities to use all learning modalities and language learning is strengthened. (Hirst & Slavik, 2012, p. 5)

CONNECTING READING-LIKE BEHAVIORS TO LATER READING

As seen through the lens of Holdaway's factors, powerful strategies of mature reading are being established as children are read to and read themselves. Reading aloud leads children to learning how to read. Reading to a child does not mean using programs to teach the child how to read.

The way reading is presented in this book is based on the premise that just as we learn language through participating in actual conversations, we learn to read and write by actually reading and writing. Understandings of written language develop over time, rather than in an all-or-nothing fashion. Novick points out that "rules for decoding and spelling words and punctuating sentences are learned through use, in the context of reading and writing meaningful texts." She cites research that states, "words and sentences are not islands, entire unto themselves" (Brown, Collins, & Duguid, 1989). Novick adds their meaning is drawn "within the context of their use" (Novick, 1996, pp. 9–10). A reader constructs the meaning of a text, while reading. This meaning is rooted in the reader's prior knowledge and past experience (Rosenblatt L. M., 1978). On-going comprehending is part of the act of reading and not an exercise that follows. In addition to learning by actually engaging in reading, readers also learn from the self-corrections they make while reading.

Reading in this interactive way is viewed as actual reading from the beginning. When children enter school, the language and literacy they have acquired up to that point is acknowledged and built upon. Traditional "reading readiness" tasks like matching circles and triangles, described by Delpit in Chapter 4 of this book, fall short in this approach. From the beginning, readers need to be seen as learning from their reading.

The idea of first learning to read and then later reading to learn is also challenged because even novice readers learn from what they read. Researcher Patricia Alexander and her colleagues have identified domain and topic knowledge as two kinds of subject matter knowledge that are relevant to reading development (Alexander, Schallert, & Hare, 1991).

Domain knowledge refers to the extensiveness of one's knowledge about reading. Topic knowledge refers to the depth of knowledge one has about specific topics. These topics are relevant to the domain and are referenced in texts. Typically, these two forms of knowledge complement each other. They become increasingly integrated as readers gain competence (Alexander, Jetton, & Kulikowich, 1995).

As individuals increase their knowledge of language, they also increase their knowledge of the ideas that print and sounds represent. Alexander provides the example that reading "c-a-t" with meaning involves some understanding of what "cat" represents. Additional readings of texts about cats not only develop readers' language facility, but their knowledge about cats as well. These processes of learning to read and reading to learn are co-facilitated, and they continue throughout development (Alexander P. A., 2005, pp. 417–418).

As readers use their developing strategies, they solve problems within the text for themselves. Approximations are expected as readers make meaning. They should not be held to word-perfect reading. As readers continue to read, they gain confidence and competence. They establish the habit of reading for meaning and they are able to express the emotions of the characters in a text. They are also able to connect the events in the stories to events in their own lives. As readers gain experience, they maintain meaning through longer and more complex language structures and less familiar texts. They enjoy reading a wide variety of prose and poetry and are able to adjust their rate of reading to the purpose. As readers gain experience with text, they are expected to read more complex texts and learn from these texts. Learning to read does not end at third grade. With support through continued interactions, readers become more skilled.

NOTES

1 From Danger in the classroom: 'Brain Glitch' research and learning to read in *Phi Delta Kappan* Volume 85, Number 5, January 2004. Usage determined by Phi Delta Kappan.

2 From Maryanne Wolf, Phi Delta Kappan Vol. 96 (3) pp 14–19, copyright 2014 by SAGE PUBLICATIONS. Reprinted by Permission of SAGE Publications, Inc.

3 From Once Upon a Time: Preschoolers and Storybook Reading in the Electronic Era by Parish-Morris, J., Mahajan, N., Hirsh-Pasek, K., Golinkoff, R., & Collins, M. in *Mind, Brain, and Education, 7(3)*, 200–211. Copyright © 2013 by the authors. Reprinted with permission of the authors.

4 From Young Children's Approaches to Books: The Emergence of Comprehension by Caitlin McMunn Dooley in *The Reading Teacher* 64(2), pp. 120–130. DOI: 10.1598/RT.64.2.4. Copyright © 2010 International Reading Association ISSN: 0034-0561print/1936-2714 online. Reprinted with permission of John Wiley & Sons Ltd.

5 From Children's emergent reading of favorite storybooks: A developmental study by Elizabeth Sulzby in *Reading Research Quarterly*, 20(4), 458–481. DOI: 10 1598/RRQ.20.4.4. Copyright © 1985 International Reading Association. Reprinted with permission of John Wiley & Sons Ltd.

6 From Assessment of emergent literacy: Storybook reading by Elizabeth Sulzby in *The Reading Teacher*, 44(7), 498–500 © International Reading Association. Reprinted with permission of John Wiley & Sons Ltd.

PART 4

THINGS THAT ARE CLEARLY BENEFICIAL: INITIATIVES AND PRACTICES THAT SUPPORT LITERACY AS A HUMAN RIGHT

CHAPTER 11

PORTRAITS OF LEARNERS IN SMALL PLACES

Words have souls. But that soul is not manifest until its word is graciously set.
—Guy de Maupassant as reflected upon by Sylvia Ashton-Warner (Ashton-Warner, 1963, p. 171)

THE WORK OF BRIAN CAMBOURNE: CONDITIONS OF LEARNING

In the previous three chapters of this book, separate modes of language have been placed in the foreground. In this chapter, these modes will be integrated as they are during actual language use.

Several decades ago, Australian researcher, Brian Cambourne, described conditions under which children learn to talk as they interact with those around them (Cambourne B., 1988). He then worked to create a theory of how these conditions relate to how children learn to read and write (Cambourne B., 1995).[1] These conditions are still relevant today. Brain researchers Stephen Rushton and his colleagues have documented the connections between Cambourne's conditions of learning and brain research.

Learning language involves interaction with other language users. Merely surrounding children with books or giving them computers to use is not enough. Learners need models and feedback. Exchanges between the child and more experienced and capable learners help the child to adapt, modify, and extend learning. Participating in demonstrations, taking risks, testing out hypotheses, and making best attempts are important and vital parts of the learning process.

When the conditions that Cambourne describes are in place, the child becomes engaged in learning. In his initial work, Cambourne described engagement as a condition of learning. Later he came to view engagement as incorporating a range of different behaviors. In order for engagement to take place, learners need to envision themselves as able to accomplish the task at hand. The task also has to be something that will be meaningful in their lives. Learners also need to be free of physical or psychological threats and be willing to take risks. They will learn from someone who is supportive, someone who will provide them with feedback that they will accept (Cambourne B., 1995).

The following chart lists Cambourne's Conditions of Learning (Cambourne B., 1995).

Cambourne's Conditions of Learning
Immersion
Demonstration
Employment
Approximation
Expectation
Responsibility
Response

CAMBOURNE'S THEORY AND CONNECTIONS TO BRAIN RESEARCH

The conditions and their connections to Rushton and his colleagues' brain research are described below. For several conditions, I have added additional information that pertains to the work of the educators described in this book. My remarks are indicated by Wilson-Keenan.

Immersion

Cambourne—"This condition refers to the state of being saturated by, enveloped in, flooded by, steeped in, or constantly bathed in that which is to be learned. From the moment of birth, young language learners are immersed in the talk they are expected to learn" (Cambourne B., 1995, p. 185).

Rushton and colleagues—"The concept of immersion is not new, and yet, it is often the first part of the learning process that is found missing in the traditional paradigm of instruction" (Rushton, Eitelgeorge, & Zickafoose, 2003, p. 13). Immersion is important because "different regions of the brain are connected through a complex system of synaptic neurological networks of dendrites" (Rushton, Eitelgeorge, & Zickafoose, 2003, p. 14). An enriched learning environment increases cell weight, branching of the dendrites, and synaptic responses (Diamond, 1998).

Wilson-Keenan—As discussed earlier in this book, brain researchers have now determined that babies are already hearing language in utero.

Demonstration

Cambourne —"This condition refers to the ability to observe (see, hear, witness, experience, feel, study, explore) actions and artifacts." It is important to note that demonstrations are not limited to observing another person doing something. "All learning begins with a demonstration of some action or artifact" (Smith F., 1981). Young learners receive thousands of these demonstrations. They are the raw data that must be used to tease out how language is structured. The concept of demonstrations can be generalized to all learning" (Cambourne B., 1995, p. 185).

Rushton and colleagues—"The brain changes physiologically as a result of experience. New dendrites are formed daily, 'hooking' new information to prior experiences" (Rushton, Eitelgeorge, & Zickafoose, 2003, p. 14). It is the job of educators and others to help connect for the child "various mental processes that they are experiencing throughout their day as they are exposed to these demonstrations" (Rushton, Eitelgeorge, & Zickafoose, 2003, p. 15).

Wilson-Keenan—The degree to which children pay attention to print, and read and write about what surrounds them, depends upon interaction with other language users. Learners of all ages require demonstrations in order to observe or experience an intended outcome. For example, children who listen to storytellers experience the stories as demonstrations and become storytellers themselves.

Employment

Cambourne—Employment "refers to the opportunities for use and practice that are provided by children's caregivers. Young learner-talkers need both time and opportunity to employ their immature, developing language skills. They seem to need two kinds of opportunity, namely those that require social interaction with other language users, and those that are done alone." These opportunities enable language learners to obtain greater control over conventional forms of language. "It's as if in order to learn language, they must first use it" (Cambourne B., 1995, p. 186).

Rushton and colleagues—Engaging in a learning experience causes "a number of areas of the brain are activated simultaneously" (Rushton, Eitelgeorge, & Zickafoose, 2003, p. 14). They add that Cambourne suggests that as a consequence of discussion and personal reflection, children will construct new knowledge. "Through the eyes of the brain, the employment condition echoes the need to see learners as unique individuals and to allow students to process information in a social setting" (Rushton, Eitelgeorge, & Zickafoose, 2003, p. 19).

Wilson-Keenan—Many of the educators whose practices are described in this book believe that "access to the process" of writing "can only be gained through involvement in that process" (Harste, Woodward, & Burke, 1984, p. 130). These educators involve children writing for real purposes.

Responsibility

Cambourne—"When learning to talk, learner-talkers are permitted to make some decisions (i.e. take responsibility) about what they'll engage with and what they'll ignore" (Cambourne B., 1995, p. 185).

Rushton and colleagues—When adults "provide opportunities" that allow learners "to have choices and make decisions about their learning," the child's "learning is often increased." In part, this is due to "an increase in self-efficacy" (Bandura, 1998). The "release of serotonin and other brain chemicals in the body help stimulate a sense of well-being, which indirectly increases the desire to want to learn" (Rushton, Eitelgeorge, & Zickafoose, 2003, p. 18).

Wilson-Keenan—George who is described in Chapter 4 of this book was not given a choice of materials or materials that matched his interests. He was waiting until someone moved him to another book so he could learn to read and write. He was denied the opportunity to take responsibility for his own learning.

Approximation

Cambourne—"When learning to talk, learner-talkers are not expected to wait until they have language fully under control before they are allowed to use it. Rather they are expected to 'have a go' (i.e., to attempt to emulate what is being demonstrated). Their childish attempts are enthusiastically, warmly, and joyously received. There is no anxiety about these unconventional forms becoming permanent fixtures in the learner's repertoire. Those who support the learner's language development expect these immature forms to drop out and be replaced by conventional forms. And they do" (Cambourne B., 1995, pp. 185–186).

Rushton and colleagues—"Each child's brain is unique. Built upon their life experiences, they are patterned to accept and process the world differently. Cambourne's concept of approximation allows for this uniqueness as the (adult) "provides feedback systems to guide, scaffold, and challenge a child's attainment of the skill" (Rushton, Eitelgeorge, & Zickafoose, 2003, p. 20). "The brain is designed to perceive and generate patterns as it tests hypotheses" (Rushton, Eitelgeorge, & Zickafoose, 2003, p. 15). Perhaps the most powerful feature of the brain is its ability to function on multiple levels and in multiple ways simultaneously (Caine & Caine, 1997).

Expectations

Cambourne—"Expectations are essentially messages that significant others communicate to learners. They are also subtle and powerful coercers of behavior. Young learner-talkers receive very clear messages that not only are they expected to learn to talk, but also that they are capable of doing it. They are not given any expectation that it is 'too difficult' or that they might fail" (Cambourne B., 1995, p. 185).

Rushton and colleagues— "Setting realistic expectations for all children is an important component of the learning process." If expectations are too low and children are not given enough responsibility for their learning, they can become apathetic toward learning. If expectations that are too high can result in frustration. "The brain's emotional center, the amygdala, is tied to the brain's ability to learn.

Emotions, learning, and memory are closely linked, as different parts of the brain are activated in the learning process (Jensen E., 1998). "Positive emotions drive attention, which in turn drives both learning and memory." Caine and Caine suggest that high levels of stress, or a perceived threat to a child, will inhibit learning (Caine & Caine, 1997) in (Rushton, Eitelgeorge, & Zickafoose, 2003, p. 18).

Wilson-Keenan—The educators described in this book expect that children will learn to read and write. They also believe that children are capable learners. They work alongside children and provide support.

Response

Cambourne—"This condition refers to the feedback or information that learner-talkers receive from the world as a consequence of using their developing language knowledge and skills. Typically, these responses are given by the significant others in the learners' lives" (Cambourne B., 1995, p. 186). Those giving the response must have more knowledge than the learner. "Response must be relevant, appropriate, timely, readily available, and nonthreatening, with no strings attached" (Cambourne B., 1995, p. 187).

Rushton and colleagues state, "Providing positive feedback to a child during the course of their learning is a necessary investment in the educational process" (Rushton, Eitelgeorge, & Zickafoose, 2003, p. 20).

Wilson-Keenan—Louise Carothers says that we should put our work down, face a child, speak to him or her, and give the child our whole attention. She adds that we should remember to follow up on the conversation at some later date. Her suggestions provide a blueprint for providing response to a child (Murray, 1991, p. 66).

In summary, new knowledge about the brain is vastly expanding our knowledge base of how children learn. As we can see from the analysis of Cambourne's work, new knowledge confirms the findings of researchers from the past regarding ways to support children's language development, learning and literacy.

STORIES FROM THE MINDS OF CHILDREN

As described in Chapter 7 of this book, between the ages of two and three years, changes take place in the brain that strengthen connections between the hippocampus, neocortex, and limbic system. This strengthening enables the brain to store long-term memories. At the same time, blood flow, that has been heavier in the right hemisphere, increases in the left hemisphere. Personal, or episodic, memories begin to form, and children from age three on are able to make sense of experiences and tell and retell stories about their lives.

After four years of age, impersonal memories that involve factual information are formed. At age five, memories become clearer and children get better at connecting past and the present events. Long-term memory also increases. It is at this time that children tell detailed stories about their experiences even after lengthy periods of time have passed since the events took place (Sprenger, 2008).

Donald Graves, professor and writing process expert, states:

> The ability to compose a story about "what happened" is one of the fundamental units of human thought and knowledge. Recounting in order with an interpretation of events is an underpinning of all human thought. Without it there would be no history, geology, chemistry, biology, or physics, to name but a few disciplines that rely on an orderly recounting of events. (Graves, 1989, p. 3)

Graves explains, "When parents tell stories and comment on the meaning of those stories, they use language to talk about language as well as about the events themselves." These actions serve as demonstrations for children, who need to understand how to use language to provide information. Graves adds, "If there are different sources of data or contrasting stories about the same event, so much the better" (Graves, 1989, p. 4).

We often talk about reading *to*, *with* and *by* children (Mooney, 1990). What we typically overlook is the potential of literacy materials that comes *from* children. We saw that talk is viewed as a brain builder and a means of developing language that is literally right in front of us. Talk and memories can also be used as resources for children's first reading materials. These are resources that surrounds us, but often we do not tap them. In schools and other settings outside the home, teachers and other adults need to recognize the linguistic, social, and cognitive resources all children bring from their homes (Dudley-Marling & Lucas, 2009).

The following section describes the work of innovative educators who honored children's language, stories, and memories and built upon them to help children create meaningful initial reading and writing experiences. Their work is a form of critical literacy because they co-constructed curriculum with children, rather than imposed curriculum. Therefore, they sustain literacy as a human right. The work of and Vivian Gussin Paley from the U.S., Sylvia Ashton-Warner from New Zealand, and Rose Duffy from England is described in this chapter. These educators did not have the information about brain development that neuroscience provides us with today, but their approaches built on children's developing language and literacy and served to support brain development.

VIVIAN GUSSIN PALEY: THE STORYTELLING CURRICULUM

Paley's storytelling curriculum connects oral and written language and memories. It consists of two "interdependent activities." The child dictates a story to the teacher, and then the class dramatizes the story (Cooper P. M., 2005, p. 230). The storytelling curriculum was written for use by teachers, but in a world of learners, other adults could become scribes, editors, and audience members for these stories as well.

Patricia Cooper conducted an analysis of Paley's dictation and dramatization activities. (Cooper P. M., 2005, p. 238) She describes their "potential impact on six essential tasks of a balanced approach" (Au, Carroll, & Scheu, 2001; Cowen, 2003; Morrow & Asbury, 1999; Morrow, 2002; Sadoski, 2004; Xue & Meisels, 2004).

The tasks are:

1. oral language: expression, home language, syntax, vocabulary, and sentence patterns
2. narrative form: knowledge of how stories work, where stories come from, what stories are composed of, sequencing, plot development, characterization, writing process, authorial intent, and use of imagination
3. conventions of print: knowledge of how print functions, including directionality, spaces between words, letters, words, and punctuation
4. code: encoding and decoding
5. word study: sight words, phonics, spelling, and decoding
6. reading for meaning

Through the curriculum, young children can gain an understanding that "what can be said can be written (encoded), that what can be written can be studied for its sub-parts (decoded), and that what can be decoded can be understood (comprehension)" (Cooper P. M., 2005, p. 243). Meaning, sentence structure, and the connections between sounds and the letters that represent them are all incorporated in the curriculum.

The dictation Paley employs is beneficial to children in many ways. It is rooted in and allows children to draw upon their oral language, and it allows young children "to talk about things they *want* to talk about" (Cooper P. M., 2005, p. 239). In considering comprehension, Cooper states, "What many literacy programs for young children fail to reflect, however, is that the ability to search for meaning is greatly enhanced by the experience of creating it. This reciprocal relationship between reading and writing is clearly fostered through the storytelling curriculum" (Cooper P. M., 2005, p. 245). One of the most powerful benefits of this curriculum is that adults help children realize that the meaning of their texts comes from their own minds (Cooper P. M., 2005).

Paley taps memories. She reinforces understanding by raising questions to make sure that what is being written down is what the child intends. Children in turn become engaged in clarifying their meanings and work at making the words match what they envision in their minds. Furthermore, since the child produces the story, and it resides in the brain, it becomes highly predictable reading material.

In addition to the benefits described above, dramatization itself is a powerful motivating force that employs both the "psychomotor domain" and the "cognitive and affective domains." The development of oral language occurs naturally, because the children both "repeat the script and ad lib." Dialogue and description are linked to action, fostering the internalization of "the nuances of language" and enabling "children to create pictures in their heads". These elements are essential to "deep reading" (Cooper P. M., 2005, p. 246). Most importantly, comprehension takes on a central role during dramatization because children may not realize what they intended to say until they see the story enacted. An author can also gain new understandings of his or her own story from the way the audience reacts to the presentation.

SYLVIA ASHTON WARNER: STORIES CREATED FROM CHILDREN'S KEY WORDS

Within her infant room, Sylvia Ashton-Warner developed close relationships with her young students and created an environment that enabled children to draw on their knowledge of oral and written language as they engaged in their work. She describes this lively classroom as "rocking like an overcrowded dinghy on high seas" (Ashton-Warner, 1963, p. 188). She also describes learning as "so mixed up with relationship that it becomes part of it." (Ashton-Warner, 1963, p. 92) It was her belief "that reading should be motivated by the deepest springs of meaning in the human heart" (Holdaway D., 1979, p. 31).

She worked "from the tradition of look-and-say and language-experience" in which children read whole words and read stories they dictated about their own experiences. When requested, she provided the students "with those words which most powerfully engaged them, words from the centre of their deepest fantasies—*kiss, fight, beer, hit, Mum, aeroplane, fast car, blood, skeleton.* These were once-seen-never-forgotten words which established an initial vocabulary for both reading and writing." Ashton-Warner did not work with individual curricular subjects, one at a time, but dismantled "subject barriers over the whole curriculum and integrated all the arts both for their own sake and in the service of literacy" (Holdaway D., 1979, p. 31). Ashton-Warner describes the reading her students did from their own words as organic. She states that organic reading is not new. She explains that "The Egyptian hieroglyphics were one-word sentences. Helen Keller's first word, 'water,' was a one-word book. Tolstoy found his way to it in his peasant school..." She explains how in 1963, in the field, UNESCO used organic reading "automatically as the only reasonable way of introducing reading to primitive people...in a famine area the teachers wouldn't think of beginning with any words other than 'crop,' 'soil,' 'hunger,' 'manure,' and the like." She views organic reading as "indispensible in conducting a young child from one culture to another, especially in New Zealand" where the Maori children with whom she worked were "obliged to make the transition at so tender an age." She also saw organic reading, however, as "universal" (Ashton-Warner, 1963, p. 25).

She believes that first words must mean something to a child. In fact, they must have "intense meaning...from which cannot help but arise a love of reading" (Ashton-Warner, 1963, p. 32). They must be part of the child's being. Similarly, first books "...must be made of the stuff of the child itself. I reach a hand into the mind of the child, bring out a handful of the stuff I find there, and use that as our first working material" (Ashton-Warner, 1963, p. 31).

Ashton Warner summarizes here beliefs about organic reading and first books in the following way:

- First words must have an intense meaning.
- First words must be already part of the dynamic life.
- First books must be made of the stuff of the child, himself, whatever and wherever the child (Ashton-Warner, 1963, p. 32).

View from a Small Place

> When Ashton-Warner provided a child with a requested word, she wrote it on a sturdy card. The child watched, and said the word as Ashton-Warner printed it. Then the child traced the word with her finger and put it in her word box. In the morning, Ashton-Warner spread the cards on the mat. The children found their own words and sat with each other saying the words. Ashton-Warner checked to see which ones were remembered. The children kept those word cards. They then wrote the words and wrote sentences that contained their words. Ashton-Warner saw that writings that came from children's words gave her the ability to draw out and preserve the child's line of thought. After a while, as their capacity increased, they wrote two sentences about themselves and their lives, then three. Six-year-olds eventually wrote half a page, and seven-year-olds wrote a page or more a day. She would then turn the children's writings into books. She thought that the earlier a book is put into children's hands, the speedier the vocabulary increases. (Ashton-Warner, 1963, p. 130)
>
> Ashton-Warner believes that the drama of these writings could never be captured in a purchased book. It could never be achieved in the most faithfully prepared reading books. No one book could ever hold the variety of subject that appeared collectively in the infant room each morning. Moreover, they were written in the language that the children use themselves. She describes these books as "the most dramatic and pathetic and colourful things I've ever seen on pages." (Ashton-Warner, 1963, p. 49)

Although it does not appear to be widely known, it is important to note that organic reading was not intended to "stand alone." Rather, it was seen as the entry into reading that was "essentially a lead up and out to all other reading…." (Ashton-Warner, 1963, p. 57). Ashton-Warner drew from children's knowledge of language and their memories as the foundation of literacy and then moved to other texts. This understanding is important for curriculum design in both developed and developing countries today. Her work aligns with the findings of neuroscientists today.

ROSE DUFFY: WRITTEN CONVERSATION

The students in Rose Duffy's classroom for five-year-olds in Manchester, UK, were accustomed to engaging in oral conversations with the adults and other children in their lives, and most likely with themselves (Duffy, 1994).[2] Therefore, it seemed natural to Duffy to allow the children to carry out the conversations in writing. In these written conversations, the children drew upon their strengths as talkers and listeners as they became readers and writers.

Duffy sat with a writing group, writing a sentence in each student's journal. She then either stayed with the group or circulated around the room writing entries in other children's journals. The children responded in the journals, and Duffy wrote replies. She tried to get in multiple turns within a day, so that the written text took "on the characteristics of conversation" (Duffy, 1994, p. 32 & 34).

Duffy's work is very much in the Freirean tradition because generally, she tried not to initiate the questions. She curbed her "natural instincts" as a teacher "to ask questions and attempted to start each exchange by making a statement…" (Duffy, 1994, p. 35). She suggested the topic, but allowed the child to ask questions and control the direction of the conversation. Duffy explains that once the children understood the nature of the journals, the children quickly took up writing the initial sentence in subsequent written conversations.

Topics were derived from everyday experiences of both participants, like cars that would not start, or pets that were not feeling well. Typical exchanges ranged between twenty and eighty words. Children did not avoid words if they did not know how to spell them. They made their best attempt, or approximation, of the spelling of the word. Duffy points out that she cares "very much about spelling," but that she did not want her students "to become spellers at the expense of being authors." She views "spelling and authorship as reciprocal experiences." The journal work "was a relatively small part" of the writing done by the children, and "those other aspects offered opportunities to explore language in more formal ways" (Duffy, 1994, p. 35).

Like Sylvia Ashton-Warner, Duffy strengthened her relationships with her students through the written conversations. The result was a written conversation that was like everyday conversation, rather than an instructional exercise. Duffy found that rather than "a typical diet of copying teacher-influenced short recount or declarative sentences," these exchanges could range "across a variety of functions." In the example below, Georgina is prepared to "hypothesise," "argue," and "respond affectively" (Duffy, 1994, p. 36). This entire exchange took place a single day. This conversation consisted of twenty-two turns. Duffy wrote sentences that averaged 5.5 words in length. Georgina's sentences were 6.9 words in length. Georgina wrote 76 words.

View from a Small Place

Here is Georgina's written conversation with Rose (Duffy, 1994, p. 34). The punctuation is presented as it appears in the text:

Me	What a nuisance! My car would not start this morning.
Georgina	My daddy had to take it to the garage.
Me	Why?
Georgina	Because the tyre wouldn't go.
Me	My tyre was flat too!

Georgina	Did you take it to the garage.
Me	I couldn't drive it there!
Georgina	You could have rung up the man who gets the cars.
Me	I'll do that the next time. I am worried about my dog.
Georgina	It could have got stolen last night.
Me	No! She was sick!
Georgina	Where was she sick.
Me	She was sick on the carpet.
Georgina	Did you have to wash it.
Me	Yes.
Georgina	Where did you put your dog after you had washed the carpet.
Me	I took her to the vet.
Georgina	What did the doctor say about her.
Me	He gave her some medicine.
Georgina	Was it nice medicine.
Me	I don't think she liked it much.
Georgina	I am worried now.

Duffy describes another child who was frequently absent and typically avoided writing, but he also became an active participant in written conversation. The written conversation journals provided undivided attention from an adult and built a supportive personal relationship. Because the journals were less formal than other kinds of writing, the relationship between the writers was more relaxed. Therefore, a sense of "jokeyness" could emerge.

The children wrote brief excerpts in a natural way, but the numerous entries resulted in the number of words written equalling the number in a longer text. These conversations not only provided opportunities for writing, but for reading as well.

Duffy sees these dialogues as opportunities for these young writers to "clarify thoughts, expressions, or knowledge" (Duffy, 1994, p. 39). Like Ashton-Warner, Duffy does not view these conversations as "a substitute for experience of writing more extended texts," but a way of offering support as children "become more experienced and competent writers" (Duffy, 1994, p. 41). The conversations serve as entry points and as valuable resources for initiating writing and reading. The written conversations increase adults' knowledge of what children know about the world in general and about written language in particular. The children participate with enjoyment and enthusiasm.

NOTES

1 Republished with permission of John Wiley and Sons, from Towards an educationally relevant theory of literacy learning: Twenty years of inquiry by Brian Cambourne, in *The Reading Teacher*, Vol. 49 (3), 1995; permission conveyed through Copyright Clearance Center, Inc.

2 From KEEPING IN TOUCH: INTERACTIVE WRITING WITH YOUNG CHILDREN, Nigel Hall and Anne Robinson (Eds.). Copyright © 1994 by Nigel Hall and Anne Robinson. Reproduced by permission of Hodder Education.

CHAPTER 12

BUILDING ON THE STRENGTHS OF FAMILIES AND COMMUNITIES

> *If you care for your own children, you must take an interest in all, for your children must go on living in the world made by all children.*—Eleanor Roosevelt to the Southern Woman's Democratic Union, New York, February 1933

DIGNITARIAN RIGHTS IN SMALL PLACES

Chapter 3 of this book recounts the Tenth Anniversary of the Universal Declaration of Human Rights, when Eleanor Roosevelt presented the guide *In Your Hands* to the United Nations. On that occasion, she put forth the challenge to all people to recognize and uphold the inherent dignity and the equal and inalienable rights of all members of the human family as the foundation of freedom, justice and peace in the world. She emphasized that in order to improve the world, the work at the local, state, and national levels needs to be continuous.

Creating literate communities is one kind of this continual work. These communities are also based on the concept of dignitarian rights that inform the Universal Declaration of Human Rights. These rights do not serve the individual alone, but perceive "...the city as a public realm where individual and community are bound together in some degree of reciprocity" (Kommers, 1991, p. 867).

Literacy for Life states:

> ...literacy is no longer exclusively understood as an individual transformation, but as a contextual and societal one. (UNESCO, 2005, p. 159)

Strong Foundations: Early Childhood Care and Education defines "literate society" in the following ways:

> A social setting within which (a) the vast majority of the population acquires and uses basic literacy skills; (b) major social, political and economic institutions (e.g. offices, courts, libraries, banks) contain an abundance of printed matter, written records and visual materials, and emphasize the reading and writing of texts; and (c) the exchange of text-based information is facilitated and lifelong learning opportunities are provided. (UNESCO, 2006, p. 350)

Collaboration has always been essential to cognitive and emotional development. However, in the 21st century, workers are expected to share responsibility with diverse, global teams working together to accomplish common goals as never before. In this chapter, I will provide descriptions of initiatives in literate communities that are based on collaboration. They fit the traditional meanings of literate communities, but they could work within mobile-based communities as well.

There are countless successful ways of fostering literacy throughout the world. UNESCO's Global Monitoring Reports describe numerous examples of successful literacy initiatives.

The practices explained in this chapter, however, stem from the kind of work undertaken by the innovators described in this book. These practices build on a person's history of language and literacy. They draw on community funds of knowledge and co-operation. Many involve parents and other community members as participants and contributors. They reflect the dignitarian rights found in the Universal Declaration of Human Rights because they are rooted in the learner's language and cultural practices and bind the community together. They also foster reciprocity.

These practices were developed decades ago. There is a resurgence of interest in them today. All involve creating written text from the learner's own language or sharing readings of texts. Most were originally designed for children, but they can be used to support adult literacy as well. Most were designed for learning to read and write in one's first language, but they have been adapted to teach additional languages as well. New technology and tools can be integrated into each practice because they all foster communication, conversation and collaboration.

Children have had exposure to a range of language and literacy experiences that have formed their preschool language capabilities. Individual children begin school "with more or less of the linguistic, social, and cultural capital required for school success." Therefore, "It is the responsibility of teachers to draw on these resources in support of school learning, including teaching language practices valued in school. If there are crucial language experiences needed for school success, then teachers must provide them" (Dudley-Marling & Lucas, 2009, p. 369). In order to support children's language learning, relationships with families are vital. Developing partnerships with families supports a reciprocal sharing of knowledge and experiences from home and school. These partnerships allow teachers to recognize and build upon what children already know. They also allow families to support learning that takes place in school.

THE SPRINGFIELD LEARNING COMMUNITY COLLABORATIVE

In 1990, Professors Judith Solsken and Jerri Willett from the Language, Literacy and Culture Program at the School of Education, University of Massachusetts, Amherst, and I began a curriculum-based action research project. The project supported two-way sharing of knowledge and understandings with families. Its purpose was to improve the education of children in urban classrooms by changing the relationships between families and school (Wilson-Keenan, Willett, & Solsken, 1993; Solsken,

Wilson-Keenan, & Willett, 1993; Wilson-Keenan, Willett, & Solsken, 2004). Our definition of "family" was broadly defined as "a circle of people who love you." Student's families were invited to come into the multiage primary classroom and share something about their families and their lives. Family visits included playing guitars and drums, showing photographs of family events, and baking bread. These visits allowed the worlds of home and school to come closer together and enabled the children to bring more of themselves into the classroom. Over two years, 83% and then 87% of the families participated in the project. This level of participation shattered the stereotype that urban families lacked interest in the education of their children.

By 1994, we attained funding from the U.S. Department of Education and the Irene E. and George A. Davis Foundation, and established the Springfield Learning Community Collaborative (SLCC). The Collaborative enabled 20 Springfield teachers from eight K-5 schools to participate in an off-campus advanced degree program. One principal, Gloria Williams from the Frank H. Freedman School, also attended the program. The courses were designed for urban teachers who wanted to foster family participation in their classrooms and learn new approaches to teaching language arts. In addition to the course work, the SLCC provided hundreds of multicultural books for classroom libraries and other resources for both home and school learning.

The SLCC involved parents and other community informants. Together we negotiated ways of teaching and learning and found innumerable ways for families to share their knowledge, talents and traditions. In some classrooms, families came in and shared their talents, family stories, or information related to their work. The students then constructed shared books and other displays based on the information provided by the families. Other teachers sent books and response journals home and engaged in written exchanges with the families. The SLCC also sponsored summer programs for children. During one summer, a family summer literacy camp was held. Families and teachers discussed learning, read and wrote together, and created books, works of art, and meals that drew upon the families' knowledge and experiences. Shared reading of both commercial titles, and books designed by students and families were a major component of SLCC classrooms. The families then shared their work with each other and others in the community. Teachers and families also traveled together on family field trips to museums and a sea aquarium. The idea of taking the trips was initiated by the families. Approximately 300 people attended the trips.

In 1997, The Annenberg Institute at Brown University in Providence, Rhode Island named the SLCC as an exemplary Public Engagement project. The Institute database notes the unusual design of the SLCC as a school-based, teacher-driven project that reaches out to parents and others in the community and values the contributions these constituencies make to schools (Annenberg Institute for School Reform, 1998).

The SLCC had four main goals:

- *Engaging in inquiry of practice*—The first goal required teachers to engage in study and reflect upon teaching practices and explore theories, models and strategies that enhance learning. SLCC teachers redefined their teaching practices through this inquiry.
- *Valuing the contributions of all constituencies*—The second goal honored partnerships with children's families. Teachers and families learned, shared, and celebrated together. Family participation was the centerpiece of the work. Some families came to school to share something about their lives. Several teachers found that written conversations in family journals were an extremely effective way of connecting families with the school. Several other models of new ways of engaging families in homework were developed by SLCC teachers as well. For example, families constructed projects on a monthly basis that were displayed on classroom bulletin boards.
- *Establishing Learning Communities in classrooms*—The third goal involved creating caring learning communities in our classrooms where all teachers, children, families, and others were accepted, valued, and challenged. Rich learning experiences that integrated language arts into all curriculum areas were implemented.
- *Implementing an on-going collaborative assessment process*—The fourth goal established assessment practices that included information from families for the purpose of informing teachers, learners, families, and the community of the strengths, development, and progress of each learner. Findings from the assessments formed the foundation of instruction. Assessments showed that children in several SLCC classrooms exceeded grade level expectations in reading and language (Wilson-Keenan J., 2015).

Although we did not call them dignitarian rights at the time, the work of the SLCC with its emphasis on family, where individuals and community were bound together in reciprocity, embodied the spirit of dignitarian rights. We tapped the language, literacies, memories, and experiences of children and their families to assist them in creating their own learning.

CONCENTRATED ENCOUNTERS: THURSDAY ISLAND 1980'S

In the 1980's, Betty Murray, an educator from Thursday Island in the Torres Straight north of Australia, designed a program to teach English to children who did "not hear English spoken around them" (Murray, 1991, p. 57). Murray described Torres Straight Islanders as speakers of "two or more languages indigenous to the region: the languages of home, ceremonial functions and local trade" (Murray, 1991, p. 58). The children had few opportunities to practice with English speakers, yet English was the official language of school.

Prior to her program, the children were expected to learn English through "teaching materials based on repetitive drills" that did not make sense to either the teachers or the pupils. Murray saw the English that the children were practicing as "utterly irrelevant to the interesting world they were exploring." She added, "For them English was dead" (Murray, 1991, p. 58).

In Murray's program, the Torres Straight English Program, children became involved in real exploration of their world in ways that allowed English to be the valid medium of communication. Murray's lessons were similar to an approach to teaching literacy called "concentrated encounters" (Murray, 1991, p. 59). This approach was developed by Dr. Brian Gray (Gray, 1984), a researcher in the Research and Development Centre of Reading at the Brisbane College of Advanced Education (GM South Africa Foundation, 2009). Murray also drew upon the work of Warwick Elley, a reading authority from New Zealand (Elley, 1982).

The program was designed for the following purposes:

- help children develop functional skills in English
- take account of the isolation of schools
- support the teachers in becoming more fluent in Standard Australian English
- provide inservice education in appropriate teaching methods
- provide content and supporting resources for teachers which would both sustain the unique cultural background of the children and introduce the culture of the language they were learning (Murray, 1991, p. 58).

The organizing principles of the program were "meaning matters," and "sense is everything" (Murray, 1991, p. 60). In this approach, books were used as the "stimulus" for the explorations of the children's world and as "scaffolds for teachers' and students' language growth." The adults were no longer simply instructors of language forms. Their role changed to being sharers of "new experiences" and supporters of "the child's exploration and explanation of his or her world." The task of the adult was a "genuine negotiation of meaning through the medium of English where this is appropriate" (Murray, 1991, p. 59). A common experience was shared through the "senses, story, pictures, song, chanting, telling stories, testimony of past experience, role play, drama" (Murray, 1991, p. 60). Parents and other community members were encouraged to participate in the sharing of the experiences that resulted from the studies. The sharing ensured that schooling did "not become distanced from the community and that the children's own cultural mores are supported and valued" (Murray, 1991, p. 64).

Since the purpose of language is communication, the program focused on "the children, their interests, their levels of maturity and their natural language learning abilities" (Murray, 1991, p. 59). The Torres Straight English Program consisted of both "work units and supporting teacher inservice materials" (Murray, 1991, p. 61). Murray used repetitive texts in the early years to provide enjoyable ways for the children to learn and use English structures.

The shared book experience was "used extensively." It gave children opportunities "to hear spoken language, to discuss their own related experiences, to make predictions and to use the language of the texts as a model as they express their own ideas and experiences" (Murray, 1991, p. 61). Learners sought meaning and learned much more than the conventions of print, although they learned these as well. It is interesting to note how Murray began with a commercial text, but connected it directly to the experiences of the children on Thursday Island.

View from a Small Place

> Murray provides a sample lesson using the shared book *There's a Hippopotamus on Our Roof Eating Cake* (Edwards H., 1980). She explains that the themes of this book are "the seeming unfairness of family rules and the desire for a world in which children might do as they wish. A secondary theme is that of approved and disapproved behaviours."
>
> Then Murray takes the children through the steps of the routine that include a first-hand experience (in this case reading the book), an opportunity to talk about the experience, time to think about what the experience shows or what learners need to clarify or understand, a response or action and an opportunity to share the new experiences. (Murray, 1991, p. 61)

Another series of lessons from Murray's program from Thursday Island is based on the shared experience of a book about turtles that are found on the islands (Murray, 1991). Talk about the book leads to a shared understanding of the life cycle of the sea turtle and the food chain, as well as the specific language used in the book. She also includes discussions that focus on why turtles leave the nest, dangers small turtles encounter, and how a turtle might feel when it reaches the sea. The study of the book leads children to engage in using language in several ways that include describing, explaining a sequence of events, and summarizing. Children talk, read, write, retell and dramatize the stories. Fiction, poetry, and informational texts are the focus of study.

Included in Murray's lessons are suggestions for suitable responses to the text. These responses include:

- telling a similar story or writing a similar book that is familiar to class members
- reminiscing, e.g., 'I remember when…'
- singing songs appropriate to the theme or incorporating language functions related to the theme
- researching/describing animals e.g. hippos
- role playing
- preparing a list of rules for the classroom (Murray, 1991, p. 64).

Earlier in this book, several of these ways of responding to the texts were explored, including reminiscing, singing songs, and telling stories. These ways honor children's language, knowledge, memories, and developing literacy. They are compatible with the findings of brain research today.

In addition to commercially published texts, there were locally produced texts that focused on the introduction of English translations of traditional Torres Straight stories and on materials that explain mainstream culture to children who were unfamiliar with that culture (Murray, 1991, p. 61). Books written by the children and adults of the Torres Straight Islands are still available today. These books contain traditional island stories, songs, recipes, and children's writings.

The Torres Straight English Program was written for the children of the Torres Straight Islands, however, Murray envisioned a far broader audience. She was "confident that its underlying rationale and the kinds of resources, activities and techniques that it employs have much wider application" (Murray, 1991, p. 65).

Murray's prediction has turned out to be correct—the idea has gone to scale.

THE CONCENTRATED LANGUAGE ENCOUNTER: GENERAL MOTORS SOUTH AFRICA 2015

Concentrated Language Encounter techniques now have much wider application. They are used to teach both children and adults in their own language as well as English. In 2009, General Motors (GM) South Africa published a teacher's guide entitled, *Concentrated Language Encounter: A proven and effective method of teaching reading* (Allen, 2009).[1] They also produced a DVD. The guide explains that the term "Concentrated Language Encounter (CLE)" came from Courtney Cazden's (Dean of the Graduate School of Education, Harvard, at the time) statement that children learn language through concentrated language encounters. The guide states that the methodology was strengthened by Dr. Brian Gray's research in the 1980's (Allen, 2009, p. 1).

By 1985, CLE had spread to Thailand. There, a CLE pilot (Thai language) was used in elementary schools where literacy teaching was failing. CLE had a high success rate in these schools, and by 1991, the Thai government extended its use into elementary schools throughout Thailand. The GM guide reports that by 2009, the CLE methodology had been "extended by Rotary to many countries throughout the world, including Brazil, the USA, several countries in Africa, the Philippines, Nepal, India, Egypt, Pakistan, Bangladesh, Laos, Cambodia, Turkey and several Pacific Island countries" (Allen, 2009, p. 1).

The CLE begins with a shared reading of a book that has a "good story line and illustrations." After the reading, participants "review the story, carry out role-plays, and talk about the story." Next, participants "recall the story in their own words" and collaborate to "develop their own class version of the story." The members of the group dictate the text to the instructor who writes each sentence on a poster-size sheet of paper. The words they speak are transformed "into written form before their eyes." As it is written, each sentence is read aloud. Changes can be negotiated by the group, and details can be added. When the text is complete, the instructor and the learners "read it aloud together." The illustrations are added to the story. Then group books and individual copies of the book are made (Allen, 2009, pp. 4–14). As a final step, learners engage in activities and games based on the text.

There are three stages of programs: Stage 1 for lower grades, Stage 2 for middle grades, and Stage 3 for upper-school grades (Allen, 2009, p. 2). Like the methods designed by Sylvia Ashton Warner and the other educators profiled in this book, the CLE is not meant to stand alone. It is described as "best applied as part of a balanced approach to literacy where other methodologies are also incorporated in the teaching of literacy" (GM South Africa Foundation, 2009, p. 1).

As the CLE guide for Stage 1 explains:

> The CLE approach to developing literacy is particularly effective in challenging environments, for example, where there are few reading books or where learners are taught in a medium of instruction other than their mother tongue. CLE literacy programmes prove their effectiveness in a remarkable short time, and they are extremely cost effective, because teachers can develop most of their own materials and learners write and make their own books. (Allen, 2009, p. 2)
>
> In addition, because local teachers decide the informational content of the programme, there is every opportunity to foster understanding of the learners own cultural heritage, to situate stories in the learner's own context, and to increase awareness of medical, nutritional, environmental and other matters that are important to the lives of the learners and the general welfare of the population and the country. Above all, CLE teaching brings high success in teaching children from illiterate populations to read and write, where other programs have failed. (Allen, 2009, p. 2)

Training materials are available online and may be downloaded at no cost by agencies interested in implementing the approach.

www.gmsouthafricafoundation.com

BREAKTHROUGH TO LITERACY

In 1979, Holdaway described a British program called Breakthrough to Literacy (BTL) in the following way:

> The most recent attempt at a radical reformulation of the literacy undertaking, and the only one which has attempted to face up squarely to language implications, arose from the application of recent linguistic theory in England. "Deeply indebted to the language experience tradition, Breakthrough to Literacy, highlights the importance of creating written language from the earliest stages." (Mackay, Thompson, & Schaub, 1970) in (Holdaway D., 1979, p. 33)

Holdaway describes Breakthrough to Literacy as employing "techniques and supporting materials" that enable "the beginner to express personal meanings in written language at the same time as he learns to read." Earlier we saw that Holdaway believed that oral language did not have to be completely in place before children began to handle books and take up reading. Here, written expression is developing at the same time the child is learning to read. Writing is not put on hold until the process of reading is completely in place.

Holdaway adds, "The major impediments to written expression—handwriting and spelling are bypassed" initially because the learner is provided with "a convenient file of printed word cards." These cards are used to construct "meaningful sentences in a 'Sentence Maker.'" Later the sentences are copied into a "personal reading book." At a later stage of development, the child manipulates letters to make words. "Grammatical understandings of syntax are facilitated by the use of prefixes and suffixes. These affixes build on base words, rather than treating each derivative as a separate word." One of the aspects of the program that Holdaway views as a limitation is that upper case letters are not presented from the beginning. Commenting on experimental situations that piloted Breakthrough in New Zealand and Australia, he cites difficulties of an organizational nature in the program. He believes it is "not easy for teachers to understand fully" (Holdaway D., 1979, p. 33).

Over the past twenty years, the Molteno Institute for Language and Literacy[2] has created the Molteno Project to disseminate the Breakthrough practices in Africa. The project consists of two approaches: Breakthrough to Literacy— for children in the primary grades; and Bridge to English—for children learning English (The Molteno Institute for Langauge and Literacy, 2012, p. 4). Breakthrough to Literacy is focused on in this chapter.

The institute describes its progress:

> Breakthrough is now available and used in all official South African languages plus the San languages of the Northern Cape Province and Namibia. To date it is available in 9 African countries, Angola, Botswana, Ghana, Lesotho, Malawi, Namibia, South Africa, Uganda, and Zambia; and fifty-one indigenous African languages. It has been extensively evaluated and found to be peerless as a mother-tongue literacy course for both children and adults, e.g. testing in Zambia in 1999 revealed that Grade One children were reading and writing at levels equivalent to Grade Four and higher. (The Molteno Institute for Langauge and Literacy, 2012, pp. 2–3)

According to the Molteno Institute, "The Breakthrough to Literacy course systematizes the Language Experience Approach to the mother tongue enliteration process…" It builds upon the listening and speaking skills "the child brings from home into the classroom as the basis of learning to read and write." The underlying belief is that the listening and speaking skills that the child brings from home are "basic to successful learning, and they constitute a starting point in the teaching of literacy through the Breakthrough methodology" (The Molteno Institute for Langauge and Literacy, 2012, p. 1).

The implementation of Breakthrough in the mother tongue is seen as providing an "ideal foundation" for learning other languages. It is not viewed as negating the value of additional languages like English, Afrikaans, French, or Spanish. Through the use of Breakthrough to Literacy, teachers develop "knowledge and skills in initial literacy teaching and in learner-centered class management." One benefit of the program is that these skills then transfer to other areas of the curriculum (The Molteno Institute for Langauge and Literacy, 2012, p. 2).

Over the past two decades, several evaluations of the project were conducted. The reports cited here focus on the results of the implementation of Breakthrough to Literacy. I cite evidence from a range of reports, because over time, the results evolve from improving literacy to showing evidence of the development of thriving literate communities.

In 1980, the British Council commissioned an evaluation conducted by R. Colet. He reported:

> Breakthrough suits local conditions and is effective in developing very early functional literacy skills. It conveys immediate benefits to pupils and teachers. "...quite simply, the Molteno Project must be acknowledged as one of the most significant, realistic and radical agencies of constructive, speedy and peaceful change in southern Africa." (Molteno 2010, p. 4)

The results were favorable from another evaluation of Breakthrough commissioned by UNESCO, and conducted in nineteen schools Botswana. The evaluation reported "a high standard of teaching, learning, motivation and organisation." The positive results of the evaluation "led to the introduction of Breakthrough in 672 schools." A follow-up evaluation in 1992 for the Overseas Development Administration found that Breakthrough had a 'powerful influence towards methodological change' (Molteno 2010, p. 5).

In 1994, Dr. P. Rea-Dickens conducted an evaluation of Breakthrough to Literacy in the Mpumalanga province of South Africa. The evaluation was commissioned by the Overseas Development Administration. Rea-Dickens "compared Molteno and non-Molteno schools and found 'extensive evidence of improved teaching and learning.'" For example, 'chorusing,' a practice of large groups chanting together, was observed in only 15% of Molteno classes, but in 93% of non-Molteno classes. Instead of chorusing, Molteno Breakthrough classes focused on collaboration. Activities included "pair and group work, pupil demonstrations, pupils' own use of language, and pupils playing language games..." These changes "were observed in significant percentages of Molteno classes but not at all in any non-Molteno classes" (Molteno 2010, pp. 5–6).

In 1999, an evaluation of the Icibemba Pilot Project in Zaire was conducted by Herman Kotze of South Africa, Cathal Higgins of Ireland, and contributed to by Geoffrey Tambulukani and Dr. Israel Chikalanga. The project was identified as an "unqualified success" for Breakthrough to Literacy. Furthermore, there was evidence that the method and teaching strategies were being transferred to other curriculum areas. The report stated that there were "clear indications that a significant new philosophy of education was evolving in project classes; specifically a growing child-centred, problem-solving approach was apparent" (Molteno 2010, p. 8).

The results led Mr. Shay Linehan, Secretary of the National Reading Committee, to remark:

> …this high degree of success would compare with more developed countries—indeed he noted that both external consultants felt that Breakthrough reading and writing levels were above what would be normally found in well-resourced Grade 2 classrooms in South Africa, UK or Ireland. He stated that this must be a major success if children in remote areas of Kasama district were outperforming children from Dublin, London and Johannesburg. (Molteno 2010, p. 8)

The report from Uganda in 2002 shows evidence of the development of a learning community. It stated that Breakthrough to Literacy (BTL) classrooms were "child-friendly." Enrollments and participation in the BTL schools surpassed enrollments in non-BTL schools. There was also a "heightened interest and participation of parents in children's learning activities and in their involvement in school activities. More important, parents have come to view school as a place that reinforces the children's cultural heritage" (Molteno 2010, p. 10).

The report adds that in these schools "learners take more responsibilities for their work and regulate their time and attention between the tasks they have to perform." Children are respected as learners in these schools. There is "evidence of mutual respect by teachers for the ability of the learners and their efforts, with teachers actively promoting leadership skills, as well as the life skills of communication and critical thinking" (Molteno 2010, pp. 10–11).

Additionally, "BTL classrooms have ushered in a new culture of co-operative learning, with evidence of having acquired a new value of democratic decision making." Teachers gave accounts of "new group dynamics in their classrooms, where leaders would unanimously vote out a leader who didn't lead them satisfactorily, and vote in someone else to lead them" (Molteno 2010, p. 11).

All of these gains would be impressive in any school, but there is a final factor here. The gains in the BTL project in Uganda are being realized in typical Ugandan schools where class size on average is eighty learners, and sometimes there are up to two hundred learners per class! (Molteno 2010, p. 10).

The 2006 report from Malawi by Frances Sampa also documents positive results. It states that Molteno Breakthrough to Literacy (MBTL) teachers were "more innovative, resourceful and committed to improving the teaching and learning than other teachers." Literacy skills improved as well. In MBTL standard 2 classrooms, "handwriting, reading and writing" all improved. These improved "skills were not stand-alone but transferred to other learning areas." Teachers here also "employed learner-centered practices in teaching MBTL." These practices had a broader impact as they "improved the teaching and learning process in schools and made children learn in an interesting way" (Molteno 2010, p. 12).

During the past five years, the Molteno Institute has also implemented the Bridges to the Future Initiative in Johannesburg. This approach utilizes "the power of interactive, easy-to-use, computer-based instruction for literacy learning in primary schools." This program has the potential to reach 30,000 children within a two-year period.

The Molteno Institute has launched a Facebook page that will "essentially" help "teachers help themselves and one another." The innovation will support teachers who have a mobile phone with Internet (The Molteno Institute for Langauge and Literacy, 2012, pp. 1–2). Historically, non-government organizations like Molteno have often "operated through initiatives" in which they "might spend three years training and supporting teachers with relevant skills for their job, or supplying them with materials to support their teaching practice" (The Molteno Institute for Langauge and Literacy, 2012, p. 1). The use of social networking changes, enhances, and expedites that process.

The learning also becomes more democratic as teachers post messages to the page. Their colleagues read and react to the messages. Subject Specialists post tips on how to teach first, or first and additional languages. Teachers download and comment on the tips. Participants can "read and write messages about topics of interest, upcoming events, questions for the field, resource sharing, research interests, or other issues that affect national and international language policy research."

The Molteno Institute sees the role it is playing to facilitate "dialogue among teachers" as "transformative and exciting." They view this initiative as a "partnership taken to higher level" that will "effectively spark positive change within a school community to define its aspirations and the means to achieve them" (The Molteno Institute for Language and Literacy, 2012, p. 2).

This chapter explored the longevity and success of the Concentrated Language Encounter and Breakthrough to Literacy. Both of these approaches honor learners' language, culture, stories, and memories. These initiatives have succeeded in places where other approaches have failed. Their success is testimony to the work of the literacy innovators who developed them.

NOTES

1. From Concentrated Language Encounter: A proven and effective method of teaching reading by Helen Allen, (Ed.), Copyright © 2009. Reprinted with permission of Roger Matlock, General Manager, The GM South Africa Foundation.
2. Quotes and descriptions of the work of the Molteno Institute for Language and Literacy used with permission of Masennya P. Dikotla, Chief Executive Officer, The Molteno Institute for Language and Literacy, Braamfontein, South Africa.

CHAPTER 13

TECHNOLOGY IN EVERYONE'S HANDS

Paper is over. —Heidi Hayes Jacobs, Learning and the Brain Conference Presentation, Boston MA—11-19-11 (Hayes Jacobs, 2011)

THE INFLUENCE OF NEW TECHNOLOGIES

Many of the materials for the initiatives described in the previous chapter of the book were originally written by hand with writing instruments and paper. Now these initiatives can be supported by the use of technology. Decisions about the use of technology will be determined within each community according to their needs and the design of their infrastructure. Some possibilities for using technology related to the initiatives described include:

- Voice-to-print technologies for dictating stories and information
- Computers for typing, illustrating, and printing books
- Small handheld devices for social networking, locating information, and accessing texts
- Video for documenting local events, interviewing local participants, and developing training programs for instructors
- Web-based searches for providing information for stories, reports, and other purposes
- E-books as a resource library
- Presentations and other documentation of learning preserved in digital archives
- Social networks for connecting with other learners throughout the world, and comparing commonalties and differences related to collaborative work

In addition to reading and writing, multiliteracies are changing the landscape in our diverse 21st century global community. These literacies acknowledge the increasing significance of cultural and linguistic diversity in a global economy. They also recognize various ways of "meaning making in different cultural, social, or domain-specific contexts." They arise "in part from the characteristics of the new information and communications media." These literacies do not rely on written text alone, rather they are "increasingly multimodal." They include "oral, visual, audio, gestural, tactile, and spatial" ways of representing meaning (Kalantzis & Cope, 2011). Harnessing new information and communication technologies can help foster literacy as a human right.

Wohlwend states that we have to gain an understanding of and "learn from new forms of literacy that children are already using" (Wohlwend, 2010, p. 149). Drawing on Millard, she explains that this knowledge is necessary in order to design curricula that support a 'literacy of fusion' (Millard, 2003) that bring together traditional and evolving literacies. It is necessary to continually explore and take up new tools and evolving ways of communicating because advancements in technology will most likely radically change our understandings of literacy in the future.

I would not have been able to write this book without combining traditional and new literacies and the use of digital technologies. In addition to conducting research through books and journals, the Web has given me access to research, practices, documents, and ideas from the U.S., and has allowed me access to small places around the world, including locations in Australia, New Zealand, the UK, South America, Africa, Asia, and Europe. Through searches, I've read writings by advocates for the Choctaw Nation in Oklahoma...accessed primary source documents from UN archives...communicated via email messages with educators in Africa... traveled not only across distances, but also through time via YouTube...watched Eleanor Roosevelt give her address at the adoption of the Universal Declaration of Human Rights in Paris...viewed video of Mary Ann Glendon talking about the Declaration...watched Noam Chomsky discuss Freire's work with Howard Gardner and Bruno della Chiesa at Harvard University...studied hours of demonstration lessons by teachers in South Africa...also read commentary on blogs and located resources on professional websites...used voice-to-print technology to record ideas and weave them into my text...learned from researchers who have employed new technologies that have uncovered groundbreaking information about the brain... accessed countless resources from a wide range of libraries and other sources.

Most of the educators that I have described in this book engaged children in traditional paper and pencil literacies. As Maya Pines, reports, however, in the 1960's, Omar Khayyam Moore, a professor of social psychology from the University of Pittsburgh headed up a "talking typewriter" project at Yale University. His invention included "a slightly modified electric typewriter, plus dictation equipment, and an exhibitor..." A human instructor had a role in the original system. A later version was completely automated. This version could be programmed to "talk, play games, read aloud, take dictation, and show pictures" (Pines, 1967, p. 95).[1] With its speech-to-print design, the "talking typewriter" was an early indicator of the potential of bringing technology and learning together in the classroom.

Children in Moore's lab worked at the typewriter voluntarily for up to a half-hour per day. The program was mainly self-regulated (Holdaway D., 1979). Moore believed, as brain researchers do today, that "...young children don't learn item by item, but by over-all search—they absorb whole patterns." (Pines, 1967, p. 112)

As Maya Pines describes, "Moore's respect for three-year-olds knows no bounds." Moore stated:

> I wouldn't pit myself against a three-year-old any day, in meeting an utterly new problem or a radically new environment...You've got your top problem solvers there. By the time a child is three, he has achieved what is probably

> the most complex and difficult task of his lifetime—he has learned to speak. Nobody has instructed him in the skill; he has had to develop it unaided. In bilingual or multilingual communities, children pick up several languages without accent at a very early age. There's plenty of information processing in a mind that can do that. (Pines, 1967, p. 112)

All of the children who worked with Moore "learned to read, write, and touch-type effortlessly," generally "in under a year." As a result of this learning, the children's first and second grade classrooms were "advanced and intellectually lively," and their program was "extremely rich" compared to that of other classrooms. Unfortunately, Moore left the program to do other research and "the project foundered on the age-old rocks of jealousy, politics, and finance" (Holdaway D., 1979, p. 60).

Technology is changing the ways both children and adults read, write, and learn. The innovations are here to stay. Traditionally, immersing children in print meant surrounding them with books, posters, charts and asking them to listen to a book on tape or on a CD. Today and in the future, the use of electronic technologies can enhance the conditions of learning. Today's preschoolers are growing up in a world where the dominant way of making meaning has shifted from print on the page to image on the screen (Jewitt C. & Kress G., 2003). Readers can be immersed in thousands of books that can be downloaded on an iPad, Kindle or similar electronic reader, some of which are specifically designed for children. These tools have the capability to increase the number of books and other texts available to readers immediately. This access is especially important in low-income communities in the U.S. and in other areas where access to texts has been limited.

Speech recognition technologies can support readers as they connect speech to print. Access to video can greatly increase the number of demonstrations available to learners, and the number of times they can replay and study the video. Email, blogs, twitter, Facebook and other social networking systems create forums for conversation and immediate response. Tools that allow writers to jot ideas that are instantly transferred to electronic text can eliminate the step of rewriting drafts. These tools also increase the amount of text a writer can produce. The spelling and grammar check capabilities of writing programs have the potential to increase writers' willingness to attempt to take risks and approximate syntax and the spelling of words. The risks can be attempted because writers know they will receive immediate feedback. Online reference materials can enhance learning vocabulary. Photographs, images and audio recordings can be stored to preserve ideas and document what learners know.

View from a Small Place

> One holiday season, I received an e-card that retold the Christmas story. It combined several social networking services and information programs including: email, googlemaps, Wikipedia, YouTube, twitter, Amazon, and

> Facebook. It ended with the message that although times change, feelings stay the same. It then wished me a Happy Digital Christmas. (Digital Christmas story, 2011)
>
> Later that day, I attended a crowded church service and had to stand in the back. Several families with young children stood there as well. In the past, I've seen children in this situation playing with rattles, dolls, small trucks, or reading books. This scene was different. One child played with a toy cell phone, another pushed the buttons on his father's smart phone, and a third child sat in a stroller and viewed a video on a handheld tablet.

As illustrated in the example above, very young children now have access to both real and toy electronic devices. Furthermore, as Wohlwend describes, when they don't have these tools that they see in use in the world around them, they create them. She points out that children do not even need the real tools. The literacy practices are so "relevant" to their lives, and "children find these technoliteracies so compelling that they pretend these digital devices into being…" She cites examples of children pretending that a "plastic carrot is a cell phone" or "by playing a video game with markers and paper" (Wohlwend K., 2009) in (Wohlwend, 2010, p. 147). Similarly, at a technology conference I attended, a presenter projected an image on the screen of an African child holding a cell phone to his ear. The child had meticulously fashioned the cell phone from mud.

When I read Wohlwend's words, I was reminded of a child I knew many years ago.

View from a Small Place

> Charlie was a student in my fourth grade classroom in 1972—my second year of teaching. Charlie taught me some of the most important lessons I ever learned as a teacher. At that time, the children in our classrooms were divided into groups by reading ability as determined by scores on reading tests. Twice a week the children in the highest reading group would leave the classroom for lessons in French —"Les riches deviennent toujours plus riches." (The rich get richer.) French lessons lasted for about forty-five minutes. Charlie was clearly not a candidate for French class. He was in the low group. He brooded. He had a difficult time getting along with other children, and he struggled with most assignments.
>
> When the students left for French class, the other children would remain in the classroom where they would work with me individually or in their small groups. At the time I belonged to a recycling center. For a charge of one dollar per student per year, I could take away all the recycling materials that I could carry and bring them back to my classroom.
>
> One day, when the group went to French class, I told the other children that when they finished their assigned work they could take a break, go to the back

> of the room and create something of their choosing out of the recycled material. As I worked with a reading group at the front of the room, Charlie made his way back to the recycling materials. He took some boxes, sheets of mylar paper, some wires coated with plastic, plastic bottle caps, and he started constructing a computer. Personal computers were not commonplace at the time. Charlie made a screen and drew some circular lines on it. It was not typical writing. It was more like a representation of an electronic signal. He worked for quite a while, mostly alone, although a few other children who were interested in his construction hovered nearby. Although I could see some things he was doing, I intentionally did not get up and go to the back of the room to direct him. I did not intervene as Charlie worked. I let him construct his computer.
>
> By the time the children in the French class came back to the room, Charlie's computer took up most of the back counter. And the kids from French class really took notice. They wanted to know where this computer had come from. They surrounded Charlie and started asking questions that required him to explain the screen, the wires, the knobs, the mylar, the dials. He nodded repeatedly and gestured and answered their questions at a rapid-fire pace. Then suddenly, Charlie, his face beaming, sprinted across the classroom to the area where I was sitting and shouted, "Ms. Wilson, Ms. Wilson, they're asking me how the computer works!"
>
> Escorted by Charlie, I walked to the back of the room to hear more of his explanation. What I saw before me was the prototype of what would be commonplace 15 years later—a desktop computer.

I believe that this was one of the few times in his school experience that Charlie saw himself as a knower, an expert, as somebody who wasn't in the bottom group, and as someone who had something of value to share with other kids. Initially, the lesson I took away from Charlie's success was that an effective way to teach is to provide a rich environment, give learners choices, allow them to draw upon what they know, and trust their desire to create and learn. I now understand that there were ways other than reading and writing, including designing, constructing, and gesturing, that allowed Charlie to express his understandings. He could have been on a level learning field with the other kids if there had been more room in the curriculum for him to use these valuable means of expression. He would have been on a more level playing field if, at the time, he had access to technology.

Researcher Perry Gilmore states that children should be seen, trusted, and evaluated as skilled language users and as individuals who have the right to instructional circumstances where pride and ownership are central features of learning (Gilmore, 1984). New literacies required by new technologies are now part of those circumstances.

As researchers Bogard and McMackin (Bogard & McMackin, 2012, p. 313) describe, ten international educators met in New London, New Hampshire, in 1994, "to discuss the future of literacy pedagogy."[2] At that time, the pedagogy was limited to reading and writing on a page and the standard form of the national language was emphasized (New London Group, 1996). This group would come to be known as New London Group. Their goal was to expand the meaning of being literate. They focused on a variety of modes of expression and placed emphasis on diversity of language and culture.

Professor of technology and learning Carey Jewitt further explains:

> The multiliteracies model highlights two interconnected changes in the communicational landscape that impinge on what it means to be literate. These are the increasing significance of cultural and linguistic diversity in a global economy and the complexity of texts with respect to nonlinguistic, multimodal forms of representation and communication, particularly, but not limited to, those affiliated with new technologies. Multiliteracies has evolved into an international pedagogic agenda for the redesign of the educational and social landscape. To this end, multiliteracies sets out to stretch literacy beyond the constraints of official standard forms of written and spoken language to connect with the culturally and linguistically diverse landscapes and the multimodal texts that are mobilized and circulate across these landscapes. (Jewitt C., 2008)[3]

In 2001, the midwinter conference of the National Council of Teachers of English (NCTE) in Berkeley, California focused on "new ways of becoming literate in new times." Application of these literacies within classrooms was a priority. The purpose of the conference supported the ideas that as "classrooms become more diverse, our notions of literacy must account for the multiple voices represented by the wide range of students we teach" (NCTE, 2000).

In their book *Multimodal Literacy*, Jewitt and Kress, challenged the predominant ideas around language, learning, and representation. Specifically, they questioned the view of literacy and learning as a primary linguistic accomplishment. Instead, they presented the multimodal nature of learning and literacy. This view encompasses representational and communicational modes involved in learning through image, animated movement, writing, speech, gesture, or gaze (Kress & Jewitt, 2003).

The 2005 position statement from the National Council of Teachers of English moved beyond calling for multiple voices to recognizing the possibilities of multimodal literacies. It states, "Young children practice multimodal literacies naturally and spontaneously. They easily combine and move between drama, art, text, music, speech, sound, physical movement, animation/gaming, etc" (NCTE, 2005). It is important to consider not only that children use these literacies, but also how they use them to communicate greater meaning to an audience.

Researchers Bogard and McMackin report that several terms began to emerge that identify practices for making meaning that transcend language. These practices include "photography, art, music, video or audio representations" (Bogard &

McMackin, 2012, p. 314). For example, several of the literacies in which Charlie engaged would be regarded as multimodal literacies.

Evolving iterations of the worldwide web have helped advance the development of new literacies. The *informational web* was developed from 1991 onwards. It was static, like a billboard or a magazine that stayed the same until it is changed by the publisher. The second generation of web applications were generated or shaped by users. Instead of being published by someone else, the people using these sites publish, market, and edit the content. The third generation of the web is a social web designed to incorporate 3d portals, avatars, integrated games, education, and business.

These new technologies require new ways of thinking and communicating. These processes include the ability to follow nonlinear text, constantly assess resources, filter out extraneous information, and create cohesive messages by employing a variety of features (Bezemer & Kress, 2008; Corio & Dobler, 2007).

Furthermore, according to researchers Karchmer-Klein & Harlow Shinas, "...there are unique social practices afforded by Information Communication Technologies (ICT)." These practices include the capacity to communicate with others "24/7 through blogs, wikis, social networking, instant messenger, multiplayer online games, and a multitude of other activities" (Karchmer-Klein & Harlow Shinas, 2012, p. 289).[4]

TECHNOLOGY AND BANKING EDUCATION

As noted in Chapter 1 of this book, even the inception of technology is not free of the grip of banking education and the pedagogy of poverty. Gorski notes that "a review of the research on how disenfranchised communities have been affected by mindless applications of computer technology in schools" shows that "these technologies, as they are being employed, appear to be contributing to inequities more than disrupting them" (Gorski, P. 2009, p. 349). As Gorski explains, rather than being the "great equalizers," these technologies more often appear to be tools that further embed "existing inequities—existing gaps of access to opportunity" (Gorski P., 2009, p. 358). Drawing on the work of others, he notes that the "pedagogical trends mirror exactly the larger discrepancies in students' access to higher-order thinking instruction" (Barton, 2004; National Commission on Teaching and America's Future, 2004) in (Gorski P., 2009, p. 355).

Gorski (Gorski P., 2009, p. 354) draws on the work of Solomon and Allen, who cite examples of teachers of children of color who tend to use the computer for "word processing, skills and drills, and other lower-order thinking activities." They contrast these classrooms with those of teachers working with predominantly White students who tend to use these technologies to encourage "critical analysis, construction of ideas and concepts and inquiry" (Solomon & Allen, 2003).

Gorski adds that "students who are least likely to have access to higher-order instruction without these technologies are also least likely to have access to such instruction when these technologies are in play." The inequities do not stop there, however, because "inequities in teachers' access to the resources and support they need also mirror larger race and class inequities in U.S. schools..." (National Commission on Teaching and America's Future, 2004) in (Gorski P., 2009, p. 355). Therefore, students of color and low-income students end up with "fewer resources, teachers with less experience, and teachers with less pedagogical training" (Gorski P., 2009, p. 355).

In a 2011 report, Zero to Eight describes what they have termed the new "app gap" that has developed among young children. The report states:

> Only 14% of lower-income parents (less than $30,000 a year) have downloaded apps for their children to use, compared to 47% of higher-income parents (more than $75,000 per year). (Common Sense Media, 2011)

The 2013/14 EFA Global Monitoring Report *Teaching and learning: Achieving quality for all*, details the inequities of Information and Communication Technologies (ICT) on low-income countries. It states:

> Effective use of ICT for learning requires careful consideration of how pupils' overall access to technology affects learning outcomes. Children from low income groups are less likely to have experience of ICT outside school, and may thus take longer to adapt to it. In low income countries, the digital divide is often extreme and strategies are needed to ensure that ICT exposure outside school does not exacerbate disparities for disadvantaged groups. (UNESCO, 2013, p. 294)

Like traditional literacy capabilities, even when children have experience and expertise with technology, there is no guarantee that knowledge will be tapped in the classroom. Researcher Wohlwend notes, "families provide children with demonstrations of important literacy practices that allow them to explore how these literacies work with and approximate digital texts." She continues, "...when young children come to school, they often have to check their technoliteracies at the classroom door" (Wohlwend, 2010, p. 145).

Wohlwend draws on the work of Jackie Marsh, a professor from the University of Sheffield who states:

> It is as if the developments in young children's lives outside of nursery and school are occurring within a self-contained, virtual bubble that has little to do with the stuff of the first years of schooling, which generally continues to focus on phonics, print-based literacy texts and canonical narratives. (Marsh, 2006, p. 23)

PROMISING TECHNOLOGIES FOR DEVELOPING COUNTRIES AND LOW-INCOME COMMUNITIES

Teaching and Learning: Achieving Quality for All, states, "A review of 15 projects showed that interactive radio instruction was associated with higher achievement of learners in English and mathematics in a range of developing countries, particularly for early grade pupils in hard-to-reach communities and schools in fragile states." The review describes "encouraging trends in narrowing of urban-rural disparities in learning outcomes, which were particularly pronounced for children in very remote areas" (UNESCO, 2013, p. 292).

View from a Small Place

> In Pakistan…the positive effects of interactive radio programming on the learning outcomes of grade 1 pupils were greatest in schools categorized as isolated. In such remote contexts, radio addresses barriers to learning raised by distance, poor access to resources, and an insufficient supply of quality teachers and of teacher supervision and support. (Ho and Thukral, 2009) in (UNESCO, 2013, p. 292)

Teaching and Learning: Achieving Quality for All also documents that by 2010 interactive radio programming was reaching "over 20,000 children on the islands of Pemba and Unguja. The project uses interactive radio instruction to build children's foundation skills and prepare them for primary school, using games, song, stories and problem-solving activities linked to the Zanzibar curriculum" (UNESCO, 2013, p. 292).

Radio is seen as supporting "education in fragile states, including those emerging from conflict, by allowing education systems with shortages of infrastructure, qualified teachers and learning materials to reach large numbers of children and provide second-chance education to returning refugees and out-of-school youth" (UNESCO, 2013, p. 292).

View from a Small Place

> …between 2006 and 2011, the South Sudan Interactive Radio Instruction project enrolled over 473,000 pupils through Learning Village audio lessons targeting grades 1 to 4. The half-hour lessons were linked to the national curriculum and included instruction in English, local language literacy, mathematics, and life skills elements such as HIV/AIDS and landmine risk awareness. In addition, the project has reached 55,000 out-of-school youth with 180 audio lessons offering the primary school curriculum, together with civics, health and English-language content, via a non-formal accelerated learning programme." (UNESCO, 2013, p. 292)

In some areas of Latin America, television-assisted instruction, similar in approach to interactive radio instruction, is popular. Several large-scale programs have been in operation for many years. "Telesecundaria in Mexico, for example, was launched in 1968 to extend access to lower secondary education; by 2010, 1.26 million students were enrolled in the programme" (UNESCO, 2012) in (UNESCO, 2013, pp. 292–293).

Prior to the inception of mobile devices, technology was too cumbersome to branch into all the small places where it could change lives. With the advent of mobile technologies, however, that is no longer the case. Because of their relatively low cost, handheld devices can help serve the pressing need to advance digital equity, reaching and inspiring populations "at the edges"—children from economically disadvantaged communities and those from developing countries.

Handheld mobile devices are important tools that have the potential to break the cycle of the pedagogy of poverty and inequitable access to education and literacy throughout the world. In a world of learners, these devices are available and in the hands of many people, parents, grandparents, siblings and other people in child's community. They move learning beyond the walls of schools. The use of these devices is widespread and they becoming increasingly popular. As noted by Hal Varian in Chapter 1 of this book, inexpensive mobile devices can have a profound effect on education throughout the world. There are people like Varian's man behind the plow, the teachers at the Ubangui River described in Chapter 1 of this book, or educators in Liberia, where paper is not well preserved in the heat, for whom handheld devices are an invaluable educational resource.

Mobile technologies have the potential to help level the playing field in gaining skills and competencies. However, they must be deployed fairly to advance digital equity. They foster communication for real purposes and allow users to engage in real world, first-hand, learning. Mobile devices allow students to transcend the barriers imposed by a classroom's four walls without losing their ability to gather, access, and process information.

Liz Kolb, author of *From Toy to Tool: Cell Phones in Learning*, said, "Mobile devices bring the real world into the classroom, and they bring the classroom into the real world" (Kolb) in (Shuler, 2009, p. 17). Shuler states, "Two key benefits of anywhere, anytime learning include promoting situated knowledge and helping to bridge barriers between home, school, and afterschool" (Shuler, 2009, p. 17).

Cell phones are of particular interest for supporting disadvantaged students. They are less costly than laptop computers and more readily available in children's homes. Shuler (Shuler, 2009, p. 21) includes the following statement from Kurt Squire, Principal Investigator for Mobile Media: Ubiquitous Learning for Global Citizenship: "Mobile devices enable kids to develop passions and interests via their own personalized, media-enhanced environments that can transport them to different times and places" (Squire, 2009).

Shuler explains:

> Not all children are alike; in an ideal world, instruction should vary and be adapted in relation to individual and diverse learners. There are significant opportunities for genuinely supporting differentiated, autonomous, and individualized learning through the use mobile of mobile devices. (Shuler, 2009, pp. 21–22)

As noted in the beginning of this book, the use of handhelds for learning is not only an American trend. Other nations are attempting to capitalize on these devices as well, and in some ways they are strikingly ahead of the United States. The Nigerian National Council for Nomadic Education was looking for ways to enhance educational opportunities for primary school-age children who do not have sufficient food, shelter, and health care. The Council integrated mobile technologies into its curricula because traditional methods of distance learning were not satisfactory. Their initial reports indicate that there has been increased literacy among the target populations. They find that mobile technologies fit nomadic lifestyles. Shuler reports, "Perhaps, the most groundbreaking mobile learning initiatives are happening in underdeveloped areas of Africa." In these places, mobile devices are less expensive and more accessible than personal computers. (Aderinoye, Ojokheta, & Olojede, 2007) in (Shuler, 2009, p. 19). Additionally, the School Empowerment Program of Kenya uses mobile technologies to remotely provide primary schoolteachers in both rural and urban areas with training, support, and materials (Traxlar, 2005) in (Shuler, 2009, p. 19).

Devices that have the capacity to download texts can be crucial resources for providing books and other reading materials for people who need them throughout the world. The users of these devices include nomadic people, refugees in developing countries, people who live in remote areas. The devices can be extremely beneficial as well to people in the low income neighborhoods in the U.S. and other developed countries who do not have equitable access to books or ways of storing books.

As described in Chapter 1, the Congolese teachers and their students, who have relocated at the Ubangui River, could also benefit from the use of handheld devices. Here is an example of how I imagine changes in their schools:

Envisioning a Small Place

> In the classes by the Ubangui River, each teacher and student has a handheld device. The boards that they nailed to a tree to record lessons is seldom used. Instead, they use mobile devices to download information, conduct research, and transcribe their ideas to print through voice-to-print technology. They also share their learning and ideas with other students across the world. They access new information through web-searches, podcasts and other electronic services. Through on-line networks, the teachers now have access to training, materials, and a means of sharing ideas.

The benefits of mobile technologies for learning both one's mother tongue and additional languages are being realized around the world. Sesame Workshop, for example, has broadcast extensive free podcasts in which Muppet characters teach "young children (and second language learner adults) the essentials of reading and language skills." The Mobile Based Interactive Learning Environment (MOBILE) has served "rural populations, where access to formal education may not be adequate." Mobile Immersion for Learning and Literacy in Emerging Economies (MILLEE) also served this population. These kinds of projects "take advantage of children's interest in mobile devices, cell phones in particular" (Shuler, 2009, p. 20). Furthermore, "Mobile devices can help overcome many of the challenges associated with larger technologies, as they fit more naturally within various learning environments" (Shuler, 2009, p. 5).

The Mobile Immersion for Learning and Literacy in Emerging Economies (MILLEE) used cell phones applications to assist children from villages and slums in the developing world to acquire language and literacy. The applications created immersive, game-like environments for learning. They focused on local learning needs and aimed to provide access to literacy resources for low-income children. The activities happened at places that were more convenient than schools. The schedule of the activities was also designed to meet the children's needs. The design methodology was informed by best practices from both commercial language learning programs and traditional village games in which children in the developing world engage (Kam, 2013).

The MOBILE project in Taiwan increased English vocabulary for elementary students. The learners were also more enthusiastic as a result of the mobile platform (Tan & Liu, 2004). The use of mobile learning apps is rapidly escalating. According to a report from the Joan Ganz Cooney Center at Sesame Street Workshop, the "market for educational apps appears to be thriving, with educational apps for preschoolers and toddlers experiencing a huge jump over the past two years" (Joan Ganz Cooney Center for Sesame Street Workshop) in (Devaney, 2012).

The market for apps continues to grow at an extremely rapid pace. There is concern that because the field is emerging so quickly, empirical studies on the effectiveness of apps for learning have not kept pace with their production and marketing. While apps are viewed as potentially important sources of learning and discovery, debate continues over the quality of apps and their impact on learners and learning (Devaney, 2012, p. 1).

Zero to Eight reports that in the U.S., "More than a quarter (29%) of all parents have down- loaded 'apps' (applications used on mobile devices) for their children to use. And more than a third (38%) of children have ever used one of these newer mobile devices, including 10% of 0- to 1-year-olds, 39% of 2- to 4-year-olds, and 52% of 5- to 8-year-olds" (Common Sense Media, 2011, p. 21).

Textbooks are also changing. They now include interactive diagrams, videos, and photographs. Three-dimensional images in these books can be manipulated and rotated on a touch screen. With the swipe of a finger, passages in a digital book can be highlighted. Digital notes can be created within a page. Textbooks can be continually up-dated by the authors. Revised reversions of books on can be viewed on mobile devices and stored in a student's digital library (Carter, 2012).

Heide Hayes Jacobs states, "Paper is over." When she makes this statement, textbooks are a resource that she focuses on in particular. She believes that giving a student hard-cover published textbooks is "old think." She argues that by the time a textbook is printed and gets into the student's hands, the information in the book is already out-of-date. The problem is compounded when a textbook adoption extends for several years because an entire generation of students relies on out-dated information from obsolete sources (Hayes Jacobs, 2014).

It is difficult to describe the benefits of specific electronic devices because these devices are changing at lightning speed. But many mobile devices embed several communication options, including voice-to-print capacity, text messaging, e-mail, and the capacity to download music and books. These options are readily available as an integrated part of the lives of many children.

Handheld devices can empower parents and caregivers as advocates for their children. Handheld devices provide parents and caregivers with opportunities to preserve the images and voices of young children. Many parents and caregivers take videos of their children talking in various settings, playing with language, singing, listening to and telling stories, reading, and writing. This documentation of what children do in their homes over time can be invaluable when children enter a childcare center or school. These videos present evidence of a range of language and literacy capabilities a child engages in during various activities with his family. These competencies can be built upon in school. More importantly, the recordings empower the parent as an advocate for the child because they document the language and literacy strengths of the child. Once these strengths are recorded, they cannot be denied. Therefore, the child cannot be categorized as "not having" language or literacy.

Teaching and Learning: Achieving Quality for All states, "One promising way of increasing the accessibility of ICT for teaching and learning is 'mobile learning' —the use of mobile phones and other portable electronic devices, such as MP3 players." In low-income countries, mobile phones are often "the only widely available technology" in low-income countries. Mobile phones have potential because they "do not require the same level of infrastructure as computers, networks are more widely available and phones increasingly have internet access and video capabilities." The report cautions, "However, while they can increase learning opportunities, these new technologies need to tailor content and delivery to the varying needs of learners, especially weaker students" (UNESCO, 2013, p. 294).

Teachers are viewed as remaining central to curriculum delivery, particularly for low achievers needing additional support. Simply introducing computers or other technology in schools is "not enough to improve learning, nor can they replace teachers as the primary source of classroom instruction." ICT is seen as "more effective as a means to improve learning and address learning disparities if it plays a complementary role, serving as an additional resource for teachers and students." *Teaching and Learning: Achieving Quality for All* further states, "In poorer countries, the availability of ICT infrastructure remains a crucial consideration. Many countries cannot yet support widespread computer-assisted learning because schools lack internet access or, in some cases, even electricity supply" (UNESCO, 2013/4, p. 293).

A LITERACY OF FUSION

As noted at the beginning of this chapter, Wohlwend (Wohlwend, 2010, p. 147) reports that we need to create a 'literacy of fusion' (Millard, 2003) that synthesizes old and new literacies. Wohlwend adds that "Anne Haas Dyson has called for a new set of basics, informed by children's lived experiences, their diverse cultural and linguistic resources, and their rapidly expanding repertoires of symbolic conventions" (Dyson A., 2006).

Wohlwend (Wohlwend, 2010, p. 147), drawing on Knobel and Wilbur, describes a new way of viewing technology that "moves away from the model of an individual interacting with a print text, off- or on- screen" (Knobel & Wilbur, 2009). This new way of viewing technology includes "global participation, multi-user collaboration, and distributed resources and knowledge." She cites examples of this technology, including "social networking sites like Facebook, fanfiction sites, wikis, massively multiplayer online games, and music- and video-sharing sites such as You Tube." Additionally, "ways of participating in vast digital networks through posting, blogging, recording, remixing, uploading, and downloading" are also included (Wohlwend, 2010, p. 147).

As new generations of the web develop, it will be necessary for the new basics to continue to evolve as well. Another major skill for effective use of technology is a person's ability to draw from his current knowledge base and problem solve how to use and derive maximum benefits from new devices. Much of this problem solving has to be done "on the fly" because the person is both using the device and learning how to use it at the same time. This skill will also need to continue to develop.

New times, technologies, and devices require knowledge and training, but new times also bring with them challenging new issues. One new issue is that many young people may have more knowledge than adults about how to use new technologies. The other side of this issue is that adults can learn a great deal from young people who use these technologies and devices regularly.

Researchers Karmarcher-Klein and Harlow Shinas, however, remind us that while is important to recognize children's knowledge and consider their perspectives of the complex relationship between literacy and technology, it is also necessary to acknowledge that "access does not guarantee use, and use does not assure deep understanding." Therefore, "it is necessary to suspend assumptions regarding the technological knowledge and experience students bring to the classroom and instead develop instruction designed to address curriculum goals and students' individual needs" (Karchmer-Klein & Harlow Shinas, 2012, p. 291).

They further explain that educators (and others) need to be aware of how rapidly both changes in technology and the ways in which it influences literacy learning come about. These changes take place so fast that "one can never know everything there is to know about technology." Therefore, teachers and other adults need to keep a "finger on the pulse of technological advancements." One way of doing this is by using "free Web-based tools that facilitate interactive information sharing in collaborative digital environments" (Karchmer-Klein & Harlow Shinas, 2012, p. 289). A blog and a technology forum are examples of these digital environments.

Since many advancements in technology are unforeseen, rather than predicting and instructing students in the next innovation in technology, it is more important for facilitators to foster life-long learning so that learners can evaluate the effects of technology and take- up ones that are beneficial and relevant.

CAUTIONS ABOUT TECHNOLOGY

In their research, Parish-Morris and her colleagues found, "Rich and diverse dialogic interactions offer children the opportunity to expand their language capabilities and tie storybook content to their own experiences." Their research suggests, however, that "the types of interactions associated with better reading outcomes are more prevalent when parents and children read traditional books together than when they read Electronic console (EC) books." The readings of the EC books showed that parents talked about the child's behavior much of the time, rather than relating the story to the child's life. Furthermore, even though the time spent reading the EC books was longer than the time spent reading traditional books, the number *distancing prompts*, (described in Chapter 10) the most potent type of dialogic language, did not increase. The researchers conclude that "if parents have only 10 minutes per day to read with a child, the richest and most condensed dialogic input can be provided by reading a traditional book" (Parish-Morris, Mahajan, Hirsh-Pasek, Golinkoff, & Collins, 2013, p. 207).

These researchers also found that 3-year-olds have fragile story comprehension when compared to five-year olds. The younger children were able to identify characters and events in EC books. Their understanding of setting, problem, characters, and resolution, however, was greater when reading traditional books with their parents. The difference may be explained by the greater number of *distancing prompts* given during the reading of the traditional books. It is also possible that distractions from games and sound effects interrupted the flow of the EC book, and therefore had a negative influence on comprehension (Parish-Morris, Mahajan, Hirsh-Pasek, Golinkoff, & Collins, 2013).

Maryanne Wolf adds that she has "great respect for colleagues who are developing interactive books," but these books are "not the answer during the first five years" (Wolf, 2014, p. 19). She also notes that pediatricians have set guidelines that advise parents "to limit technology in the early years" (Wolf, 2014, p. 18).

Additionally, Krashen states, "It is often suggested that technology can solve the problem of access to books, through high-powered computers with internet access and through e-books and e-readers." He cautions, however, that "jumping in without proper preparation wastes our students' time and will cost more money in the long run." Instead, he advocates for providing access to books. He states, "…we already have an astonishing amount of evidence that providing access to interesting, comprehensible books has a strong impact on literacy development" (Krashen S., 2014, p. 7). When given access to these kinds of books, "most students will read them" (Krashen S., 2001; Krashen S., 2004). When students engage in this reading, "their vocabulary, grammar, writing style, and knowledge of the world will improve" (Krashen S., 2014, p. 7).

Nicholas Carr (Carr, 2010/11), author of *The Juggler's Brain*, cites the work of researcher Patricia Greenfield who raises the concern that while the use of the Internet and other screen-based technologies strengthens some skills, it weakens others. She states that use of these technologies has brought about "widespread and sophisticated development of visual-spatial skills (Greenfield, 2009). One example of this development is that we can now "rotate objects in our minds better than we used to be able to" (Carr, 2010/11, p. 13).[5] But as Greenfield cautions, these "new strengths in visual-spatial intelligence" are accompanied by a weakening of our ability to engage in the kind of "deep processing" that supports "mindful knowledge acquisition, inductive analysis, critical thinking, imagination and reflection" (Greenfield, 2009, pp. 69–71).

Carr (Carr, 2010/11, p. 13) points out that researchers Small and Vorgan find "many of us are developing neural circuitry that is customized for rapid and incisive spurts of directed attention" (Small & Vorgen, 2008). Carr cautions, "We can assume that the neural circuits devoted to scanning, skimming, and multitasking are expanding and strengthening, while those used for reading and thinking deeply, with sustained concentration, are weakening or eroding" (Carr, 2010/11, p. 14). Carr adds that other researchers voice concerns as well. For example, Jordan Grafman, head of the cognitive neuroscience unit at the National Institute of Neurological Disorders and Stroke, states, "The more you multi-task, the less deliberative you become; the less able to think and reason out a problem" (Tapscott, 2009).

Research is also showing that increasingly, young people's reading is focusing on online resources. A study from the Henry J. Kaiser Family Foundation shows that while time spent reading books has remained relatively steady, time spent reading newspapers and magazines has decreased (Generation M2: Media use in the lives of 8- to 18-year-olds, 2010). Often, online reading revolves around skimming and scanning text as described above, rather than the deeper more sustained reading needed to absorb a complicated text such as a novel. It's important, however, that readers engage in both kinds of reading, in a sense, becoming ambidextrous readers (Alexander F., 2010).

Shuler describes other reasons for concerns about the use of mobile technologies:

> Though mobile technologies offer rich opportunities to promote children's healthy development and learning, the devices pose potential pitfalls. There are a number of cognitive, social, and physical challenges to surmount when these devices are incorporated into children's learning. Some of these serious

concerns, which have led to controls such as cell phone bans in many school districts, include:

- Increasing the "screen time" that is already so prevalent in children's lives.
- Difficulty monitoring children's access to and sharing of inappropriate content.
- Potential for students to become distracted, diminishing educational engagement.
- Growing acceptance of texting slang/abbreviations and concern about the negative effects on children's writing.
- Enablement of cheating via text messaging.
- Possibility that the devices will be used for "cyberbullying."
- Concern, largely speculative, over whether too much cell phone use may negatively affect children's health.
- Data privacy issues, such as concern from schools that assessment and other proprietary data could leak onto children's personal devices. (Shuler, 2009, p. 25)

Unless mobile learning initiatives actively attempt to understand, take into account, and counteract these disadvantages, the devices could potentially do greater harm than good (Shuler, 2009). Some observers have asserted that immersion in mobile technologies can be detrimental to a child's social interactions. They draw a picture of an isolated child, alone in her room, focused solely on her cell phone, or a classroom of children sitting quietly at their desks, heads hunched over individual small screens.

On the contrary, research has shown that, if used properly, mobile technologies have the power to promote and foster collaboration and communication, which are deemed essential for 21st-century success. Hayes Jacobs states that the use of technology should be "strategic and selective," not simply "balanced," but implemented in a careful and thoughtful manner that meets the needs of the learners and works within the specific situations of their learning communities (Hayes Jacobs, 2014).

Technology can enhance learning or the purpose of assuring literacy as a human right. The traditional language and literacy practices described in this book emphasize the importance of human interaction. These ways of interacting include: playing with language; singing together; writing to or with a child; responding to the explanations, requests, or demands embedded in first scribbles; reading books or telling stories together. The new technologies and new literacies center around conversation, and they enhance the practices described in this book. Shuler (Shuler, 2009, p. 20) points out that mobile technologies facilitate what researchers Naismith and colleagues "call 'conversational learning' in that they naturally support an environment where people 'can converse with each other, by interrogating and sharing their descriptions of the world' " (Naismith, Lonsdale, Vavoula, & Sharples, 2004).

Hayes Jacobs also believes that there will always be a role for classic texts and ways of reading that preserve texts from the past and traditional ways of interacting with readers and books (Hayes Jacobs, 2014).

Using technology does not have to be a case of choosing digital vs. human interaction. In 1984 Donald Graves wrote a monograph entitled, "The Enemy is Orthodoxy." In this piece, he warns that orthodoxies can "come from people who try to take shortcuts with very complex processes." He views orthodoxies as "substitutes for thinking" (Graves, 1984, p. 153). In our evolving globalized world, neither an orthodoxy of using only books or only electronic texts will advance literacy as a human right. What is needed at this time is the thoughtful, responsible, and strategic combination of the two.

What is most important is that through whatever means, all readers have access to a wide variety of informational and fictional texts and opportunities to realize the benefits of engaging in them. As Lucia Quiñonez Sumner writes:

> In today's globalized world there are no excuses for failing to provide literacy for our children. In fact there have never been any valid excuses. All human beings have the right to enjoy poetry, legends and stories, not only through oral tradition but through the written form. I dream of a day in which little children all over the world would have the time, the education and safety to read the myriads of literary works of art from around the world. Reading provides stimulation for the mind, extends knowledge and stimulates curiosity, provides escape from tragic situations and is indeed a human right. (Quiñonez Sumner L., 2015)

As social networking and new devices continue to be implemented, ways of interacting with children may change. Studies that could be taken up as technology advances in the 21st century include:

- How children learn language, learn to write, learn to read, and learn to employ and express their ideas through a fusion of new and traditional means
- How technology affects the conditions of learning (Cambourne) so that children are immersed in learning; see demonstrations of how tasks are accomplished; attempt approximations that are acknowledged and given feedback; and engage in learning with other learners who enjoy being with them
- How to preserve the rare words found in books, songs, and spoken stories that go beyond the level of words in everyday conversations
- How to preserve the complexity of language forms found in books
- How to engage learners in inquiry and in-depth study that goes beyond quick searches

NOTES

1 Brief quotes from pp. 95, 112 from REVOLUTION IN LEARNING by MAYA PINES. Copyright ©1967 by Maya Pines. Reprinted by permission of HarperCollins Publishers. Reprinted also by permission of Maya Pines.

[2] From Combining traditional and new literacies in a 21st-century writing workshop by Jennifer M. Bogard and Mary C. McMackin in *The Reading Teacher* vol. 65 Issue 5, pp. 313–323. DOI: 10.1002/TRTR.010048 Copyright © 2012 International Reading Association. Reprinted with permission of John Wiley & Sons Ltd.

[3] From Mulitmodality and Literacy in School Classrooms, by Carey Jewitt, in Review of Research in Education, Vol. 32(1), pp. 241–267. Copyright ©2008 by SAGE Publications. Reprinted by Permission of SAGE Publications.

[4] From Rachel Karchmer-Klein and Valerie Harlow-Shinas in *The Reading Teacher* Vol 65, Issue 5, pp. 288–29.3 DOI.10.1002/TRTR 01044 Copyright © 2012 International Reading Association. Reprinted with permission of John Wiley & Sons Ltd.

[5] From The Juggler's Brain by Nicholas Carr in *Phi Delta Kappan* Volume 92, Number 4, December 2010/January 2011. Usage determined by Phi Delta Kappan.

CHAPTER 14

TOWARD THE REALIZATION OF LITERACY AS A HUMAN RIGHT

Where, after all, do universal human rights begin? In small places, close to home. —Eleanor Roosevelt (Roosevelt, Speech to UN on Tenth Anniversary of the Adoption of the Universal Declaration of Human Rights, 1958a)

SPRINGFIELD TODAY

Returning to my small place, Springfield, today we see that people there are taking the future into their own hands and are mobilizing to write the next chapter for their literate community. Irene Sege, Director of communications for Boston-based Strategies for Children, reports the progress of the Springfield initiative. She describes a groundbreaking 2010 memorandum of understanding between the school system and the state's Department of Early Education and Care. This memorandum that aims at aligning community-based early learning programs with the public schools has led to regular collaboration and joint professional development. Sege also states that the Hampden County Regional Employment Board is helping early educators pursue college degrees and other credentials (Sege, 2012).

Sege reports on other steps that are being taken in Springfield. Promising place-based programs for children (birth to 9) and their families have been established in two public- housing developments. Springfield is one of six school districts in the country to receive a Closing the Achievement Gap grant from the NEA Foundation and is using part of its \$1.2 million award to expand an elementary school home-visiting program. Local English- and Spanish-language media run literacy tips for parents. Springfield is the nation's largest Reach Out and Read "bookend" city, enlisting all pediatric providers to give books to children, age 6 months to 5 years, and to talk to parents about the importance of reading aloud. The Hasbro Summer Learning Initiative (HSLI) provides rich literacy-based curriculum programs for children during the summer months (Sege, Early childhood education: Springfield tackles a benchmark, 2012). The Irene E. and George A. Davis Foundation supports these efforts.

After advocating for preschool for many years, Springfield has now acquired a four-year federal Preschool Development Grant: Expansion Grant that will allow public and private early childhood educators to develop a program for 350 children – from infants to preschoolers. The grants are being provided to high-need communities. Springfield's allocation will be \$3.56 million in the first year, giving preschool access to 195 four-year olds. The public schools, Head Start, and private providers will be involved in the effort. The Davis Foundation is also supporting this project (Robbins, 2014).

In the summer of 2014, students participating in the Hasbro Summer Learning Initiative (HSLI) were assessed on a variety of reading competencies before and after their participation in the program. Various analyses of the data indicate that a substantial number of student participants, approximately 80% assessed, either maintained their reading proficiency levels over the summer program or actually demonstrated improvements in oral or silent reading comprehension. HSLI serves over 25 community based or school sites. At no site was there a statistically significant loss of achievement among the group of readers who were assessed. At two particular sites significant gains were found. Based on the evaluation of the data, it was concluded that the HSLI program is successful and effective in ameliorating summer reading loss (Rasinski, 2014).

According to Jean M. Canosa Albano (Canosa Albano, 2015), Manager of Public Services for the Springfield City Library (SCL), for several decades, the SCL has sponsored a Summer Reading Club that offers the opportunity for local children to read during the summer months. The SCL has now partnered with the Hasbro Summer Learning Initiative (HSLI) so that children who attend summer programs can obtain library cards and become reading club members. As members, children are expected to read for a minimum of 20 minutes per day and report the amount of reading they do to the library during the summer. There is also a "read to me" component of the club for those children who are not yet reading on their own. As they progress, children are given books that they can keep. On a designated day each week, HSLI programs visit the branch library in their neighborhood. During the visit, children report their progress to the librarian, select new books, and participate in a literacy-related craft, or other, activity. Before the end of the visit, librarians provide incentive for the children to attend the give next visit by giving a preview of coming events. Additionally, the City of Springfield expanded branch library hours from 18.5 to 30 hours per week, making it possible for more people to access library services. The combined efforts of the city, the library, and HSLI have led to success. This summer membership in the SCL Summer Reading Club rose from approximately 550 members to 948 members, an increase of 72%!

Furthermore, Superintendent, Daniel Warwick of the Springfield Public Schools has visited Puerto Rico to learn about the home and culture of many Springfield students. Currently, sixty-one percent of the students in Springfield are Latino. While in Puerto Rico, Warwick met with school leaders and other local officials. His visit followed a cultural exchange with the Puerto Rican Philharmonic Orchestra that came to Springfield and performed at Symphony Hall for Springfield school children and their families (Roman, 2013).

Warwick's visit and the performance are important because they show that Springfield is committed to acknowledging and honoring the culture and heritage of its students. Earlier in this book, we saw teachers who were learning about the home lives of the children that they teach. When administrators engage in this kind of learning, teachers and others in the community receive a powerful message about the importance of valuing children, their language, culture, memories, and lives.

> School attendance in Springfield is currently at its highest rate, 92.8 percent, as compared to an average rate of 91.8 percent a year ago. The superintendent views attendance as a key factor in pushing for stronger graduation rates and academic performance. (Goonan, 2014)

Additionally, the Springfield Parent Academy, a community-driven initiative, has been designed to provide educational resources to help parents and caring adults become engaged in their child's education. The Academy offers families free educational opportunities that help students succeed and to help parents attain their personal and professional goals. By presenting a variety of workshops, one-day seminars, and courses, the Academy addresses issues that parents and families have identified as being important to them.

Springfield, my small place, is an example of a community in which citizens are working together to acknowledge and build upon children's culture, language, literacy, experiences, and memories. When many people in a community begin to view children from a position of strength rather than a position of deficit, good things happen. Springfield is taking the right steps in that direction.

HOPE FOR THE REALIZATION OF LITERACY AS A HUMAN RIGHT

Throughout this book, I've attempted to follow the example of Eleanor Roosevelt and Paulo Freire. The ideas presented here support literacy as a human right in small places around the world. I have worked to try to dispel the myth that children who are economically poor do not have language. I have argued that language and literacy begin at birth, and the learning that first occurs within a child's home needs to be honored as the basis of all future learning. It is my belief that the language and literacy capabilities of all children need to be acknowledged and built upon. I have also linked the work of literacy theorists and innovators to current brain research.

In order to build upon children's understandings, there is a need to undertake extensive study and become a world of learners. In this world of learners, knowing not only what should be done, but why we do specific things will lead to the realization of literacy as a human right.

The steps suggested here to help young children develop language and literacy are simple, timeless, and inexpensive. They require engagement on the part of adults and children. They include talking, singing, storytelling, reading, writing, language play, and the possibilities of new technologies. Parents, caregivers, and other members of a child's community can support young learners by understanding the ways in which they interact with and use print. They can use technology to advance collaboration and literacy learning. Parents and others can also use technology to document the language and literacy capabilities of young children and share that information with others to advocate for children outside the home. When they do these things, they will be advocating for literacy as a human right.

Policy makers need to undertake deep study as well. They should not be lured by the promise of quick fixes. These solutions usually draw upon banking education practices that keep the pedagogy of poverty entrenched. Instead, leaders should explore and implement rich practices, such as the Concentrated Language Encounter and Breakthrough to Literacy. These practices support the right to literacy for both children and adults within a community. They also advance the language and literacy development of children and adults learning their first language or additional languages.

I continue to work in small places to help support the language, literacy, and human rights of the children they serve. In the spirit of Eleanor Roosevelt and the framers of the Universal Declaration of Human Rights, I see this book as a "milestone in a long and difficult journey." Like them, I do not believe that I have uncovered the "whole truth" or that this book states the "last word." I hope that this book furthers the "quest" of the realization of literacy as a human right and that the "experiences gained in implementing" the ideas of this book will bring about a "deeper understanding in the future" (Glendon, 2001, p. 231).

In the words of Alfred Bandura, I believe:

> As a society, we enjoy the benefits left by those before us who collectively fought inhumanities and worked for social reforms that permit a better life. Our own collective efficacy will, in turn, shape how future generations will live their lives. The times call for social initiatives that build people's sense of collective efficacy to influence conditions that shape their lives and the lives of future generations. (Bandura, 1998, p. 69)

I believe that this book can help make it possible for people across the world to "cross the bridge that enables the disinherited to gain their dignity and true image," as envisioned by Reverend Prince Wreh (Wreh, 2011) of Monrovia, Liberia, or to set their feet on the first step of the "escalator" that lifts them up from poverty, as envisioned by New York Times columnist Nicholas Kristof (Kristof, 2011). When those things happen, "sufficient numbers of men and women in 'small places close to home' can imagine and, then begin to live, the reality of freedom, solidarity, and peace" (Glendon, 2001, p. 241)—and we will all live in a more compassionate world. I trust, as Eleanor Roosevelt did, that hope for that vision is "in the air" (Roosevelt, 1958b, p. 73).

A Last View from a Small Place

> From Boston to Beijing, parents are discussing what their children learn from the time of birth until the time they go to school. They share this information with others through social media and other platforms. At small gatherings in

Sao Paulo, Malawi, and on Thursday Island, teachers discuss child's brain development and growth in language and literacy. At homes in Liberia and in early childhood centers in Nepal, children's own words are being honored as their first reading material. Policy makers in Washington are questioning the findings of broad-stroke research studies, and they are seeking to understand the ways in which people within the small places in their communities tell and scribe the stories of their lives. A mother in the south Sudan downloads information on a mobile phone that has been charged with a solar battery. She shares the information with her daughters. Children in after-school and summer programs in Springfield relax and read together. Parents sit in parks in Moscow, Madrid, and New York and share papers stored in manila envelopes. On these papers are shopping lists, stories, notes, and drawings by children that show their growth in literacy. Fathers in Austin, Seoul, and Queensland send images of children's written language to grandparents over mobile devices. The parents will share these images at school screenings at the time of enrollment as evidence of a child's strengths. Children across the world sing in churches and schools, and their songs are heard as valuable ways of expressing language. Every child's language and literacy is viewed from a perspective of strength rather than deficit. People in small places across the world view literacy as a human right. The conversation is continuing. A global literacy community dedicated to the realization of literacy as a human right is coming into being.

Jo-Anne Wilson-Keenan, Ed.D.
East Dennis, Massachusetts
June 2, 2015

APPENDICES

Universal Declaration of Human Rights

PREAMBLE

Whereas recognition of the inherent dignity and of the equal and inalienable rights of all members of the human family is the foundation of freedom, justice and peace in the world,

Whereas disregard and contempt for human rights have resulted in barbarous acts which have outraged the conscience of mankind, and the advent of a world in which human beings shall enjoy freedom of speech and belief and freedom from fear and want has been proclaimed as the highest aspiration of the common people,

Whereas it is essential, if man is not to be compelled to have recourse, as a lastresort, to rebellion against tyranny and oppression, that human rights should be protected by the rule of law,

Whereas it is essential to promote the development of friendly relations between nations,

Whereas the peoples of the United Nations have in the Charter reaffirmed their faith in fundamental human rights, in the dignity and worth of the human person and in the equal rights of men and women and have determined to promote social progress and better standards of life in larger freedom,

Whereas Member States have pledged themselves to achieve, in cooperation with the United Nations, the promotion of universal respect for and observance of human rights and fundamental freedoms,

Whereas a common understanding of these rights and freedoms is of the greatest importance for the full realization of this pledge,

Now, therefore,

The General Assembly
Proclaims this Universal Declaration of Human Rights as a common standard of achievement for all peoples and all nations, to the end that every individual and every organ of society, keeping this Declaration constantly in mind, shall strive by teaching and education to promote respect for these rights and freedoms and by progressive measures, national and international, to secure their universal and effective recognition and observance, both among the peoples of Member States themselves and among the peoples of territories under their jurisdiction.

Article 1

All human beings are born free and equal in dignity and rights. They are endowed with reason and conscience and should act towards one another in a spirit of brotherhood.

Article 2

Everyone is entitled to all the rights and freedoms set forth in this Declaration, without distinction of any kind, such as race, colour, sex, language, religion, political or other opinion, national or social origin, property, birth or other status.

Furthermore, no distinction shall be made on the basis of the political, jurisdictional or international status of the country or territory to which a person belongs, whether it be independent, trust, non-self-governing or under any other limitation of sovereignty.

Article 3

Everyone has the right to life, liberty and security of person.

Article 4

No one shall be held in slavery or servitude; slavery and the slave trade shall be prohibited in all their forms.

Article 5

No one shall be subjected to torture or to cruel, inhuman or degrading treatment or punishment.

Article 6

Everyone has the right to recognition everywhere as a person before the law.

Article 7

All are equal before the law and are entitled without any discrimination to equal protection of the law. All are entitled to equal protection against any discrimination in violation of this Declaration and against any incitement to such discrimination.

Article 8

Everyone has the right to an effective remedy by the competent national tribunals for acts violating the fundamental rights granted him by the constitution or by law.

Article 9

No one shall be subjected to arbitrary arrest, detention or exile.

Article 10

Everyone is entitled in full equality to a fair and public hearing by an independent and impartial tribunal, in the determination of his rights and obligations and of any criminal charge against him.

Article 11

1. Everyone charged with a penal offence has the right to be presumed innocent until proved guilty according to law in a public trial at which he has had all the guarantees necessary for his defence.
2. No one shall be held guilty of any penal offence on account of any act or omission which did not constitute a penal offence, under national or international law, at the time when it was committed. Nor shall a heavier penalty be imposed than the one that was applicable at the time the penal offence was committed.

Article 12

No one shall be subjected to arbitrary interference with his privacy, family, home or correspondence, nor to attacks upon his honour and reputation. Everyone has the right to the protection of the law against such interference or attacks.

Article 13

1. Everyone has the right to freedom of movement and residence within the borders of each State.
2. Everyone has the right to leave any country, including his own, and to return to his country.

Article 14

1. Everyone has the right to seek and to enjoy in other countries asylum from persecution.
2. This right may not be invoked in the case of prosecutions genuinely arising from non-political crimes or from acts contrary to the purposes and principles of the United Nations.

Article 15

1. Everyone has the right to a nationality.
2. No one shall be arbitrarily deprived of his nationality nor denied the right to change his nationality.

Article 16

1. Men and women of full age, without any limitation due to race, nationality or religion, have the right to marry and to found a family. They are entitled to equal rights as to marriage, during marriage and at its dissolution.
2. Marriage shall be entered into only with the free and full consent of the intending spouses.
3. The family is the natural and fundamental group unit of society and is entitled to protection by society and the State.

Article 17

1. Everyone has the right to own property alone as well as in association with others.
2. No one shall be arbitrarily deprived of his property.

Article 18

Everyone has the right to freedom of thought, conscience and religion; this right includes freedom to change his religion or belief, and freedom, either alone or in community with others and in public or private, to manifest his religion or belief in teaching, practice, worship and observance.

Article 19

Everyone has the right to freedom of opinion and expression; this right includes freedom to hold opinions without interference and to seek, receive and impart information and ideas through any media and regardless of frontiers.

Article 20

1. Everyone has the right to freedom of peaceful assembly and association.
2. No one may be compelled to belong to an association.

Article 21

1. Everyone has the right to take part in the government of his country, directly or through freely chosen representatives.
2. Everyone has the right to equal access to public service in his country.
3. The will of the people shall be the basis of the authority of government; this will shall be expressed in periodic and genuine elections which shall be by universal and equal suffrage and shall be held by secret vote or by equivalent free voting procedures.

Article 22

Everyone, as a member of society, has the right to social security and is entitled to realization, through national effort and international co-operation and in accordance with the organization and resources of each State, of the economic, social and cultural rights indispensable for his dignity and the free development of his personality.

Article 23

1. Everyone has the right to work, to free choice of employment, to just and favourable conditions of work and to protection against unemployment.
2. Everyone, without any discrimination, has the right to equal pay for equal work.
3. Everyone who works has the right to just and favourable remuneration ensuring for himself and his family an existence worthy of human dignity, and supplemented, if necessary, by other means of social protection.
4. Everyone has the right to form and to join trade unions for the protection of his interests.

Article 24

Everyone has the right to rest and leisure, including reasonable limitation of working hours and periodic holidays with pay.

Article 25

1. Everyone has the right to a standard of living adequate for the health and well-being of himself and of his family, including food, clothing, housing and medical care and necessary social services, and the right to security in the event of unemployment, sickness, disability, widowhood, old age or other lack of livelihood in circumstances beyond his control.
2. Motherhood and childhood are entitled to special care and assistance. All children, whether born in or out of wedlock, shall enjoy the same social protection.

Article 26

1. Everyone has the right to education. Education shall be free, at least in the elementary and fundamental stages. Elementary education shall be compulsory. Technical and professional education shall be made generally available and higher education shall be equally accessible to all on the basis of merit.
2. Education shall be directed to the full development of the human personality and to the strengthening of respect for human rights and fundamental freedoms. It shall promote understanding, tolerance and friendship among all nations, racial

or religious groups, and shall further the activities of the United Nations for the maintenance of peace.
3. Parents have a prior right to choose the kind of education that shall be given to their children.

Article 27

1. Everyone has the right freely to participate in the cultural life of the community, to enjoy the arts and to share in scientific advancement and its benefits.
2. Everyone has the right to the protection of the moral and material interests resulting from any scientific, literary or artistic production of which he is the author.

Article 28

Everyone is entitled to a social and international order in which the rights and freedoms set forth in this Declaration can be fully realized.

Article 29

1. Everyone has duties to the community in which alone the free and full development of his personality is possible.
2. In the exercise of his rights and freedoms, everyone shall be subject only to such limitations as are determined by law solely for the purpose of securing due recognition and respect for the rights and freedoms of others and of meeting the just requirements of morality, public order and the general welfare in a democratic society.
3. These rights and freedoms may in no case be exercised contrary to the purposes and principles of the United Nations.

Article 30

Nothing in this Declaration may be interpreted as implying for any State, group or person any right to engage in any activity or to perform any act aimed at the destruction of any of the rights and freedoms set forth herein.

INTERNATIONAL SYMPOSIUM FOR LITERACY

Persepolis
3-8 September 1975
Declaration of Persepolis

The number of illiterates is constantly growing.

This reflects the failure of development policies that are indifferent to man and to the satisfaction of his basic needs.

In spite of the progress made in some countries as a result of far-reaching social changes, there are close to one thousand million illiterates in the world, and many more under-nourished people.

In many cases, moreover, even people who have become literate have not yet acquired to a sufficient degree the means of becoming aware of the problems of the societies in which they live and of their own problems, nor the means of solving them or of playing a real part in their solution.

There is even a tendency to a decline in literacy in the industrialized countries.

Successes were achieved when literacy was linked to meeting man's fundamental requirements, ranging from his immediate vital needs to effective participation in social change.

Successes were achieved when literacy programmes were not restricted to learning the skills of reading, writing and arithmetic, and when they did not subordinate literacy to the short-term needs of growth unconcerned with man.

Tribute should be paid to those mass campaigns that have already brought about the complete or almost complete eradication of illiteracy in certain countries and to regional or more limited experiments, which have helped to prepare innovative methods with regard to the programming, means and organization of literacy activities linked to development aims. These experiments, and in particular functional literacy pro-programmes and projects, have made a valuable contribution to the common stock of practical methods in the field of literacy and basic education. Greater use should be made of them in future efforts.

The International Symposium for Literacy meeting in Persepolis from 3-8 September 1975, in unanimously adopting this Declaration, considered literacy to be not just the process of learning the skills of reading, writing and arithmetic, but a contribution to the liberation of man and to his full development. Thus conceived, literacy creates the conditions for the acquisition of a critical consciousness of the contradictions of society in which man lives and of its aims; it also stimulates initiative and his participation in the creation of projects capable of acting upon the world, of transforming it, and of defining the aims of an authentic human development. It should open the way to a mastery of techniques and human relations. Literacy is not an end in itself. It is a fundamental human right.

It is true that all social structures give rise to the type of education which can maintain and reproduce them, and that the purposes of education are subordinated to the purposes of the dominant groups; but it would be incorrect to conclude that there is nothing to be done within the existing system.

Literacy, like education in general, is not the driving force of historical change. It is not the only means of liberation, but it is an essential instrument for all social change.

Literacy work, like education in general, is a political act. It is not neutral, for the act of revealing social reality in order to transform it, or of concealing it in order to preserve it, is political.

Consequently, there are economic, social, political and administrative structures that favor the accomplishment of literacy projects, others that hinder them.
The most favourable structures would be:

- Those that, from the political point of view, tend to bring about the effective participation of every citizen in decision-making at all levels of social life: in economics, politics and culture.
- Those that, from the economic point of view, aim at an endogenous and harmonious development of society, and not at blind and dependent growth.
- Those that, from the social point of view, do not result in making education a class privilege and a means of reproducing established hierarchies and orders .
- Those that, from the professional point of view, provide communities with genuine control over the technologies they wish to use.
- Those that, from the institutional point of view, favour a concerted approach and permanent co-operation among the authorities responsible for basic services (agriculture, welfare, health, family planning, etc.).

Experience has shown that literacy can bring about the alienation of the individual by integrating him in an order established without his consent. It can integrate him, without his participation, in a foreign development model or, on the contrary, help to expand his critical awareness and creative imagination, thereby enabling every man to participate, as a responsible agent, in all the decisions affecting his destiny.

The success of literacy efforts is closely connected with national political will.

Ways exist of attaining the objectives which result from the definition of literacy on which the Symposium based its work.

The ways and means of literacy activities should be founded on the specific characteristics of the environment, personality and identity of each people. True education must be rooted in the culture and civilization of each people, aware of its unique contribution to universal culture and open to a fertile dialogue with other civilizations.

Literacy is effective to the extent that the people to whom it is addressed, in particular women and the least privileged groups (such as migrant workers), feel the need for it in order to meet their most essential requirements, in particular the need to take part in the decisions of the community to which they belong.

Literacy is therefore inseparable from participation, which is at once its purpose and its condition. The illiterate should not be the object but the subject of the process whereby he becomes literate. A far-reaching mobilization of human resources implies the commitment of literacy students and teachers alike. The latter should not form a specialized and permanent professional body, but should be recruited as close as possible to the masses undergoing literacy training and should belong to the same or to a related social and professional group in order to make dialogue easier.

The effectiveness of this mobilization will be increased if greater respect is paid to the initiative of the populations concerned and to consultation with them, instead of abiding by bureaucratic decisions imposed from outside and above. The motivation of those involved will be stronger if each community is itself given the opportunity of carrying out the literacy project.

The methods and material means should be diversified, flexible and suited to the environment and needs of the new literates, as opposed to a uniform and rigid model.

Literacy work of this kind would constitute the first stage of basic education designed to bring about the individual development of men and women through continuing training and to improve the environment as a whole. It would permit the development of non-formal education for the benefit of all those who are excluded by the present system or are unable to take advantage of it. Finally, it will imply a radical reform of the structures of the education system as a whole.

The importance of audio-visual aids for literacy was fully recognized. However, attempts to take over these aids on grounds of technical necessity by economic or political forces beyond the control of the peoples concerned, and their use as instruments of cultural colonization, should be rejected. Uses of audio-visual aids that would hinder active participation and human dialogue should be banned. Programmes should be drawn up in consultation with those concerned, through an exchange of information on significant experiences.

Literacy work should encourage the participants to acquire a wide range of communication skills.

The accomplishment of these tasks calls for a priority claim on national and local financial and human resources. In certain situations, the appeal of countries for complementary international financial cooperation supplied, *inter alia,* by international and regional institutions, may be justified in the light of special needs, particularly with regard to equipment and to the training of personnel. The use of complicated equipment which the recipient community could not fully control should not be encouraged, and such assistance should under no circumstances be allowed to influence national policies.

Literacy work is of world-wide concern, requiring that ideological, geographical and economic distinctions be transcended .

While its primary field of operation is in the Third World, the new international order gives it a universal dimension, through which the concrete solidarity of nations and the common destiny of man must find expression.

EDUCATION FOR ALL (EFA)

OVERVIEW

Education is a right, like the right to have proper food or a roof over your head. Article 26 of the 1948 Universal Declaration of Human Rights states that "everyone has the right to education". Education is not only a right but a passport to human development. It opens doors and expands opportunities and freedoms. It contributes to fostering peace, democracy and economic growth as well as improving health and reducing poverty. The ultimate aim of Education for All (EFA) is sustainable development.

In the year 2000, the world's governments adopted the six EFA goals and the eight Millennium Development Goals (MDGs), the two most important frameworks in the field of education. The education priorities of the United Nations Educational, Scientific and Cultural Organization (UNESCO) are shaped by these objectives (United Nations, 2015).

The two sets of goals are an ambitious roadmap for the global community to follow. They offer a long-term vision of reduced poverty and hunger, better health and education, sustainable lifestyles, strong partnerships and shared commitments.

The EFA goals and MDGs are complementary: as Irina Bokova, UNESCO's Director-General, says: "When you fund education, you are securing progress towards all the Millennium Development Goals."

EDUCATION FOR ALL GOALS

- Goal 1: Expand early childhood care and education
- Goal 2: Provide free and compulsory primary education for all
- Goal 3: Promote learning and life skills for young people and adults
- Goal 4: Increase adult literacy
- Goal 5: Achieve gender parity
- Goal 6: Improve the quality of education

THE DAKAR FRAMEWORK FOR ACTION GOALS AND STRATEGIES

The Dakar Framework for Action
Education for All:
Making Our Collective Commitments
Text adopted by
the World Education Forum
Dakar, Senegal, 26-28 April 2000

1. Meeting in Dakar, Senegal, in April 2000, we the participants in the World Education Forum, commit ourselves to the achievement of education for all (EFA) goals and targets for every citizen and for every society.
2. The Dakar Framework is a collective commitment to action, Governments have an obligation to ensure that EFA goals and targets are reached and sustained, This is a responsibility that will be met most effectively through broad-based partnerships within countries, supported by the cooperation with regional and international agencies and institutions.
3. We re-affirm the vision of the World Declaration on Education for All (Jomtien, 1990), supported by the Universal Declaration of Human Rights and the Convention on Rights of the Child, that all children, young people and adults have the human right to benefit from an education that will meet their basic learning needs in the best and fullest sense of the term, an education that includes learning to know, to do, to live together and to be. It is an education geared to tapping each individual's talents and potential, and developing learners' personalities, so that they can improve their lives and transform their societies.
4. We welcome the commitments made by the international community to basic education throughout the 1990's, notably at the World Summit for Children (1990), the Conference on Environment and Development (1992), the World Conference on Human Rights (1993), the World Conference on Special Needs Education: Access and Quality (1994), The International Conference on Population and Development (1994), the World Summit for Social Development (1995), the Fourth World Conference on Women (1995), the Mid-Term Meeting of the International Consultative Forum on Education for All (1996), the Fifth International Conference on Adult Education (1997), and the International Conference on Child Labour (1997). The challenge now is to deliver on these commitments.
5. The EFA 2000 Assessment demonstrates that there has been significant progress in many countries. But it is unacceptable in the year 2000 that more that 113 million children have no access to primary education, that 880 million adults are

illiterate, gender discrimination continues to permeate education systems, and the quality of learning and acquisition of human values and skills fall far short of the aspirations and needs of individuals and societies. Youth and adults are denied access to the skill and knowledge necessary for gainful employment and full participation in their societies. Without accelerated progress towards education for all, national and internationally agreed targets for poverty reduction will be missed, and inequalities between countries and societies will widen.

6. Education is a fundamental human right. It is the key to sustainable development and peace and stability within and among countries, and thus an indispensible means for effective participation in the societies and economies of the twenty-first century, which are affected by rapid globalization. Achieving EFA goals should be postponed no longer. The basic learning needs of all can and must be met as a matter of urgency.
7. We hereby collectively commit ourselves to the attainment of the following goals:
   (i) expanding and improving comprehensive early childhood care and education, especially for the most vulnerable and disadvantaged children;
   (ii) ensuring that by 2015 all children, particularly girls, children in difficult circumstances and those belonging to ethnic minorities, have access to and complete free and compulsory primary education of good quality;
   (iii) ensuring that the learning needs of all young people and adults are met through equitable access to appropriate learning and life skills programmes;
   (iv) achieving a 50 per cent improvement in levels of adult literacy by 2015, especially for women and equitable access to basic and continuing education for all adults;
   (v) eliminating gender disparities in primary and secondary education by 2005, and achieving gender equality in education by 2015, with a focus on ensuring girls' full access to and achievement in basic education of good quality;
   (vi) improving all aspects of the quality of education and ensuring excellence of all so that recognized and measurable learning outcomes are achieved by all, especially in literacy, numeracy, and essential life skills.
8. To achieve these goals, we the governments, organizations, agencies, groups and associations represented at the World Education Forum pledge ourselves to:
   (i) mobilize strong national and international political commitment for education for all, develop national action plans and enhance significantly investment in basic education;
   (ii) promote EFA policies within a sustainable and well-integrated sector framework clearly and linked to poverty elimination and development strategies;
   (iii) ensure the engagement and participation of civil society in the formulation, implementation and monitoring of strategies for educational development;
   (iv) develop responsive, participatory and accountable systems of educational governance and management;

(v) meet the needs of education systems affected by conflict, national calamites and instability and conduct educational programmes in ways that promote mutual understanding, peace and tolerance, and help prevent violence and conflict;

(vi) implement integrated strategies for gender equality in education which recognize the need for changes in attitudes, values and practices;

(vii) implement as a matter of urgency education programmes and actions to combat the HIV/AIDS pandemic;

(viii) create safe, healthy, inclusive and equitably resourced educational environments conducive to excellence in learning with clearly defined levels of achievement for all;

(ix) enhance the status, morale and professionalism for teachers;

(x) harness new information and communication technologies to help achieve EFA goals;

(xi) systematically monitor progress towards EFA goals and strategies at the national, regional and international levels; and

(xii) build on existing mechanisms to accelerate the progress of education for all.

THE MILLENNIUM DEVELOPMENT GOALS

In September of the year 2000, leaders of 189 countries met at the United Nations in New York and endorsed the Millennium Declaration, a commitment to work together to build a safer, more prosperous and equitable world. The Declaration was translated into a roadmap setting out eight time-bound and measurable goals to be reached **by 2015**, known as the Millennium Development Goals, namely:

1. Eradicate extreme poverty and hunger
   - Reduce by half the proportion of people whose income is less than $1 a day
   - Achieve full and productive employment and decent work for all, including women and young people
   - Reduce by half the proportion of people who suffer from hunger
2. Achieve universal primary education
   - Ensure that all boys and girls complete a full course of primary schooling
3. Promote gender equality and empower women
   - Eliminate gender disparity in primary and secondary education preferably by 2005, and in all levels of education no later than 2015
4. Reduce child mortality
   - Reduce by two thirds the mortality of children under five
5. Improve maternal health
   - Reduce maternal mortality by three quarters
   - Achieve universal access to reproductive health
6. Combat HIV/AIDS, malaria and other diseases
   - Halt and reverse the spread of HIV/AIDS
   - Achieve, by 2010, universal access to treatment for HIV/AIDS for all those who need it
   - Halt and reverse the incidence of malaria and other major diseases
7. Ensure environmental sustainability
   - Integrate principles of sustainable development into country policies and programmes;
   - reverse the loss of environmental resources
   - Reduce biodiversity loss, achieving, by 2010, a significant reduction in the rate of loss

- Halve the proportion of people without access to safe drinking water and basic sanitation
- Improve the lives of at least 100 million slum dwellers by 2020

8. Develop a global partnership for development

- Develop further an open, rule-based, predictable, non-discriminatory trading and financial system
- Address special needs of the least developed countries, landlocked countries and small island developing States
- Deal comprehensively with developing countries' debt
- In cooperation with pharmaceutical companies, provide access to affordable essential drugs in
- developing countries
- In cooperation with the private sector, make available the benefits of new technologies, especially information and communications technologies

BIBLIOGRAPHY

2012 Common Core Standards Committee. (n.d.). *English Language Arts Standards*. Retrieved March 21, 2013, from Common Core State Standards Initiative http://corestandards.org/ELA-Literacy/RF/introduction

Aderinoye, R., Ojokheta, K., & Olojede, A. (2007). Integrating mobile learning into nomadic education programmes in Nigeria: Issues and perspectives. *International Review of Research in Open and Distance Learning, 8*(2), 1–17. Retrieved from http://www.irrodl.org/index.php/irrodl/article/view/347/928

Alexander, F. (2010, June/July). *Deep reading often gets short shrift: International reading association*. Retrieved June 7, 2011, from http://www.reading.org/General/Publications/ReadingToday/RTy_June_2010/RTy_10Jun_summer_slide.aspx

Alexander, P. A. (2005). The path to competence: A lifespan developmental perspecitve on reading. *Journal of Literacy Research, 37*(4), 413–436.

Alexander, P., Schallert, D., & Hare, V. (1991). Coming to terms: How researchers in learning and literacy talk about knowledge. *Journal of Literacy Research, 61*(3), 315–343.

Alexander, P., Jetton, T., & Kulikowich, J. (1995). Interrelationship of knowledge, interest, and recall: Assessing a model of domain learning. *Journal of Educational Psychology, 87*(4), 559–575.

Allen, H. E. (2009). *Concentrated language encounter: Instruction guide*. Port Elizabeth, South Africa: GM South Africa Foundation.

Amnesty International Publications. (2012). *Convention on the rights of the child*. Retrieved February 6, 2012, from http://www.amnestyusa.org

Anderson, A., & Stokes, S. (1984). Social and institutional influences on the development and practices of literacy. In H. O. Goelman (Ed.), *Awakening to literacy* (pp. 24–37). Exeter, NH: Heinemann.

Anderson, B. (1998). Developmental skills for ages 9–12 months. *Thera Notes*. Retrieved March 26, 2012, from http://www.pearsonassessments.com/hai/Images/resource/techrpts/TheraNotes/TN_EI_pdf_/Ages9_12Mos.pdf

Annenberg Institute for School Reform. (1998). *Reasons for hope, voices for change: A report of the Annenberg instituite on public engagement for public education*. Providence, Rhode Island: Annenberg Instituite for School Reform.

Anyon, J. (1981). Elementary schooling and distinctions of social class. *Interchange on Educational Policy, 12*(2–3), 118–132.

Anzuldúa, G. (2007). *Borderlands / La Frontera: The new mestiza* (3rd ed.). San Francisco, CA: Aunt Lute Books.

Arnold, D., & Whitehurst, G. (1994). Accelerating language development through picture book reading. A summary of dialogic reading and its effect. In D. K. Dickinson (Ed.), *Bridges to literacy: Approaches to supporting child and family literacy* (pp. 103–128). Cambridge, MA: Blackwell.

Ashton-Warner, S. (1963). *Teacher*. New York, NY: Simon and Schuster.

Au, K., Carroll, J., & Scheu, J. (2001). *Balanced literacy instruction*. Norwood, MA: Christopher-Gordon.

Bailey, D. (2002). Are critical periods critical? The role of timing in early childhood pedagogy. *Early Childhood Researach Quarterly, 17*, 281–294.

Bailey, P. (1998, December). The creation of the Universal Declaration of Human Rights. *Universal rights network*. Retrieved February 5, 2012, from http://www.universalrights.net/main/creation.htm

Bandura, A. (1998). Personal and collective efficacy in human adaptation and change. In J. G. Adair, D. Belanger, & K. L. Dion (Eds.), *Advances in psychological science: Personal, social and cultural aspects* (Vol. 1, pp. 51–71). Hove, UK: Psychology Press.

Barnhart, J. E., & Sulzby, E. (1986). *How Johnny can write: Kindergarten children's uses of emergent writing systems*. Chicago, Illinois, USA: American Educational Research Association.

Barron, M. (1990). *I laen to raed and wrt the wa I laen to tak*. Katonah, NY: Richard C. Owen.

Barton, P. (2004). Why does the gap persist? *Educational Leadership, 62*(3), 8–13.

Bassetti, B. (2008, October 7). *Learning second language writing systems: Centre for Languages, Linguistics and Area Studies (LLAS)*. Retrieved February 24, 2014, from https://www.llas.ac.uk//resources/gpg/2662

Beck, I. L., McKeown, M. G., & Kucan, L. (2008). *Creating robust vocabulary: Frequently asked questions and extended examples*. New York, NY: Guilford Press.

Bergen, D., & Coscia, J. (2001). *Brain research and childhood education: Implications for educators*. Olney, Maryland: Association for Childhood Education International.

Berk, L. (2006). *Child development* (7th ed.). New York, NY: Pearson.

Berk, L. (2012). *Infants, children, adolescents*. Boston, MA: Pearson, Allyn & Bacon.

Bernard, S. (2010, December 1). Neuroplasticity: Learning physically changes the brain. *Edutopia*. Retrieved February 17, 2013, from http://www.edutopia.org/neuroscience-brain-based-learning-neuroplasticity

Berninger, V. W., & Winn, W. D. (2006). Implications of advancements in brain research and technology for writing development, writing instruction, and educational evolution. In C. A. MacArthur, S. Graham, & J. Fitzgerald (Eds.), *Handbook of writing research* (pp. 96–114). New York, NY: Guilford Press.

Bezemer, J., & Kress, G. (2008). Writing in multimodal texts: A social semiotic account of designs for learning. *Written Communication, 25*(2), 166–195. doi: 0.1177/0741088307313177

Bissex, G. (1980). *Gyns at wrk: A child learns to read and write*. Cambridge, MA: Harvard University Press.

Black, A. (1999). *Courage in a dangerous world*. New York, NY: Columbia University Press.

Black, A. (2007). *The Eleanor Roosevelt papers: The human rights years* (Vol. 1). Detroit, Canada: Thomson Gale.

Bloome, D., Carter, S., Christian, B., Otto, S., & Shuart-Farris, N. (2005). *Discourse analysis and the study of classroom language and literacy events: A microethnographic perspective*. Mahwah, NJ: Erlbaum.

Bogard, J., & McMackin, M. (2012). Combining traditional and new literacies in a 21st century writing workshop. *Reading Teacher, 65*(5), 313–323.

Booth, S. (2005, September). *Developing children's emergent literacy*. Auckland, New Zealand: University of Auckland Faculty of Education. Retrieved February 11, 2012, from http://www.education.auckland.ac.nz/uoa/ace-issue16

Brittain, W. (1979). *Creativity, art, and the young child*. New York, NY: Macmillan Publishing Company.

Britton, J. (1973). *Language and learning*. Harmondsworth, England: Pelican Books.

Brock, C., McMillon, G., Pennington, J., Townsend, D., & Lapp, D. (2009). Academic English and African American Vernacular English: Exploring possibilities for promoting literacy learning in all children. In L.M. Morrow, R. Rueda, & D. Lapp (Eds.), *Handbook of research on literacy instruction: Issues of diversity, policy, and equity* (pp. 137–157). New York, NY: Guilford.

Brown, J., Collins, A., & Duguid, P. (1989). Situated cognition and the culture of learning. *Educational Researcher, 18*(1), 32–42.

Bruner, J. (1983). *Children's talk: Learning to use language*. New York, NY: Norton.

Bruner, J. (1984). Language, mind, and reading. In H. Goelman, A. Oberg, & F. Smith (Eds.), *Awakening to literacy* (p. 196). Portsmouth, NH: Heinemann.

Burnett, N. (2009, September 7). *Learning from history*. Paris, France: UNESCO International Institute for Educational Planning. Retrieved February 4, 2012, from http://www.iiep.unesco.org/fileadmin/user_upload/Info_Services_Newsletter/pdf/eng/2009/2009_2En.pdf

Burns, M., & Casbergue, R. (1992). Parent-child interaction in a letter-writing context. *Journal of Reading Behavior, 24*(3), 289–312.

Bus, A., Both-de Vries, A., de Jong, M., Sulzby, E., de Jong, W., & de Jong, E. (2001). *Conceptualizations underlying emergent readers' story writing*. Ann Arbor, MI: Center for the Improvement of Early Reading Achievement (CIERA).

Caine, R., & Caine, G. (1990). Understanding a brain-based approach to learning and teaching. *Educational Leadership, 48*, 66–69.

Caine, R., & Caine, G. (1997). *Education on the edge of possibility*. Alexandria, VA: Association for Supervision and Curriculum Development.

Cambourne, B. (1987). Language, learning, and literacy. In A. Butler & J. Turbill (Eds.), *Towards a reading and writing classroom* (pp. 5–9). Portsmouth, NH: Heinemann.

Cambourne, B. (1988). *The whole story: Natural learning and the acquisition of literacy in the classroom*. New York, NY: Ashton Scholastic.

Cambourne, B. (1995). Towards an educationally relevant theory of literacy learning. *The Reading Teacher*, *49*(3), 182–192.

Canosa-Albano, J. (2015, January 2). Personal email correspondence. Springfield, MA.

Carr, N. (2010/11). The juggler's brain. *Phi Delta Kappan*, *92*(4), 8–14.

Carrington, V., & Luke, A. (1997). Literacy and Bourdieu's sociological theory: A reframing. *Language and Education*, *11*(2), 96–112.

Carroll, L. (1865). The walrus and the carpenter. In *Through the looking glass and what Alice found there*. London, UK: Macmillan & Co.

Carter, D. (2012, January 19). *Apple unveils interactive textbooks, revamped iTunes U*. Bethesda, MD: eSchool news. Retrieved January 20, 2012, from http://www.eschoolnews.com/2012/01/19/apple-unveils-interactive-textbooks-revamped-itunes-u/

Casey, B. G. (2000). Structural and functional brain development and its relation to cognitive development. *Biological Psychology*, *54*, 241–257.

Cazden, C. (1992). *Whole language plus: Essays on literacy in the United States and New Zealand*. New York, NY: Teachers College Press.

Center for Early Education and Brain Development. (2002). *Talking reasonably and responsibly about early brain development*. Minneapolis, Minnesota, MN: University of Minnesota.

Chan, L. (1998). Children's understanding of the formal and functional characteristics of Chinese. *Applied Psycholinguistics*, *19*(1), 115–131.

Chapman, M. (1996). More than spelling: Widening the lens on emergent writing. *Reading Horizons*, *36*, 317–339.

Cherry, K. (n.d.). 10 facts about memory. *About.com: Psychology*. Retrieved October 4, 2013, from http://psychology.about.com/

Children's Defense Fund. (2007). *America's cradle to prison pipeline*SM*: A report of the children's defense fund*. Washington, DC: Author.

Choi, S.-H. (2006). *Ensuring equitable access to preschool education: Kazakhstan's experience*. Paris, France: UNESCO Policy Brief on Early Childhood.

Chomsky. (1976, May). Approaching reading through invented spelling. *Conference on theory and practice*. Pittsburgh, Pennsylvania, USA: University of Pittsburgh, Learning Research and Development Center.

Church Peace Union (Carnegie Council for Ethics in International Affairs). (1958). *In your hands: A guide for community action*. New York, NY: The Church Peace Union.

Clark, M. (1976). *Young fluent readers: What can they teach us?* London, UK: Heinemann.

Clay, M. (1977). Exploring with a pencil. *Theory Into Practice*, *16*(5), 334–341.

Clay, M. (1982). *What did I write: Beginning writing behaviour*. Exeter, NH: Heinemann.

Clay, M. (1991). Developmental learning puzzles me. *Australian Journal of Reading*, *14*(4), 263–275.

Clay, M. (2001). *Change over time in children's literacy development*. Portsmouth, NH: Heinemann.

Coiro, J., Knobel, M., Lankshear, C., & Leu, D. (2008). Central issues in new literacies and new literacies research. In J. Coiro, M. Knobel, C. Lankshear, & D. J. Leu (Eds.), *Handbook of research on new literacies* (pp. 1–22). New York, NY: Routledge.

Coiro, J., Knobel, M., Lankshear, C., & Leu, D. (2010). *Handbook of research on new literacies*. New York, NY: Erlbaum.

Coles, G. (2004). Danger in the classroom: 'Brain Glitch' research and learning to read. *Phi Delta Kappan*, *85*(5), 344–351.

Committee on Econonic Social and Cultural Rights. (1999, August 12). *General comment 13: ESCR-Net*. Retrieved September 30, 2014, from http://www.escr-net.org/docs/i/425236

Committee, U. D. (1947). Report of the drafting committee. Paris, France: U.N.

Common Sense Media. (2011, October 25). *Zero to Eight: Children's media use in America*. Common Sense Media. Retrieved May 1, 2012, from http://www.commonsensemedia.org/sites/default/files/research/zerotoeightfinal2011.pdf

Common Sense Media. (2013, October 25). *Zero to Eight: Children's media use in America 2013*. Common Sense Media. Retrieved November 13, 2014, from https://www.commonsensemedia.org/sites/default/files/research/zero-to-eight-2013.pdf

Cooper, P. M. (1993). *When stories come to school: Telling, writing, and performing stories in the early childhood classroom*. New York, NY: Teachers and Writers Collaborative.

Cooper, P. M. (2005). Literacy learning and pedagogical purpose in Vivian Paley's storytelling curriculum. *Journal of Early Childhood Literacy*, *5*(3), 229–251.

Corson, D. (1985). *The lexical bar*. Oxford, UK: Pergamon Press.

Cowen, J. (2003). *A balanced approach to beginning reading instruction: A synthesis of six major U.S. research studies*. Newark, DE: International Reading Association.

Crystal, D. (1998). *Language play*. London, UK: Penguin Books, Ltd.

Darling-Hammond, L. (1995). Inequality and access to knowledge. In J. A. Banks & C. Banks (Eds.), *Handbook on research on multicultural education* (pp. 465–483). New York, NY: Macmillan.

Delpit, L. (2006). *Other people's children: Cultural conflict in the classroom*. New York, NY: The New Press.

Devaney, L. (2012, January 17). *Educational apps for early learners see huge jump*. eSchool news. Retrieved January 20, 2012, from http://www.eschoolnews.com/2012/01/17/educational-apps-for-early-learners-see-huge-jump/

Di Loreto, C., & Tse, L. (1999). Seeing is believing: Disparity in books in two Los Angeles area public libraries. *Public Library Quarterly*, *17*(3), 31–36.

Diamond, M., & Hopson, J. (1998). *Magic trees of the mind: How to nurture your child's intelligence, creativity and healthy emotions from birth through adolescence*. New York, NY: Penguin Putnam.

Dickinson, D. (2002). Shifting images of developmentally appropriate practices as seen through different lenses. *Educational Researcher*, *31*, 26–32.

Digital Christmas Story. (2011, December). Retrieved December 24, 2011, from http://www.flixxy.com/digital-christmas-story.htm

Discussion of Pedagogy of the Oppressed. (2013, May 1). *Noam Chomsky, Howard Gardner, Bruno della Chiesa*. Askwith Forum. Cambridge, MA: Harvard University.

Doake, D. (1985). Reading-like behavior: Its role in learning to read. In A. Jagger & M. Smith-Burke (Eds.), *Observing the language learner* (pp. 82–97). Newark, Delaware: National Council of Teachers of English and the International Reading Association.

Donald, M. (2001). *A mind so rare: The evolution of human consciousness*. New York, NY: Norton.

Donaldson, M. (1978). *Children's minds*. Glasglow, Scotland: William Collins Sons.

Dudley-Marling, C. (2007, Winter). Return of the deficit. *Journal of Educational Controversy*, *2*(1). Retrieved November 23, 2014, from http://wce.wwu.edu/REsourcces/CEP/eJournal/v002n001/Index.shtml

Dudley-Marling, C., & Lucas, K. (2009). Pathologizing the language and culture of poor children. *Language Arts*, *86*, 362–370.

Duffy, R. (1994). It's just like talking to each other: Written conversation wiht five-year-old children. In N. Hall & A. Robinson (Eds.), *Keeping in touch* (pp. 31–42). Portsmouth, NH: Heinemann.

Duke, N. (2000a). For the rich it's richer: Print experiences and environments offered to children in very low- and very high-socioeconomic status first-grade classrooms. *American Educational Research Journal*, *37*(2), 441–478.

Duke, N. (2000b). 3.6 minutes per day: The scarcity of informational texts in first grade. *Reading Research Quarterly*, *35*(2), 202–224.

Durkin, D. (1966). *The children who read early*. New York, NY: Teachers College Press.

Dwyer, J. (1991a). Talking in class. In J. Dwyer (Ed.), *A sea of talk* (pp. 2–8). Portsmouth, NH: Heinemann.

Dwyer, J. (1991b). Talking with Aboriginal children. In J. Dwyer (Ed.), *A sea of talk* (pp. 44–56). Portsmouth, NH: Heinemann.

Dyson, A. H. (1984, January). Emerging alphabetic literacy in school contexts: Toward defining the gap between curriculum and child mind. *Written Communication, 1*(1), 5–55.

Dyson, A. H. (1993). *Social worlds of children learning to write in an urban primary school.* New York, NY: Teachers College Press.

Dyson, A. H. (1997). *Writing superheroes: Contemporary childhood, popular culture, and classroom literacy.* New York, NY: Teachers College Press.

Dyson, A. H. (2003). *The brothers and sisters learn to write: Popular literacies in childhood and school cultures.* New York, NY: Teachers College Press.

Dyson, A. H. (2006). On saying it right (write): "Fix-its" in the foundation of learning to write. *Research in the Teaching of English, 41*, 8–42.

Dyson, A. H. (2007). School literacy and the development of a child culture: Written remnants of the "Gusto of Life". In D. Thiessen & A. Cook-Sather (Eds.), *International handbook of student experience in elementary and secondary school* (pp. 115–142). Dordrecht, The Netherlands: Springer.

Dzaldov, B., & Peterson, S. (2005). Book leveling and readers. *The Reading Teacher, 59*(3), 222–229.

Edelsky, C. (1985). Learning about language in the classroom. *Volta Review, 87*(5), 57–72.

Edelsky, C., Altwerger, B., & Flores, B. (1991). *Whole language: What's the difference.* Portsmouth, NH: Heinemann.

Edwards, H. (1980). *There's a hippopotamus on our roof eating cake.* London, UK: Hodder & Stoughton.

Edwards, P. (2011, April/May). Access to books makes a difference. *Reading Today, 28*(6), 16.

Edwards, P., Thompson McMillon, G., & Turner, J. (2008). *Change is gonna come.* New York, NY and Newark, DE: Teachers College Press and the International Reading Association.

Eighty-ninth Meeting of the Third Committee. (1948, September 30). United Nations.

Eliot, L. (1999). *What's going on in there: How the brain and mind develop in the first five years of life.* New York, NY: Bantam.

Elley, W. (1982). Bridging the gap between 1st and 2nd language learning. In L. Ruth & D. Burnes (Eds.), *Aboriginal literacy: Bridging the gap* (pp. 110–128). Adelaide, South Australia: Australian Reading Association.

Elley, W. (1992, July). *How in the world do children read?* (pp. 136). Hamburg, Germany: The International Association for Evaluation of Educational Achievement.

Fernald, A. (2013, October 15). In *Talking directly to toddlers strengthens their language skills.* Stanford, California: Stanford research shows-Stanford report.

Fernald, A., Marchman, V., & Weisleder, A. (2012). *SES differences in language processing skill and vocabulary are evident at 18 months.* Oxford, UK: Blackwell Publishing Ltd.

Fernandez, B. (2005, May 8). *UNESCO: Background paper prepared for the education for all Global Monitoring Report 2006, education for all.* Retrieved March 16, 2014, from http://unesdoc.unesco.org/images/0014/001459/145985e.pdf

Ferreiro, E., & Teberosky, A. (1982). *Literacy before schooling.* Exeter, New Hampshire: Heinemann.

Fitzgerald, J. (1999). What is this thing called balance? *The Reading Teacher, 53*(2), 100–107.

Foley Cusumano, K. (2008). Every mark on the page: Educating family and community members about young children's writing. *Language Arts, 86*(1), 9–17.

Foley, D. (1997). Deficit thinking models based on culture: The anthropological protest. In R. Valencia (Ed.), *The evolution of deficit thinking* (pp. 113–131). London, UK: Falmer.

Fox, B., & Saracho, O. (1990). Emergent writing: Young children solving the written language puzzle. *Early Childhood Development & Care, 26*(4), 81–90.

Franklin and Eleanor Roosevelt Institute. (2008, December 5–6). Conference program for the 60th Anniversary of the UDHR. *Bringing human rights home.* Hyde Park, New York, USA: Franklin and Eleanor Roosevelt Institute.

Fredericks, L. (1997). *Developing literacy skills through storytelling.* Resource center: Tools and training for volunteer and service programs. Retrieved April 7, 2012, from http://www.nationalserviceresources.org/literacy-storytelling

Freeman, E., & Sanders, T. (1989). Kindergarten children's emerging concepts of of writing functions in the community. *Early Childhood Research Quarterly, 4*(3), 331–338.

Freire, P. (1993). *Pedagogy of the city*. New York, NY: Continuum.

Gamse, B., Jacob, R. T., Horst, M., Boulay, B., & Unlu, F. (2008). *Reading first impact study final report (NCEE–4038)*. Washington, DC: National Center for Education Evaluation and Regional Assistance, Institute of Educational Sciences, U.S. Department of Education.

Gardner, H. (1980). *Artful scribbles: The significance of children's drawings*. New York, NY: Basic Books.

Gbowee, L., & Mithers, C. (2011). *Mighty be our powers; How sisterhood, prayer and sex changed a nation at war*. New York, NY: Beast Books.

Gee, J. (1996). *Social linguistics and literacies: Ideology in discourses* (2nd ed.). Philadelphia, PA: Routledge/Falmer.

Gee, J. P. (2004). *Situated language and learning: A critique of traditional schooling*. New York, NY: Routledge.

Genesee, F. (2012). Simultaneous bilingual acquisition. *In Encyclopedia of literacy and language development, 17*(44), p. 30.

Genesee, F. H. (2007). French immersion and at-risk students: A review of the research findings. *Canadian Modern Language Review, 63*, 655–688.

Gibson, E., & Levin, H. (1980). *The psychology of reading*. Cambridge, MA: MIT Press.

Gilmore, P. (1984). Subrosa skills in children's language. *Langauge Arts, 61*, 384–391.

Glasswell, K., & Ford, M. (2011). Let's start leveling about leveling. *Language Arts, 88*(3), 208–216.

Glendon, M. A. (2001). *A world made new: Eleanor Roosevelt and the Universal Declaration of Human Rights*. New York, NY: Random House.

GM South Africa Foundation. (2009). *Concentrated Language Encounter*. Port Elizabeth, South Africa: Author. Retrieved October 10, 2011, from http://gmsouthafricafoundation.com/project_default.asp?ProjectII

Goldman, A. (2011, November 29). *New Springfield Institute voter participation analysis: Severe disparites persist, lots of factors*. The Springfield Institute. Retrieved December 5, 2011, from http://www.springfieldinstitute.org/?p=5077

Gonzalez, N., Moll, L., & Amanti, C. (2005). *Funds of knowledge: Theorizing practices in households and classrooms*. Mahwah, NJ: Erlbaum.

Goodman, K., & Goodman, Y. (1983). Reading and writing relationships: Pragmatic functions. *Language Arts, 60*(5), 590–599.

Goodman, Y. (1982). El desarrollo de la escritura en ninos muy pequenos [The development of writing in very small children]. In E. Ferreiro & M. Gomez Palacio (Eds.), *Nuevas perspectivas sobre los procesos de lectura y escritura* [New perspectives on the process of reading and writing] (pp. 107–128). Mexico City, Mexico: Siglo XXI.

Goonan, P. (2014, April 3). *Springfield schools celebrate outstanding attendance during 'Stay in School' awards ceremony*. Massachusetts, MA: Masslive. Retrieved November 30, 2014, from http://www.masslive.com/news/index.ssf/2014/04/springfield_students_celebrate.html

Gorski, P. (2008). The myth of the "culture of poverty". *Educational Leadership, 65*(7), 32–36.

Gorski, P. (2009, May 6). Insisting on digital equity: Reframing the discourse on multicultural education and technology. *EdChange*, SAGA. Retrieved February 8, 2012, from http://www.edchange.org/publications/Digital-Equity-as-published.pdf

Graves, D. (1979). *Let children show us how to help them write* (Unpublished manuscript). Dover, New Hampshire.

Graves, D. (1984). *A researcher learns to write*. Portsmouth, NH: Heinemann.

Graves, D. (1989). *Investigate nonfiction*. Portsmouth, NH: Heinemann.

Gray, B. (1984). *Helping children to become language learners in the classroom*. Darwin, Australia: Northern Territory Department of Education.

Greene, J., & Winters, M. (2005). *Public high school graduation and college readiness rates: 1991–2002*. New York, NY: Manhattan Instiitiute.

Greenfield, P. (2009). Technology and informational education: What is taught, what is learned. *Science, 323*(5910), 69–71.

Greer, T., & Lockman, J. (1998). Using writing instruments: Invariances in young children and adults. *Child Development, 69*, 888–902.

Gumperz, J. J. (1982). *Discouse strategies*. Cambridge, UK: Cambridge Univesity Press.

Haberman, M. (1991). The pedagogy of poverty versus good teaching. *Phi Delta Kappan, 73*(4), 290–294.

Haberman, M. (2010). 11 Consequences of failing to address the pedagogy of poverty. *Phi Delta Kappan, 92*(2), 45.

Hale, J. (2001). *Learning while black: Creating educational excellence for African American children*. Baltimore, MD: Johns Hopkins Press.

Hall, L. (2005). *It's not just the text: Transactions between content-area teachers and struggling readers DAI-A 66/04* (Unpublished doctoral dissertation). East Lansing, Michigan: Michigan State University.

Hansen, C. (2004). Teacher talk: Literacy development through response to story. *Journal of Research in Early Childhood Education, 19*(2), 115–124.

Harry S. Truman Library and Museum. (1947, October). *To secure these rights: The report of the President's committee on civil rights*. Independence, MO: Author. Retrieved January 12, 2015, from http://www.trumanlibrary.org/civilrights/srights2.htm

Harste, J., & Kress, G. (2012). Image, identity, and insights into language. *Language Arts, 89*(3), 205–210.

Harste, J., Woodward, V., & Burke, C. (1984). *Language stories & literacy lessons*. Portsmouth, NH: Heinemann.

Hart, B., & Risley, T. (1995). *Meaningful differences in the everyday experiences of young American children*. Baltimore, MD: Paul H. Brookes Publishing Company.

Hart, B., & Risley, T. (2003). The early catastrophe: The 30 million word gap. *American Educator, 27* (1), 4–9.

Hayes Jacobs, H. (2011, November 19). Curriculum 21: Essential Education for a Changing World. *Preparing 21st Century minds: Using brain research to enhance cognitive skills for the future*. Boston, Massachusetts: Learning and the Brain.

Hayes Jacobs, H. (2014, December 31). Phone conversation.

Hayes, D., & Ahrens, M. (1988). Vocabulary simplification for children: A special case of "motherese"? *Journal of Child Language, 15*(2), 395–410.

Heath, S. (1983). *Ways with words: Language, life, and work in communities and classrooms*. Cambridge, UK: Cambridge University Press.

Heath, S. B. (2010). Family literacy or community learning. In K. Dunsmore & D. Fisher (Eds.), *Bringing literacy home* (pp. 15–41). Newark, DE: International Reading Association.

Herschkowitz, N., & Herschkowitz, E. (2002). *A good start in life*. Washington, DC: Joseph Henry Press.

Herschkowitz, N., & Herschkowitz, E. (2006, May). *Intense brain development between four & eight years and its impact on preschool and school years*. Cambridge, Massachusetts, USA: Learning and the Brain Conference Presentation.

Hess, K. (1974). The nonstandard speakers in our schools: What should be done? *The Elementary School Journal, 74*(5), 280–290.

Hirst, L., & Slavik, C. (2012, February 17). *Cooperative approaches to language learning: Effective language education practices*. Arizona, AZ: Northern Arizona University. Retrieved February 17, 2012, from http://jan.ucc.nau.edu/~jar/NALI10.html

Hoff, E., & Elledge, C. (2003). Bilingualism as one of many environmental variables that affect language development. Proceedings of the 4th international symposium on Bilingualism. Tempe, AZ.

Hoff, E., & McKay, J. (2005a) *Phonological memory skill in monolingual and bilingual 23- month-olds*. Florida: Atlantic University. Retrieved March 18, 2012, from http://www.lingret.com/isb.4.079ISB4.PDF

Hoff, E., & McKay, J. (2005b). Phonological memory skills in monolingual and bilingual 23-month-olds. In J. Cohen, K. McAlister, K. Rolstad, & J. MacSwan (Eds), *Proceedings of the 4th International symposium of bilingualism* (pp. 1041–1444). Somerville, MA: Cascadilla Press.

Holdaway, D. (1979). *The foundations of literacy*. Sydney: Ashton Scholastic.

Holdaway, D. (1982). Shared book experience: Teaching reading using favorite books. *Theory Into Practice, 21*, 293–300.

Hollie, S. (2001). Acknowledging the language of African American students: Instructional strategies. *English Journal, 90*, 54–59.

Holt, J. (1975). *Escape from childhood: The needs and rights of children reported.* Harmondsworth, England: Penguin Books (first published in 1974).

Hooks, B. (1994). *Teaching to transgress: Education as the practice of freedom.* London, UK: Routledge.

Horton, J. (2001). Critical periods in the development of the visual system. In D. B. Bailey (Ed.), *Critical thinking about critical periods* (pp. 27–44). Baltimore, MD: Paul Brookes.

Howard Hughes Medical Institute. (2013, January 1). *The next generation of brain scans.* Retrieved February 16, 2013, from www.hhmi.org/senses/e210html

Hruby, G., & Goswami, U. (2011). Nueroscience and reading: A review for reading educators. *Reading Research Quarterly, 46*(2), 156–172.

Hull, G., & Nelson, M. (2005). Locating the Semiotic Power of Multimodality. *Written Communication, 22*(2), 224–261.

Hurwitz, S. (2001). The teacher who would be Vivian. *Young Children, 56*(5), 89–91.

International Symposium for Literacy. (1975). Declaration of Persepolis: International symposium for literacy. *Persepolis 3–8 September.* Paris, France: UNESCO.

IRIN 2010. (n.d.). *In depth: Congo's refugee crisis, Nairobi, Office of the United Nations for the coordination of humanitarian affairs.* Retrieved September 15, 2010, from www.irinnews.org/IndepthMain.aspx?InDepthID=86&ReportID=88469

Jamaica UNICEF. (2010). *Jamaica UNICEF—Advocacy public policy and partnerships.* 20th anniversary convention on the rights of the child. Retrieved April 12, 2012, from http://www.unicef.org/jamaica/promoting_child_rights_15284.htm

Jensen, E. (1998). *Teaching with the brain in mind.* Alexandria, VA: Association for Supervision and Curriculum Development.

Jensen, E. (2000). *Music with the brain in mind.* Thousand Oaks, CA: Corwin Press.

Jewitt, C. (2008, February). Mulitmodalities and literacy in school classrooms. *Review of Research in Education, 32*, 241–267. Retrieved February 20, 2012, from http://rre.sagepub.com/content/32/1/241.full

Jewitt, C., & Kress, G. (Eds.). (2003). *Multimodal literacy.* New York, NY: Peter Lang.

Joan Ganz Cooney, Center for sesame street workshop.

Johnson, D., & Sulzby, E. (1999). *Critical issue: Addressing the literacy needs of emergent and early readers. Pathways to school improvement* [Online]. Retrieved February 12, 2012, from http://www.ncrl.org/sdrs/areas/issues/content/cntareas/reading/li100.htm

Jones, P. (1990). UNESCO and the politics of global literacy. *Comparative Education Review, 34*(1), 41–60.

Judge, S., Puckett, K., & Cabuk. B. (2004). Digital Equity: New findings from the early childhood longitudinal study. *Journal of Research on Technology in Education, 36*(4), 383–396.

Justice, L. (2004). Creating language-rich preschool classroom environments. *Teaching Exceptional Children, 37*(2), 36–44.

Justice, L. M., & Kadervak, J. N. (2002). Shared storybook reading as an intervention context: Practices, potentials, and pitfalls. *American Journal of Speech-Language Pathology, 11*(4), 395–406.

Kagan, J., & Herschkowitz, N. (2005). *A young mind in a growing brain.* Mahwah, NJ: Lawrence Erlbaum.

Kaiser Family Foundation. (2010, January 20). *Generation M2: Media use in the lives of 8- to 18-year-olds.* Retrieved September 27, 2012, from http://www.kff.org/entmedia/mh012010pkg.cfm

Kalantzis, M., & Cope, B. (2011). New Learning: Transformational designs for pedagogy and assessment. Expanding the scope of literacy pedagogy. Retrieved March 30, 2012, from http://newlearningonline.com/multiliteracies/

Kam, M. (2013). Mobile learning games for low-income children in India: Lessons from 2004–2009. In Z. Berg & L. Muilenburg (Eds.), *Handbook of mobile learning.* New York, NY: Routledge.

Kamberelis, G., & Sulzby, E. (1988). Transitional knowledge in emergent literacy. *National Reading Conference Yearbook, 37*, 95–106.

Karchmer-Klein, R., & Harlow Shinas, V. (2012). Guiding principles for supporting new literacies in your classroom. *Reading Teacher, 65*(5), 288–293.

Katch, J. (2001). *Under deadman's skin.* New York, NY: Beacon Press.

Katch, J. (2003). *They don't like me: Lessons on bullying and teasing from a pre-school classroom.* New York, NY: Beacon Press.

Kato-Otani, E. (2008). *Writing development of a bilingual child: Japanese and English.* Osaka, Japan: Osaka Jogakuin College.

Kell, C. (1996). Literacy practices in an informal settlement. In M. Prinsloo & M. Breier (Eds.), *The social uses of literacy: Theory and practice in contemporary South Africa* (pp. 235–256). Bertsham, South Africa: Sacred Books and John Benjamins Publishing Company.s

Kelly, J. (2012). *The graves are walking.* New York, NY: Henry Holt.

Kenner, C. (2003). Embodied knowledges: Young children's engagement with the act of writing. In C. Jewitt & G. Kress (Eds.), *Multimodal literacy* (pp. 88–106). New York, NY: Peter Lang.

Kiefer, B., & De Stefano, J. (1985). Cultures together in the classroom: What you sayin'? In A. Jagger & S.-B. Trika (Eds.), *Observing the language learner* (pp. 159–172). Newark, Delaware: National Council of Teachers of English and the International Reading Association.

King, K., & Fogle, L. (2006). *Raising bilingual children: common parental concerns and current research.* Washington, DC: Center for Applied Linguistics.

King, M. (1985). Language and language learning for kid watchers. In A. Jagger & M. T. Smith-Burke (Eds.), *Observing the language learner* (pp. 19–38). Newark, Delaware: National Council of Teachers of English and the International Reading Association.

Knobel, M., & Wilbur, D. (2009). Let's talk 2.0. *Educational Leadership, 66*(6), 20–24.

Kolb, L. (n.d.). *Interview with Carly Shuler.* Joan Ganz Cooney foundation.

Kommers, D. (1991). German constitutionalism: A prolegomenon. *Emory Law Journal (40 Emory LJ 837)*, 867.

Krashen, S. (1982). *Principals and practices in second langauge acquisition.* New York, NY: Pergamon.

Krashen, S. (2001). More smoke and mirrors: A critique of the National Reading Panel Report on fluency. *Phi Delta Kappan, 83*, 119–123.

Krashen, S. (2004a). *Free voluntary reading: New research, applications, and controversies.* Vladivostok, Russia: PAC 5 Pan Asian Conference.

Krashen, S. (2004b). *The power of reading.* Portsmouth, NH: Heinemann.

Krashen, S. (2008, December). The case for libraries and librarians. *Invited paper, submitted to the Obama-Biden Working Policy Group.* Washington, DC, USA: Obama-Biden Policy Working Group.

Krashen, S. (2014, February 11). *Why invest in libraries.* Retrieved November 30, 2014, from https://www.youtube.com/watch?v=JAui0OGfHQY

Krashen, S., Lee, S. Y., & McQuillan, J. (2008). *Is the library important?* Presented at the 37th annual meeting of the international association of school librarianship, Berkeley, CA.

Kress, G., & Jewitt, C. (2003). *Multimodal literacy.* Retrieved September 27, 2012 from http://www.amazon.com/Multimodal-Literacy-Literacies-Digital-Epistemologies/dp/0820452246

Kristof, N. D. (2011, October 20). Occupy the classroom. *New York Times*, p. A29.

Labov, W. (1970). *The study of nonstandard English.* Urbana, IL: National Council of Teachers of English.

Ladson-Billings, G. (1999). Preparing teachers for diverse student populations: A critical race theory perspective. In A. Iran-Nejad & P. D. Pearson (Eds.), *Review of Research in Education* (Vol. 24, pp. 211–247). Washington, DC: American Educational Research Association.

Lance, K. (2004). The impact of school library media centers on academic achievement. In C. E. Kuhlthau (Ed.), *School library media annual* (pp. 188–197). Westport, CT: Libraries Unlimited.

Lange. (2013). *Survey of middle and low income households.* Paris, France: UNESCO.

Lanza, E. (1992). Can bilingual two-years-olds code-switch? *Journal of Child Language, 19*, 633–658.

Lesaux, N. K. (2010). Turning the page: Refocusing Massachusetts for reading success. *Strategies for improving children's language and literacydevelopment, birth to age 9.* Springfield, Massachusetts: Strategies for Children.

Leu, D., Karchmer, R., & Leu, D. (1999). The Miss Rumphius effect: Envisionments for literacy learning that transform the internet. *The Reading Teacher, 52*, 636–642.

Liberia, & UN. (2004). *Republic of Liberia: Millenium development goals report.* Monrovia, Liberia: Liberia Government/United Nations.

Liberman, I. (1973). Segmentation of the spoken word and reading acquisition. *Bulletin of the Orton Society, XXIII*, 65–77.

Liberman, M. (2006, November 26). *Word counts*[Web log post]. Retrieved February 8, 2012, from http://itre.cis.upenn.edu/~myl/languagelog/archives/003831.html

Lindfors, J. (1985). Understanding the development of language structure. In A. Jaggar & M. T. Smith-Burke (Eds.), *Observing the language learner* (pp. 41–56). Newark, Delaware: National Council of Teachers of English and the International Reading Association.

Lindfors, J. (1991). *Children's language and learning* (2nd. Ed.). Boston, MA: Allyn & Bacon.

Lindfors, J. (2008). *Children's language: Connecting reading, writing, and talk.* New York, NY: Teachers College Press.

Long, R. (2012). The limitations of instruction-focused funding strategies. *Reading Today, 29*(4), 27–28.

Lopez-Robertson, J., Long, S., & Turner-Nash, K. (2010). First steps in constructing counter narratives of young children and their families. *Language Arts, 88*(2), 93–103.

Mackay, D., Thompson, B., & Schaub, P. (1970). *Breakthrough to literacy: Programme in linguistics and English teaching.* London, UK: Schools Council/Longman.

Malan, L. (1996). Literacy learning and local literacy practice in Bellville South. In M. Prinsloo & M. Breier (Eds.), *The social uses of literacy: Theory and use in contemporary South Africa* (pp. 141–155). Bertsham, South Africa: Sacred Books and John Benjamins Publishing Company.

Marsh, J. (2006). *Global, local/public/private: Young children's engagement in digital literacy practices at home*. San Francisco, CA: American Educational Research Association.

Martin, B. J., & Brogan, P. (1975). *Teaching suggestions for "Sounds Jubilee" and "Sounds Freedomring".* Winnipeg, Manitoba, Canada: *Peguis Publishing.*

Martin, B., Archambault, J. & Ehlert, L. (1989). *Chicka chicka boom boom.* New York, NY: Simon and Schuster.

Mason, P., & Galloway, E. (2012). What children in poverty do bring to school: Strong oral skills. *Reading Today, 29*(4), 29–30.

Massachusetts Department of Elementary and Secondary Education (ESE). (2014a, September 18). *2014 MCAS results by subgroup by grade and subject.* Massachusetts, MA. Retrieved October 21, 2014, from http://profiles.doe.mass.edu/mcas/subgroups2.aspx?linkid=25&orgcode=02810000&fycode=2014&orgtypecode=5&

Massachusetts Department of Elementary and Secondary Education. (2014b). *Spring 2014 MCAS tests: Summary of state results.* Malden, MA: Massachusetts Department of Elementary and Secondary Education.

Mayer, K. (2007). Emerging knowledge about emergent writing. *Young Children, 62*(1), 34–40.

McGee, L., & Purcell-Gates, V. (1997). So what's going on in research on emergent literacy? *Reading Research Quarterly, 32*(3), 310–318.

McGee, L., & Richgels, D. (1996). *Literacy's beginnings: Supporting young readers and writers* (2nd ed.). Boston, MA: Allyn and Bacon.

McMunn Dooley, C. (2010). Young children's approaches to books: The emergence of comprehension. *The Reading Teacher, 64*(2), 120–130.

McNamee, G., McLane, J., Cooper, P., & Kerwin, S. (1985). Cognition and affect and early literacy development. *Early Childhood Development and Care, 20*(4), 229–244.

McQuillan, J. (1998). *The literacy crisis: False claims and real solutions.* Portsmouth, NH: Heinemann.

Michaels, S. (1981). Sharing time: Children's narrative styles and differential access to literacy. *Language in Society, 10*(3), 423–442.

Michaels, S. (1991). The dismanting of narrative. In A. McCabe & C. Peterson (Eds.), *Developing narrative structure* (pp. 303–351). Hillside, NJ: Erlbaum.

Michaels, S. (2005). Can the intellectual affordances of working-class storytelling be leveraged in school? *Human Development, 48*, 137.

Millard, E. (2003). Toward a literacy of fusion: New times, new teaching and learning. *Reading, Literacy, and Language, 37*(1), 3–8.

Miller, P., & Mehler, R. (1994, January 1). Personal storytelling, socialization, and self-construction at home and in kindergarten. In A. H. Dyson & C. Genesi (Eds.), *The need for story: Cultural diversity in classroom and community*. Urbana, IL: National Council of Teachers of English.

Miller, P., Cho, G., & Bracey, J. (2005). Working class children's experience through the prism of personal storytelling. *Human Development, 48*(3), 115–135.

Mills, H., O'Keefe, T., & Stephens, D. (1992). *Looking closely: Exploring the role of phonics in one whole language classroom*. Urbana, Illinois: National Council of Teachers of English.

Mills, K. (2010). A review of the "digital turn" in the new literacy studies. *Review of Educational Research, 80*(2), 246–271.

Milroy, L., & Muysken, P. (1995). *One speaker, two languages: Cross-disciplinary perspectives on code-switching*. Cambridge, UK: Cambridge University Press.

Mooney, M. E. (1990). *Reading to, with, and by children*. Katonah, NY: Richard C. Owen Publishers, Inc.

Morrow, L. (2002). *Literacy development in the early years: Helping children to read and write* (4th ed.). New York, NY: Allyn and Bacon.

Morrow, L., & Asbury, E. (1999). Best practices for a balanced early literacy program. In L. M. Gambrell (Ed.), *Best practices in literacy instruction* (pp. 49–67). New York, NY: Guilford Press.

Morrow, L., & Sharkey, E. (1993). Motivating independent reading and writing in the primary grades through social cooperative literacy experiences. *The Reading Teacher, 47*(2), 162–165.

Murray, B. (1991). Talking when English is a foreign language. In J. Dwyer (Ed.), *A sea of talk* (pp. 57–66). Portsmouth, NH: Heinemann.

Mustard. (2002). Early childhood development and the brain—The base for health, learning & behavior throughout Life. In M. Young (Ed.), *From early childhood development to human development* (pp. 23–61). Washington DC: World Bank.

Mustard. (2005, May 25). *Behavior (affect), literacy, & early childhood development*. Monterrey, Mexico: The Founder's Network, Early Childhood.

Naismith, L., Lonsdale, P., Vavoula, G., & Sharples, M. (2004). *Literature review in mobile technologies and learning*. London, UK: FutureLab.

National Commission on Teaching and America's Future. (2004). *Fifty years after Brown v. Board of education: A two-tiered education system*. Washington, DC: National Commission on Teaching and America's Future.

NCTE (National Council of Teachers of English). (2005, November). *NCTE position statement on multimodal literacies*. Retrieved February 21, 2012, from http://www.ncte.org/positions/statements/multimodalliteracies

NCTE Midwinter Conference Call for Papers. (2000). *New literacies for New Times: Bakhtinian Perspectives on language and literacy learning*. Berkeley, CA: NCTE.

Neddermeyer, D. M. (n.d.). *E-learning solutions*. skillsoft.com. Retrieved March 5, 2014, from http://ezinearticles.com/?Silence---Important-Aspect-of-Communication&id=5409097

Nel, E. (2000). Academics, literacy, and young children. *Childhood Education, 76*(3), 136–141.

Neuman, S. B., & Celano, D. (2001). Access to print in low-income and middle-income communities. *Reading Research Quarterly, 36*(1), 8–26.

New London Group. (1996). A pedagogy of multiliteracies: Designing social futures. *The Harvard Educational Review, 66*(1), 60–92.

Ngala Family Services. (2009). *Help your baby to learn*. Retrieved March 26, 2012, from http://www.ngala.com.au/You-and-Your-Family/For-Dads/Help-Your-Baby-to-Learn

Niccolopolu, A., Scales, B., & Weintraub, J. (1994). Gender differences and symbolic imagination in the stories of four-year-olds. In A. H. Dyson & C. Genishi (Eds.), *The need for story: Cultural diversity in the classroom* (pp. 102–123). Urban, IL: National Council of Teachers of English.

Nieto, S. (2000). *Affirming diversity: The sociopolitical context of multicultural education* (3rd ed.). New York, NY: Addison Wesley Longman.

Nieto, S., & Bode, P. (2008). *Affirming diversity: The sociopolitical context of multicultural education* (6th ed.). Boston, MA: Allyn and Bacon.

Nkutu, A., Bang, T., & Tooman, D. (2010). *Protecting children's rights to education: Evaluation of NRC's accelerated learning programme in Liberia*. Oslo, Norway: Norwegian Refugee Council

Noguera, P. (2012). Saving Black and Latino boys: What schools can do to make a difference. *Phi Delta Kappan, 93*(12), 8–12.

Nolte, J. (2010). *Essentials of the human brain.* Philadelphia, PA: Mosby Elsevier.

Norweign Nobel Committee. (2011, October 7). *The nobel peace prize 2011.* Retrieved February 14, 2012, from http://www.nobelprize.org/nobel_prizes/peace/laureates/2011/press.html

Novick, R. (1996). *Developmentally appropriate and culturally responsive education.* Portland, Oregon: Northwest Regional Educational Laboratory.

Obama, B. (2009, July 16). *Speech to the N.A.A.C.P. on the 100th anniversary of the organization.* New York, NY.

Obama, B. (2013, January 21). *President Barack Obama's second inagural address.* Washington, DC.

Ochs, E. (1982). Talking to children in Western Samoa. *Language in Society, 11*, 77–104.

Office of the UN High Commissioner for Human Rights—General Comments. (n.d.). *Committee on economic, social and cultural rights.* Retrieved February 4, 2012, from http://www2.ohchr.org/english/bodies/cescr/comments.htm

Office of the United Nations High Comissioner for Human Rights. (n.d.). *International covenant for economic, social and cultural rights.* Retrieved September 26, 2012, from http://www2.ohchr.org/english/law/cescr.htm

Ohanian, S. (2011, May 31). *The pedagogy of poverty versus good teaching.* Retrieved February 8, 2012, from http://susanohanian.org/show_commentary.php?id=937--retrieved 2-8-12

Opitz, M. (2000). *Rhymes and reasons: Literature and language play for phonological awareness.* Portsmouth, NH: Heinemann.

Opitz, M. F., Ford, M. P., & Erekson, J. A. (2011). *Accessible assessment: How 9 sensible techniques can power data-driven instruction.* Portsmouth, NH: Heinemann.

Ornitz, E. M. (2002). Developmental aspects of neurophysiology. In M. Lewis (Ed.), *Child and adolescent psychiatry* (pp. 60–74). Philadelphia, PA: Lippincott.

Parish-Morris, J., Mahajan, N., Hirsh-Pasek, K., Golinkoff, R., & Collins, M. (2013). Once upon a time: Preschoolers and storybook reading in the electronic era. *Mind, Brain, and Education, 7*(3), 200–211.

Paus, T. C. (2001). Maturation of white matter in the human brain: A review of magnetic resonance studies. *Brain Research Bulletin, 54*(3), 255–266.

Pearson, B. Z. (1993). Predictive validity of the Scholastic Aptitude Test for Hispanic bilingual students. *Hispanic Journal of Behavioral Sciences, 15*, 342–356.

Pearson, B. Z., Fernandez, S. C., Lewedeg, V., & Oller, D. K. (1997). The relation of input factors to lexical learning in bilingual infants. *Applied Linguistics, 18*, 41–58.

Pearson, P. (2006). Foreword. In K. Goodman (Ed.), *The truth about DIBELS: What it is, what it does* (pp. v–xix). Portsmouth, NH: Heinemann.

Phinney, M. (1987). Whole reading. *Mothering* (winter issue), 79–82.

Piasta, S. B., Justice, L. M., McGinty, A. S., & Kadervak, J. N. (2012). Increasing young children's contact with print during shared reading: Longitudinal effects on literacy achievement. *Child Development, 83*(3), 810–820.

Pines, M. (1967). *Revolution in learning: The years from birth to six.* New York, NY: Harper & Row, Publishers.

Polakow, V. (1993). *Lives on the edge: Single mothers and their children in the other America.* Chicago, IL: University of Chicago Press.

Porter, P. (2007, May 3). *Early brain development: What parents and caregivers need to know.* Educarer. org. Retrieved March 26, 2010, from http://www.educarer.com/brain.htm

Pullen, P., & Justice, L. M. (2003). Enhancing phonological awareness, print awareness, and oral language skills in preschool children. *Intervention in School and Clinic, 39*, 87–98.

Quiñonez Summer, L. (2014). Language acquisition for the bilingual child: A perspective on raising bilingual children in the United States. In L. R. Schmeltz (Ed.), *The NCHAM eBook: A resource guide for early hearing detection* (pp. 17.1–17.12). Logan, Utah: The National Center for Hearing Assessment and Management.

Quiñonez Summer, L. (2015, January 2). Personal email correspondence.

Ranker, J. (2008). Composing across multiple media: A case of digital video production in a fifth grade classroom. *Written Communication, 25*(2), 196–234.

Rasinski, T. (2014). *Executive summary: Hasbro summer learning initiative report.* Springfield, MA: Hasbro Summer Learning Intiative.

Ravitch, D. (2010). *The death and life of the great American school system.* Perseus Books Group.

Riggs, M. (2014, January 8). *Nearly 50 percent of Black Men have been arrested by 23.* The Atlantic Cities. Retrieved January 27, 2014, from http://www.theatlanticcities.com/politics/2014/01/n http://www.citylab.com/politics/2014/01/nearly-50-percent-black-males-have-been-arrested-age-23/8042/

Robbins, C. (2014, December 12). *Springfield early childhood advocates plan Mason Square child care center.* Masslive.com. Retrieved January 28, 2015, from http://nl.newsbank.com/nl-search/we/Archives?p_action=doc&p_docid=1527200058FA8FD0&p_docnum=1&s_trackval=&s_subexpires=12/14/2015%2023:59%20PM&s_dlid=DL0115012819210802677&s_accountid=AC0115012819190702558&s_referrer=&s_siteloc=&s_orderid=NB01150128192106

Rogers, R., & Schaenen, I. (2014). Critical discourse analysis in literacy education: A review of the literature. *Reading Research Quarterly*, 121–143.

Roman, E. (2013, April 23). *Springfield school superintendent Daniel Warwick, other school officials visit Puerto Rico.* Mass Live. Retrieved November 30, 2014, from http://www.masslive.com/news/index.ssf/2013/04/springfield_superintendent_of_3.html

Roosevelt, E. (1946). *If you ask me.* New York, NY: D. Appleton -Century Company Inc.

Roosevelt, E. (1947, February 12). *My day.* New York, NY, USA: United Feature Syndicate.

Roosevelt, E. (1948, December 10). *On the adoption of the Universal Declaration of Human Rights. American rhetoric.* Retrieved May 22, 2008, from http://www.americanrhetoric.com/speeches/eleanorrooseveltdeclarationhumanrights.htm

Roosevelt, E. (1958a). Speech to UN on 10th anniversary of the adoption of the universal declaration of human rights. New York, NY.

Roosevelt, E. (1958b, March 27). *In your hands* (E. Roosevelt, Performer). United Nations, New York, USA.

Roosevelt, E. (1958c). *On my own.* New York, NY: Dell.

Roosevelt, E. (1992). *The autobiography of Eleanor Roosevelt.* New York, NY: Da Capo Press.

Roosevelt, E. (2001). *My day.* Cambridge, MA: Da Capo Press, A Member of the Perseus Book Group.

Rose, P. (2009, September 7). *The impact on poverty.* UNESCO International Instiitute for Educational Planning, Paris, France. Retrieved August 30, 2012, from http://www.iiep.unesco.org/fileadmin/user_upload/Info_Services_Newsletter/pdf/eng/2009/2009_2En.pdf

Rosemary, C. A., & Roskos, K. (2002). Literacy conversations between adults and childen at childcare: Desciptive observations and hypotheses. *Journal of Research in Childhood Education, 16*(2), 212–231.

Rosenblatt, L. M. (1978). *The reader, the text, the poem: The transactional theory of the literary work.* CArbondale, IL: Southern Illinois University Press.

Rushton, S., Eitelgeorge, J., & Zickafoose, R. (2003). Connecting Brian Cambourne's conditions of learning theory to brain/mind principles: Implications for early childhood educators. *Early Childhood Education Journal, 31*(1), 11–19.

Saddler, C. (2005). The impact of Brown on African-American students: A critical race theoretical perspective. *Educational Studies, 37*(1), 41–55.

Sadoski, M. (2004). *Conceptual foundations of teaching reading.* New York, NY: Guilford Press.

Sapon-Shevin, M. (1998). Everyone here can play. *Educational Leadership, 56*(1), 42–45.

Sapon-Shevin, M., Dobbelaere, A., Corrigan, C., Goodman, K., & Mastin, M. (1998). Promoting inclusive behavior in inclusive classrooms: You can't say you can't Play. In I. H. Meyer, H. S. Park, M. Grenot-Scheyer, I. S. Schwartz, & B. Harry (Eds.), *Making friends: The influences of culture and development* (pp. 105–132). Baltimore, MD: Paul H. Brookes.

Saxton, M. (2010). *Child language: Acquisition and development.* London, UK: Sage Publications Ltd.

Schickedanz, J. (1986). *More than ABC's.* Washington, DC: National Association for the Education of Young Children.

Schickedanz, J. A. (1999). *Much more than ABC's: The early stages of reading and writing*. Washington, DC: NAEYC.

Schickedanz, J. A., & Casbergue, R. M. (2004). *Writing in preschool: Learning to orchestrate meaning and marks*. Newark, DE: International Reading Association.

Schmithorst, V., Wilke, M., Dardzinski, B., & Holland, S. (2002). Correlation of white matter diffusivity and anisotropy with age during childhood and adolescence: A cross-sectional diffusion-tensor MR imaging study. *Radiology*, *222*, 212–218.

Schutz, D. (2009, February 12). *The non-impact of reading first—Where to go from here*. New York, NY: Teachers College Record, Columbia University. Retrieved February 8, 2012, from http://www.tcrecord.org/search.asp?kw=non-impact+of+reading+first&x=15&y=11

Scribner, S., & Cole, M. (1981). *The psychology of literacy*. Cambridge, MA: Harvard University Press.

Sears, J. (2008). *Eleanor Roosevelt and the Universal declaration of human rights*. Hyde Park, New York, NY: Franklin and Eleanor Roosevelt Institute—The Task Force Celebrating Eleanor Roosevelt 2008.

Sege, I. (2011, September 8). *No improvement in MA third grade reading*. Boston, Massachusetts: Eye on education. Retrieved September 15, 2011, from http://eyeonearlyeducation.org/2011/09/08/2011-mcas-shows-no-improvement-in-third-grade

Sege, I. (2012). Early childhood education: Springfield tackles a benchmark. *Communities and banking*. Boston, MA: Federal Reserve Bank of Boston.

Sendak, M. (1963). *Where the wild things are*. New York, NY: Scholastic.

Shannon, P. (1992). Commercial reading materials, a technological ideology, and the deskilling of teachers. In P. Shannon (Ed.), *Becoming political: Readings and writings in politics of literacy education* (pp. 182–207). Portsmouth, NH: Heinemann.

Shor, I. (1992). *Empowering education: Critical teaching for social change*. Chicago, IL: University of Chicago Press.

Shuler, C. (2009). *Pockets of potential: Using mobile technologies to promote children's learning*. New York, NY: The Joan Ganz Cooney Center at Sesame Workshop.

Small, G., & Vorgen, G. (2008). *iBrain: Surviving the technological alteration of the modern mind*. New York, NY: Harper Collins Publishers.

Smith, A. (2014, January 6). *African Americans and technology use*. Washington, DC: Pew Research Internet Project. Retrieved February 21, 2014, from http://www.pewinternet.org/2014/01/06/detailed-demographic-tables/

Smith, C., Constantino, R., & Krashen, S. (1996). Differences in print environments for children in Beverly Hills, Compton and Watts. *Emergency Librarian*, *24*(4), 4–5.

Smith, F. (1971). *Understanding reading: A psycholinguistic analysis of reading and learning to read*. New York, NY: Holt, Rinehart & Winston.

Smith, F. (1982). *Writing and the writer*. London, NY: Heinemann.

Snow, C., Burns, S., & Griffin, P. (Eds.). (1998). *Preventing reading difficulties in young children*. Washington DC: National Academic Press.

Solomon, G., & Allen, N. (2003). Introduction: Educational technology and equity. In G. Solomon, N. Allen, & P. E. Resta (Eds.), *Toward digital equity: Bridging the divide in education* (pp. xxiv–xxvi). Boston: Allyn and Bacon.

Solsken, J., Wilson-Keenan, J., & Willett, J. (1993). Interweaving stories: Creating a multicultural classroom through school/home/university collaboration. *Democracy and Education Fall 1993*, 16–21.

Sousa, D. A. (2005). *How the brain learns to read*. Thousand Oaks: Corwin Press.

Sousa, D. A. (2006). *How the brain learns to read* (3rd ed.). Thousand Oaks, CA: Corwin Press.

Sousa, D. A. (2011). *How the brain learns* (4th ed., pp. 216). Thousand Oaks, CA: Corwin/A Sage Company.

Speaker K. M., Taylor, D., & Kamen, R. (2004). Storytelling: Enhancing language acquisition in young children. *Education*, *125* (1), 3–14.

Speaker, K. M., Taylor, D., & Kamen, R. (2003). Storytelling: Enhancing language acquisition in young children. *Education*, 3–14.

Spears-Bunton, L., & Powell, R. (2009). *Toward a literacy of promise: Joining the African American struggle*. Oxon, NY: Routledge.

Sprenger, M. (2008). *The developing brain: Birth to age eight*. Thousand Oaks, CA: Corwin Press.

Squire, K. (2009). Interview with Shuler. Joan Ganz Cooney Foundation.

Stamm, J. (2007). *Bright from the start*. New York, NY: Gotham Books.

Stine, S. (1980). Beginning reading—naturally. *Claremont reading conference yearbook* (pp. 144–155). Claremont, CA: Center for Developmental Studies.

Street, B. (1996). Preface. In M. Prinsloo & M. Breier (Eds.), *The social uses of literacy* (p. 4). Bertsham, South Africa: Sached Books and John Benjamins Publishing Company.

Street, B. (1997). The implications of new literacy studies for literacy education. *English in Education, 31*(3), 45–59

Street, B. (2005a). At last: Recent applications of new literacy studies in educational contexts. *Research in the Teaching of English, 39*, 417–423.

Street, B. (2005b). *Understanding and defining literacy*. New York, NY: UNESCO.

Strickland, D. (2005). Educating African American learners at risk: Finding a better way. In B. Hammond, M. E. R. Hoover, & I. P. McPhail (Eds.), *Teaching African American learners to read: Perspectives and practices* (pp. 147–160). Newark, DE: International Reading Association.

Strickland, D., & Morrow, L. (1991). Fostering independent learning. *The Reading Teacher, 44*(9), 694–697.

Strunk, W., & White, E. (1979). *The elements of style* (3rd ed.). New York, NY: Macmillan.

Sulzby, E. (1985a). Children's emergent reading of favorite storybooks: A developmental study. *Reading Research Quarterly, 20*(4), 458–481.

Sulzby, E. (1985b). Kindergarteners as writers and readers. In M. Farr (Ed.), *Advances in writing research: Children's early writing development* (Vol. 1, pp. 127–199). Norwood, NJ: Ablex.

Sulzby, E. (1991, March). Assessment of emergent literacy. *The Reading Teacher, 44*(7), 498–500.

Sweeney, S. (2010). Writing for the instant messaging and text messaging generation: Using new literacies to support writing instruction. *Journal of Adolescent and Adult Literacy, 54*(2), 121–130.

Tallal, P. (2007, March). *Better living through neuroscience*. Presentation at annual conference of the association of supervision and curriculum development. Anaheim, CA, USA.

Tan, T., & Liu, T. (2004). *The mobile-based interactive learning environment (MOBILE) and a case study for assisting elementary school English learning*. In proceedings of 2004 IEEE International conference on Advanced Learning Technologies (ICALT 2004) (pp. 530–534). Joensuu, Finland.

Tannen, D. (1981, March 30). *Talking New York: It's not what you say, It's the way that you say it*. New York, NY.

Tapscott, D. (2009). *Grown up digital: How the net generation is changing your world*. New York, NY: McGraw-Hill.

Tatum, A. (2005). *Teaching reading to Black adolescent males*. Portland, Maine: Stenhouse.

Taylor, N. (1986). Developing beginning literacy concepts: Content and context. In D. Yaden & S. Templeton (Eds.), *Metalinguistic awareness and literacy: Conceptualizing what it means to read and write* (pp. 173–184). Portsmouth, NH: Heinemann.

Teale, W. (1995). Young children and reading: Trends across the 20th century. *Journal of Education, 177*, 95–128.

Thatcher, R. (1992). Cyclical cortical reorganization in early childhood. *Brain and Cognition* 20, *20*(1), 24–50.

The Consultative Group on Early Childhood Care and Development. (1993/1994). *The world declaration on education for all: Meeting basic learning needs. Coordinators' Notebook, 14*. Washington, DC: The Consultative Group Secretariat.

The History Place. (2000). *Irish potato famine: The great hunger*. Retrieved September 10, 2012, from http://www.historyplace.com/worldhistory/famine/hunger.htm

The Molteno Institute for Langauge and Literacy. (2012, February 17). Break through to literacy. Retrieved February 17, 2012, from http://www.molteno.co.za/index.php?option=com_content&view=article&id=46&Itemid=53

The Molteno Institute for Language and Literacy (2010). *Molteno programme testimonials*. Retrieved September 13, 2012, from http://www.molteno.co.za/index.php?option=com_content&view=article&id=51&Itemid=60

The Schott Foundation for Public Education. (2008). *Given half a chance: The Schott 50 state report on public education and black males: Executive Summary*. Cambridge, MA: Schott Foundation for Public Education. Retrieved September 15, 2009, from http://blackboysreport.org

The Schott Foundation for Public Education. (2010). *Yes, we can: The 2010 Schott 50-state report on public education of black males*. Cambridge, MA: Schott Foundation for Public Education. Retrieved from www.blackboysreport.org

The Schott Foundation for Public Education. (2012, September 19). *The urgency of now: The 2012 Schott 50-state report on public education of Black males*. Cambridge, MA: Schott Foundation for Public Education. Retrieved February 20, 2015, from http://blackboysreport.org/theurgencyofnow/2012.pdf

The Schott Foundation for Pubic Education. (2015, February). *Black lives matter: The 2015 Schott 50-state report in the public education of Black males*. Cambridge, MA: Schott Foundation for Public Education. Retrieved February 20, 2015, from http://blackboysreport.org/bbreport 2015 pdf

Third committee—Eighty-ninth meeting. (1948, September 30). *Meeting notes: Eighty-ninth meeting*. UN official documents. Retrieved March 25, 2015, from http://www.un.org/en/ga/search/view_doc.asp?symbol=A/C.3/SR.89

Thompson, R. A. (2001, Spring/Summer). Development in the first years of life. *The Future of Children, 11*(1), 21–33. Retrieved January 9, 2015, from http://www.princeton.edu/futureofchildren/publications/journals/article/index.xml?journalid=44&articleid=186&sectionid=1212

Tolchinsky, L. (2006). The emergence of writing. In C. A. MacArthur, S. Graham, & J. Fitzgerald (Eds.), *Handbook of writing research* (pp. 83–95). New York, NY: Guilford Press.

Tough, P. (2008). *Whatever it takes: Geoffrey Canada's quest to change Harlem and America*. Boston, MA: Houghton Mifflin.

Toynbee, P. (2004, January 2). *We can break the vice of the great unmentionable*. UK: The Guardian. Retrieved February 12, 2012, from http://www.theguardian.com/politics/2004/jan/02/society.schools

Traxlar, J. (2005). *Mobile learning in developing countries*. Vancouver, Canada: Commonwealth of Learning. Retrieved from http://www.col.org/colweb/webdav/site/myjahiasite/shared/docs/KS!""'_mlearn.pdf

Uganda UNICEF. (2014). *Convention on the rights of the child*. Kampala, Uganda: Uganda UNICEF. Retrieved October 3, 2014, from http://www.unicef.org/uganda/aboutus_7646.html

UN. (1947, June 17). International bill of rights to be drafted. *UN Weekly Bulletin*, 639–643.

UN. (2000, September 8). *Millennium Summit (6–8 September, 2000)*. Presented at United Nations conferences and meetings. Retrieved October 1, 2014, from https://www.un.org/en/events/pastevents/millennium_summit.shtml

UN General Assembly. (1948, December 10). *Universal Declaration of Human Rights 217 A (III)*. Paris, France: United Nations.

UN General Assembly. (1989, November 20). Full text of the convention on the rights of the child. *United Nations treaty series (Vol. 1577*, p. 3). New York, NY: UNICEF. Retrieved September 26, 2012, from www.unicef.org/magic/media/crc_word_format_english.doc

UN Secretary General. (2014, December 4). *UN—The road to dignity by 2030: Ending poverty, transforming lives, and protecting the planet*. Retrieved January 25, 2015, from http://www.un.org/disabilities/documents/reports/SG_Synthesis_Report_Road_to_Dignity_by_2030.pdf

UN Summit on Millennium Development Goals. (2010, September 20–22). *UN Summit: UN millennium development goals 2015*. New York, NY: UN. Retrieved January 25, 2015, from http://www.un.org/en/mdg/summit2010/

UNESCO. (1975). *The declaration of Persepolis*. Paris, France: UNESCO.

UNESCO. (1990). *World declaration on education for all*. Paris, France: UNESCO.

UNESCO. (2000). *The dakar framework for action*. Paris, France: UNESCO.

UNESCO. (2005). *EFA global monitoring report 2006: Literacy for life*. Paris, France: UNESCO.

UNESCO. (2006). *Global monitoring report 2007: Strong foundations—Early childhood care and education*. Paris, France: UNESCO.

UNESCO. (2010). *EFA Global monitoring report 2011: The hidden crisis—Armed conflict and education summary*. Paris, France: UNESCO.

UNESCO. (2012). *Telesecundaria, Mexico: Lower secondary school learning with television support*. Paris, France: UNESCO. Retrieved from http://www.unesco.org/education/educprog/lwf/doc/portfolio/abstract8.htm

UNESCO. (2013/2014). *EFA global monitoring report 2013/14: Teaching and learning—Achieving quality for all*. Paris, France: UNESCO.

UNESCO. (n.d.). *Education for all (EFA) documents*. Bangkok, Thailand: UNESCO. Retrieved February 6, 2012, from http://www.unescobkk.org/education/efa/efa-in-asia-pacific/efa-documents/

UNESCO-Education. (2010, January 1). *Ten things you need to know about education for all*. Retrieved May 2, 2012, from http://www.unesco.org/en/efa/the-efa-movement/10-things-to-know-about-efa/

UNICEF Uzbekistan. (2006). *Overview: Convention the Rights of the Child (CRC)*. Uzbekistan, Central Asia: UNICEF. Retrieved November 13, 2014, from http://www.unicef.org/ceecis/1583.html

United Nations. (2002). *Resolution 56/116 on United Nations literacy decade*. New York, NY: United Nations.

United Nations. (2012). Convention on the Rights of the Child (CRC). *United Nations Treaty Collection*. Retrieved March 30, 2012, from http://treaties.un.org/Pages/ViewDetails.aspx?src=TREATY&mtdsg_no=IV.11&chapter=4&lang=en

United Nations. (2015, March 20). *Resources for speakers on global issues*. Retrieved March 20, 2015, from http://www.un.org/en/globalissues/briefingpapers/efa/

United States History. (n.d.). *Eleanor Roosevelt*. US: United States History.com. Retrieved October 20, 2009, from http://www.u-s-history.com/pages/h1590.html

U.S. Congress. (2003). The critical need for evidence-based programs. Retrieved from http://olpa.od.nihh.gov/hearings/108/session1/testimonies/headstart.asp

Varian, H. (2014, March 11). *The future of the internet*. Pew center's internet & American life. Retrieved October 5, 2014, from http://www.pewinternet.org/2014/03/11/digital-life-in-2025

Vasudevan, L., Schulta, K., & Bateman. J. (2010). Rethinking composing in a digital age: Authoring literate identities through multimodal storytelling. *Written Communication, 27*(4), 442–468.

Vygotsky, L. (1978). *Mind in society*. Cambridge, MA: Harvard University Press.

Wagner, D. A. (2010). What happened to literacy? Historical and conceptual perspectives on literacy in UNESCO. *International Journal of Educational Development, 31*, 319–323.

Weisleder, A., & Fernald, A. (2013). Talking to children matters: Early language experience strengthens processing and builds vocabulary. *Sage/Psychological Science, 24*(11), 2143–2152.

Wells, G. (1986). *The meaning makers: Children learning language and using language to learn*. Portsmouth, NH: Heinemann.

What Is My IP Address.com. (2014, October 14). How you connect to the world. Retrieved from http://www.whatismyipaddress.com/broadband

Whitehurst, G. (2014, October 9). Personal communication via email.

Widdowson, J. (2001). Rhyme, repetition and rhetorical: Learning language in the school playground. In J. Bishop, Bishop, & M. Curtis (Eds.), *Play today in the primary school: Life, learning and creativity* (pp. 135–151). Buckingham, UK: Open University Press.

Williams, L. (1992). Historical and philosophical roots of early childhood practice. In L. Williams & D. Fromberg (Eds.), *Encyclopedia of early childhood education* (pp. 7–10). New York, NY: Garland Publishing.

Willingham, D. (2009). *Why don't students like school? A cognitive scientist answers questions about how the mind works and what it means for the classroom*. San Francisco, CA: Jossey-Bass.

Wilson, J.-A. (1988). *Multiple contexts: Tapping the writing abilities of innerciity writers* (Unpublished dissertation). Amherst, Massachusetts, USA.

Wilson-Keenan, J. (2015, January 1). *Personal notes* (Unpublished). East Dennis, Massachusetts, USA.

Wilson-Keenan, J., Willett, J., & Solsken, J. (1993). Focus on research: Constructing an urban village: School/home collaboration in a multicultural classroom. *Language Arts, 70*(3), 204–214.

Wilson-Keenan, J., Willett, J., & Solsken, J. (2001). Families as curriculum partners in an elementary inclusion classroom. In J. Murphy & P. Byrd (Eds.)., *Understanding the courses we teach: Local perspectives on English language teaching* (pp. 92–114). Ann Arbor, IN: University of Michigan Press.

Wiltz, N., & Fein, G. (1996). Evolution of a narrative curriculum: The contributions of Vivian Gussin Paley. *Young Children, 51*(3), 61–68.

wisegeek. (2013). What is semantic memory? Retrieved October 4, 2013, from http://www.wisegeek.org/what-is-semantic-memory.htm

Wodak, R., & Meyer, M. (2009). *Methods of critical discourse analysis* (2nd ed.). London, UK: Sage.

Wohlwend, K. E. (2009). Early adopters: Playing new Literacies and pretending new technologies in print-centric classrooms. *Early Childhood Literacy, 9*(2), 119–143.

Wohlwend, K. E. (2010). A is for avatar: Young children in literacy 2.0 worlds and literacy 1.0 schools. *Language Arts, 88*(2), 144–152.

Wolf, M. (2007). *Proust and the squid: The story and science of the reading brain.* New York, NY: Harper, an Imprint of Harper Collins Publishers; and London, UK: Icon Books.

Wolf, M. (2014, November). Balance technology and deep reading to create biliterate children. *Phi Delta Kappan, 96*, 14–19.

Wolfram, W. (2005). Do you speak American? *Social identity: What is sociolinguistics?* Arlington, Virginia, VA: Public Broadcasting Service (PBS). Retrieved February 17, 2013, from http://www.pbs.org/speak/speech/sociolinguistics/socialbehavior/

Women's Commission for Refugee Women and Children. (2004, February). *Global survey on education in emergencies.* New York, NY: www.womenscommission.org

Woodham-Smith, C. (1962). *The great hunger, Ireland 1845–1849.* New York, NY: Harper and Row.

World Conference on Education. (1990). *World declaration on education for all.* Jomtien, Thiland: United Nations.

Wreh, P. (2011, December 25). Personal email message. Monrovia, Liberia.

Xue, Y., & Meisels, S. J. (2004). Early literacy instruction and learning in kindergarten: Evidence from the early childhood longitudinal study—Kindergarten class of 1998–1999. *American Education Research Journal, 41*(1), 191–229.

Yaden, D. (2008, September). Reported personal communication to Foley Cusumano. *Every mark on the page: Educating family and community members about young children's writing.* Urbana, Illinois, IL: National Council of Teachers of English.

Young, S. K., Fox, N. A., & Zahn-Waxler, C. (1999). The realtionship between temperament and empathy in 2-year-olds. *Developmental Psychology, 35*, 1038–1047.

Zentella, A. C. (2005). *Building on strength: Language and literacy in Latino families and communities.* New York, NY: Teachers College Press.

Zero to Three-National Center for Infants, Toddlers and Families. (2012, February 18). *Early experiences matter.* Retrieved from http://main.zerotothree.org/site/PageServer?pagename=ter_key_brainFAQ

Zevenbergen, A., Whitehurst, G., & Zevenbergen, J. (2003). Effects od shared-reading intervention on the inclusion of evaluative devices in narratives of children from low-income families. *Journal of Applied Developmental Psychology, 24*, 1–15.

INDEX

CPSIA information can be obtained at www.ICGtesting.com
Printed in the USA
BVOW06s1913060815

412225BV00006B/40/P

9 789463 001342